Understanding Psychology

Paul R. Robbins

J. WESTON
WALCH
PUBLISHER
Portland, Maine

1 2 3 4 5 6 7 8 9 10

ISBN 0-8251-2706-8

Copyright © 1984, 1995
J. Weston Walch, Publisher
P. O. Box 658 • Portland, Maine 04104-0658

Printed in the United States of America

Contents

Acknowledgments

The author would like to thank Dr. Blair Webb for his comments on the chapter dealing with biology and behavior, Dr. Jean McKeithen for her reactions to the chapters on human development, Dr. Sharon Hauge for her comments on the treatment of statistics and measurement, and Dr. Roland Tanck for his reactions to the entire manuscript. He would also like to thank Shirley Lucas for typing the manuscript.

We wish to acknowledge permission to reprint excerpts from the following sources:

American Psychiatric Association, *Diagnostic and Statistical Manual of Mental Disorders*. Third edition. Washington, DC: APA, 1980.

Cohen, Arthur R., "Cognitive Tuning as a Factor Affecting Impression Formation." *Journal of Personality*, 29:2, pp. 235–245, Duke University Press, 1961.

Foa, E.B., "Failure in Treating Obsessive-compulsives." *Behavior Research and Therapy*, Vol. 17, Pergamon Press, 1979.

International Journal of Clinical and Experimental Hypnosis. Society for Clinical and Experimental Hypnosis, October 1979.

Journal of Personality Assessment. (Table 1), Vol. 43, pp. 396–400, 1979.

Kohler, W., *The Mentality of Apes*. London: Routledge & Kegan Paul PLC.

Psychotherapy, Vol. 15, pp. 27–33, 1978.

Psychotherapy: Theory, Research, and Practice. Vol. 17, pp. 143–150, 1980.

Robbins, Paul R., *Marijuana: A Short Course*. Second edition. Brookline, MA: Branden Press, 1983.

Rogers, Carl R., *Counseling and Psychotherapy*. Boston: Houghton Mifflin, 1942.

About the Author

Dr. Robbins has a background in both research and therapy. He has been on the staff of the National Institute of Mental Health and the Department of Psychiatry of the George Washington University School of Medicine. He has also served as director of a consultation project for the California Department of Public Health, as a con-sultant on drug abuse for the Washington, D.C. Veterans Adminis-tration Hospital, and as a consultant on the problems of the aged. He has contributed many papers to professional journals and is currently a practicing therapist in Silver Spring, Maryland.

To the Teacher

This book is intended as a general introduction to the study of psychology. It is divided into eleven chapters, beginning with an overview of the field of psychology and its historical roots and ending with a discussion of psychotherapy. The chapters introduce such topics as perception, learning, motivation, personality, child development, adolescence, dating and marriage, and abnormal psychology.

Questions and activities are provided at the end of each chapter. A true-false quiz also follows each chapter. A glossary defining a number of unfamiliar or technical terms is included for students' use. Terms included in the glossary are printed in boldface the first time they appear in the text. An answer key, a bibliography, and some suggestions for further reading are also included.

—*Paul R. Robbins*

Introduction to Psychology

What is psychology? The answer is not as obvious as you might think, and psychologists have disagreed among themselves as to exactly what the answer is. If we ask the question somewhat differently—for example, if we ask: what do psychologists deal with? or, What problems are psychologists concerned about?—it may be a better way to begin looking at what psychology is all about.

Psychologists are interested in behavior, primarily the behavior of human beings—though many psychologists are interested in the behavior of animals as well. Psychologists are also interested in mental processes—the thoughts, ideas, and understandings of human beings. These mental processes, sometimes called **cognitions**, are very important to clinical psychologists who are trying to help persons with emotional problems or severe mental illnesses, and to educational psychologists who are trying to develop better ways of teaching. Clearly, psychologists are also interested in feelings and emotions. The feelings of anxiety and depression are perhaps the most frequent problems that a clinical psychologist encounters.

Psychology as we will present it deals with the behavior, thoughts, and emotions of individuals. The focus of psychology has always been on individuals. This makes it different from sociology or anthropology, where the focus is on groups of people and the way people are organized into societies.

Psychology is not the only field of study that deals with human behavior, thoughts, and emotions. For example, philosophy, religion, and literature are deeply concerned with these subjects. The basic difference between psychology and these other important forms of human inquiry is that psychology is a branch of modern science. Whatever is accepted as fact or principle in psychology must be established using scientific methods. This usually means carrying out large numbers of carefully controlled studies and experiments.

Psychology as a scientific discipline is not very old. Some writers date it to the latter part of the nineteenth century, when Wilhelm Wundt founded the first major psychology laboratory in Leipzig, Germany. The interest of men and women in the problem areas of psychology, however, dates back to the time of early written records and probably to the dawn of human history. For example, there are records from the ancient lands of Mesopotamia revealing that people there puzzled about the nature of dreams. Where did dreams come from? What did they mean? This is a problem that psychologists are still very much concerned with. But today they approach the problem with the aid of sleep laboratories with electronic equipment that monitors eye movements and brain waves.

The ancient Greeks, who seem to have been interested in almost everything—sports, mathematics, government, the arts—were deeply interested in the problems of psychology. Plato talked about discords of the mind, and Aristotle distinguished between various psychological states such as perceiving, thinking, and imagining. The basic approach of Aristotle was one of observation and reasoning—one might say armchair reasoning. This is fine as far as it goes, but it doesn't go very far. It stops short of a very important step—*verification*, or testing your ideas to see if they are correct.

Armchair reasoning in psychology is something like taking a preseason poll in sports before the season actually begins. Sports experts analyze the talent of different teams (say, college basketball teams), look at the strengths and weaknesses of the players, and then decide which team is the best, second best, and so forth. The preseason poll is published in the newspapers. Then, the season begins. It often turns out some highly rated teams don't perform as well as expected, and some teams which were not expected to perform well do better than expected. As the season progresses, the preseason polls are sometimes dramatically revised.

Now imagine a situation where the preseason polls are carried out as usual. However, this time the polls are accepted by everyone as fact—what the experts said is taken as true. Under these circumstances, there would be no point in playing any games. Imagine that all the games are cancelled and the championship is decided by the experts' preseason reasoning. Wouldn't that be an easy way of settling the question of which team is best? The only problem, of course, is that the experts could be dead wrong in their conclusions.

Aristotle's prestige was so great that his carefully reasoned view of the world, science, and human nature was accepted as the standard of knowledge for centuries. Until the nineteenth century, armchair reasoning was the basic approach used in the study of psychology. Scholars continued to draw distinctions between various mental processes and seldom went beyond this speculation.

During this prescientific period of psychology, there were a number of philosophers who expressed thoughtful ideas about human behavior. And there were great writers like Shakespeare who offered penetrating descriptions of human actions and motivations. There are also records showing that many people had enlightened views about mental illness, seeing its origin in psychological and physical causes. At the same time, however, there was a great deal of misinformation about human behavior particularly about the symptoms of mental illness. One time-honored way of explaining abnormal behavior was to say it was caused by possession by evil spirits or devils. This was particularly true of the symptoms which were finally identified in the mid-nineteenth century as a mental illness called **hysteria**. One sees little of hysteria these days, but in earlier centuries, it seemed to be more widespread. Some of the symptoms of hysteria are apparent paralysis, apparent loss of sight or hearing, amnesia (loss of memory), anesthesia (insensitivity to pain), tics, tremors, and convulsions. These symptoms occur in hysteria without any medical basis— nothing is physically wrong with the patient that would account for such symptoms.

Until the mid-nineteenth century, many people believed that such symptoms were caused by witchcraft or possession by devils. One treatment that was used was exorcism. During the exorcism rites, the afflicted person might go into convulsions. Some of the reports describing these convulsions sound grisly enough to rival a Hollywood horror film (for example, "her teeth rattled and sound came out of her throat . . . her face became completely unrecognizable, her glance furious, her tongue prodigiously large . . ."). It sometimes happened that the person who was supposed to be bewitched might go into convulsions at the sight of the alleged witch. This, of course, could be taken as proof of the witch's guilt. The unfortunate people who were thus accused risked burning at the stake.

The Forerunners of Modern Psychology

Modern science as we know it began during the Renaissance. The story of Galileo and the Leaning Tower of Pisa is often told as an example. Tradition has it (and it may or may not be true) that Galileo stood atop the tower and dropped a heavy weight and a lighter weight at the same time. Galileo wanted to test the then-accepted idea that the heavy weight would hit the ground first. Using simple experiments, he was able to show that this was not the case. When Galileo began these demonstrations, he introduced an essential part of the scientific method as well—an attitude which seems to say "show me" or "prove it."

The natural sciences made great progress following the Renaissance. The social and behavioral sciences lagged far behind.

Eventually, the idea began to take hold that if experimentation and the scientific method were producing dividends in the study of nature, such methods might also work in the study of the mind's workings.

In nineteenth-century Germany, a number of people whose original training was in physiology, medicine, or physics began to cross the frontiers of these sciences into the then-unknown realm of psychology. The man who took the radical step of actually setting up a laboratory to study psychological problems was Wilhelm Wundt. Trained as a physician and in physiology, Wundt set up a laboratory in 1879 in Leipzig. There, he and his students began to "open up" the study of psychology.

Wundt believed that the study of psychology should start with **introspection**—looking carefully at and analyzing one's own conscious experiences. While this approach did not prove to be very fruitful, Wundt also believed in the importance of experimental studies. His laboratory carried out research on such topics as vision, hearing, touch, space perception, reaction time, and word association. In these experiments, Wundt and his students showed that psychological problems could be studied in the laboratory. Some of the important early figures in psychology in the United States studied in Wundt's laboratory, and when they returned home, set up laboratories of their own. With this kind of influence, Wundt certainly qualifies as one of the founding fathers of modern psychology.

One major branch of modern psychology had its origins in the nineteenth-century interest in hypnosis, sleepwalking, and amnesia. These mysterious happenings seemed to point towards the existence of **unconscious** mental processes. The discovery of hypnosis is linked with the name of an eighteenth-century Austrian physician, Franz Mesmer, who treated patients with a technique he called *animal magnetism.*

Mesmer believed that one's state of health was influenced by an invisible fluid that filled the universe. For a person to maintain good health, this fluid had to be properly distributed in the body. Illness could be cured by redistributing the fluid. Mesmer claimed he could do this by transmitting magnetic fluid from himself to the patient. The patient sat in what seems like a forerunner of a "hot tub," with metal bars stuck into its side to assist in the transfer of the magnetism. What Mesmer actually did was to hypnotize his patients, some of whom then went into convulsions. As if by the power of suggestion, convulsions in some patients were quickly followed by convulsions in others. After this treatment, in any of the patients reported that they felt better. Have you ever heard the word *mesmerized*? That's where it comes from.

Mesmer's procedure was striking and was observed by, among others, Benjamin Franklin. In the latter part of the nineteenth century, the famous French neurologist Jean-Martin Charcot began to use hypnosis in the study of hysteria. In his clinics, Charcot was able to show that, under hypnosis, he could produce in normal people the classic symptoms of hysteria: paralysis, tremors, and anesthesia. The symptoms produced in normal people under hypnosis appeared remarkably similar to those of his hysterical patients.

This was a very exciting development and a milestone in the development of *psychiatry.*

In the fall of 1885, a young Viennese doctor spent four months visiting Charcot's clinics in Paris, making the rounds in the hospital. He was very interested in Charcot's ideas about hysteria and continued with his own study of the subject when he returned to Vienna. Working with an older colleague named Josef Breuer, the young doctor began to develop a revolutionary approach to the treatment of hysteria. Instead of relying on hypnosis, he began to listen with great care to his patients and to interpret their thoughts and experiences. The younger doctor was a man with a remarkable intellect. His name was Sigmund Freud, and he was the father of **psychoanalysis.**

Freud's approach to psychological data was very different from that of modern psychology. He did not test out his theories with carefully done experiments. Freud's approach brings to mind the method of the fictional detective Sherlock Holmes. Freud looked at small details of behavior that might normally be overlooked and asked: What do they mean? What do slips of the tongue mean? Freud wondered. What do the details of dreams mean? He listened endlessly to patients, and formulated and reformulated theories of how the mind works. Eventually, he came up with the theories and methods of psychoanalysis.

Psychoanalysis is both a theory about human behavior and a method of treating patients with emotional difficulties. As such, it continues to influence many present-day psychologists. But psychology and psychoanalysis are far from identical. As we shall see, the methods and standards of evidence used in psychology and psychoanalysis are very different.

Another branch of modern psychology owes much of its direction to a Russian physiologist who did research on the digestive system. The name of the scientist was Ivan Petrovich Pavlov. Pavlov won a Nobel prize in physiology in 1904 and continued his research right through the Russian Revolution. It is said that he was a very punctual, no-nonsense type of man and expected his co-workers to be the same way. When one of his colleagues was late, dodging an exchange of gunfire on the street, Pavlov was said to have commented that a revolution shouldn't make any difference when there's work to be done in the laboratory.

Pavlov's important contribution to psychology was the discovery of the **conditioned reflex.** Pavlov noticed that his laboratory animals (dogs) would salivate when food was placed in their mouths. This was a natural—unconditioned—response or reflex. Pavlov also noticed that the dogs began to salivate at the mere sight of the food or the person who usually carried the food into the room. His curiosity was aroused. How did this come about? Pavlov began to experiment. For example, he began to sound a bell when the food appeared. What Pavlov found was that the dogs would begin to salivate when they heard the bell. He soon found that he could sound the bell without presenting any food and the animals would salivate. A new, learned reflex had been established—the bell which in the beginning had no effect on salivation now produced salivation. This new reflex—bell produces salivation—had been established by pairing the bell with the natural, unconditioned reflex—food produces salivation. The new reflex was called a conditioned reflex.

Pavlov and other scientists who followed him thought that conditioned reflexes might be important building blocks in learning, and his discovery led to much research and theorizing.

Also important to the beginnings of modern psychology was the development of intelligence testing. The principal name to remember here is that of Alfred Binet, a turn-of-the-century French psychologist who became interested in the problem of measuring intelligence. Around 1900, the Ministry of Education in France wanted to set up a program of special education for slow learners. They asked Binet if he could find a way to pick out these children. Working with Theodore Simon, Binet made up a number of tasks that seemed to measure a variety of mental abilities in children. (For example, a child might be asked to identify the meaning of a particular word.) The more difficult the tasks the child could do, the higher the mental age the child was believed to have. If two children had the same actual age and one appeared to have a higher mental age, he or she was thought to be the more intelligent, or, as we might say today, to have a higher *I.Q.* (intelligence quotient).

The Binet-Simon tests were revised in the United States into the Stanford-Binet intelligence scale. These tests were used routinely for many years, but have now been replaced in the main by another set of intelligence scales developed by David Wechsler. Binet's pioneering contribution to psychology was to show that one could measure important psychological traits (mental abilities) in an objective way and that these measures could have important uses in society.

The development of the early intelligence tests caused psychologists to ask: If we can measure intelligence, why can't we measure other psychological traits as well? And so efforts were made to develop "tests" for special aptitudes like music and art, and all kinds of measures of personality. These tests helped expand the field of applied psychology, since psychologists could now tell people more about themselves. The tests also helped spur basic research in psychology. For example, if there are objective ways to measure depression, it is much easier to study questions like which kinds of treatment help most in reducing levels of depression.

Psychology had many other pioneers in the late nineteenth and early twentieth centuries. All of them played important roles in the development of the field. As you read more deeply in psychology, you will come across the names of these men, so we have listed some in the next column. Along with Freud, Wundt, Pavlov, and Binet, they would be candidates for a "Psychology Hall of Fame."

Ten Candidates for a Psychology Hall of Fame

1. **Wilhelm Wundt**   1832–1920
    Established first significant psychological laboratory.

2. **William James**   1842–1910
    Wrote one of the first influential books on psychology, *Principles of Psychology*.

3. **Ivan Pavlov**   1849–1936
    Discovered and studied the conditioned reflex.

4. **Hermann Ebbinghaus**   1850–1909
    Carried out pioneering studies on memory.

5. **Alfred Binet**   1857–1911
    Developed measures of intelligence.

6. **Sigmund Freud**   1856–1939
    Developed theories and methods of psychoanalysis.

7. **Edward Thorndike**   1874–1949
    Developed the reinforcement theory of learning and the "law of effect."

8. **John B. Watson**   1878–1958
    Emphasized behavior over thought processes.

9. **Carl Rogers**   1902–1987
    Developed an approach to psychotherapy different from psychoanalysis.

10. **B. F. Skinner**   1904–1990
    Carefully studied the effects of reinforcement on behavior.

From these beginnings, the field of psychology expanded into many other areas. Experimental techniques were devised to study perception, learning, memory, motivation, and the emotions. Studies of social behavior and of personality were begun. Psychologists began to apply their knowledge and techniques to problems in education, health, criminology, business, and defense.

The broad interests of current psychology are illustrated by papers presented at conventions of The American Psychological Association. For example, at recent meetings psycchologists discussed such subjects as treating elderly depressed patients, studying pilot performance in flight simulators, reducing cigarette smoking, training for disabled children, ways of helping people deal with loneliness, evaluations of teaching methods, spouse battering, and adolescent sexual behavior.

Careers in Psychology

Have you ever wondered about what psychologists do on the job? Or have you perhaps considered going into psychology as a career? In either event, you may want to know more about careers in psychology.

There are now about 77,000 members of The American Psychological Association and over 40,000 student affiliates. That's a huge increase from the 31 people who founded the association back in 1892 and points to the growth and vitality of the profession. Most licensed psychologists hold a Ph.D. (a Doctor of Philosophy degree) in psychology, and have also completed some additional supervised experience. However, there are many people who work in psychology with a master's degree. They may be doing such things as giving psychological tests, participating in research projects, or counseling in drug treatment programs.

The profession of psychology offers careers that have attracted both men and women. The number of women receiving doctoral degrees in psychology began to increase steadily in the 1970's, and by 1989 more women than men were receiving doctorates. While women have gone into every area of psychology, they have shown a special interest in developmental psychology—the branch of psychology that focuses largely on child development. In 1989, almost four out of every five degrees in this specialty were awarded to women.

The most likely careers for a psychologist today are as a clinical psychologist or as a teacher of psychology. Clinical psychologists work with people who are having emotional problems. This work is called *therapy* or **psychotherapy**. Clinical psychologists also do psychological testing. According to a survey of people who had recently completed their training in psychology, 44 percent found jobs doing clinical work. Another 30 percent of these recent graduates took teaching jobs at universities, colleges, and medical schools. The remaining graduates took jobs as psychologists in school systems, or found jobs in industry or government. Some of the psychologists in government do research. They may work, for example, for the National Institutes of Health.

Many clinical psychologists work in hospitals, community mental health centers, or university counseling centers. Others have private practices, either by themselves or along with other therapists. As we indicated, the major activities of a clinical psychologist are testing and therapy. Tests may include measures of intelligence, aptitude, and personality. Therapy may be done on a one-to-one basis with a client, with a couple who are having problems, with an entire family, or with a group of unrelated individuals—this last is called **group therapy**.

In a hospital or clinic, the psychologist often works as part of a team, reporting his or her findings and conferring with other staff members (for example, psychiatrists or social workers) about the client. In a counseling center at a university, the psychologist tries to help students cope with both academic and adjustment problems. He or she may also offer guidance in career choice. In private practice, the psychologist tries to help clients deal more effectively with a variety of emotional problems, such as anxiety, depression, and difficulties with relationships.

In therapy, the psychologist must be a very good listener, trying to discover what things are bothering the client, what has caused this state of affairs, and what can be done about it. The psychologist is not a physician. The psychologist may suggest to the client that he or she might consider medications, but only a physician can prescribe them.

A school psychologist uses his or her training within the school system, providing services and consultation. Unlike many clinical psychologists, who do therapy intensively with a small number of people, the school psychologist may serve a large population (perhaps 2,000 students). You may find the school psychologist traveling from school to school on a rotating basis.

One of the main jobs of the school psychologist is to help students with special needs (e.g., children with learning disabilities, students with emotional problems, students who are under-achievers, and unusually gifted children) get the kind of special services they need. The psychologist may give tests to help diagnose problems and then confer with parents, teachers, and other professionals about steps that can be taken to deal with the problems. The school psychologist may also work directly with some students, offering counseling or therapy.

As the employment survey of psychologists suggests, a great many psychologists become teachers of psychology. These individuals find positions in community colleges, four-year colleges, universities, or medical schools. Their primary job, of course, is teaching, and this usually means giving lectures. To prepare for a lecture, the professor reads through the psychological literature (books and journal articles) on a topic. Then he or she tries to put together this information with his or her own professional experience, and present this to the students in a way that stimulates their interest. On the graduate school level, the professor may conduct seminars. These are smaller groups of advanced students where each student may have the task of presenting topics for discussion.

In addition, psychology professors are often called on to reach out to the community. They may be asked to give advice on specific problems or make speeches about their areas of special knowledge to community groups. Psychology professors are usually expected to carry out and publish the results of research.

Careers doing full-time research in psy-chology are unusual. More typically, people who are teaching in universities or colleges do research on the side. Sometimes the research is supported by grants which permit the teacher to spend more time on the research project and to hire student assistants to help with the work.

The researcher, whether full time or part time, usually goes through several stages of activity: planning, collection of data, analyses of results, and writing up of the study for publication in a professional journal. We shall learn more about how research is carried out in the next chapter.

The Relevance of Psychology to the Student

Sometimes students wonder why a certain course is offered in school. They may ask what the value of the course is to them. Will the course have any relevance to them in their daily lives? While the purposes of education go far beyond the immediate concerns of students, offering a balanced, long-range program of knowledge and skills, these are fair questions that deserve consideration. So, let us ask, how is a course in psychology relevant to the student?

You might be curious how students themselves answer this question and how these answers might compare with your own thoughts. A colleague of mine posed the question to a college class studying psychology. Here are some typical responses:

Psychology teaches you about yourself and how similar you are to others. It helps you understand how and why your mind works in the fashion it does. It can explain inner feelings in an easy, logical way.

Psychology is relevant to me in that it is helping me to better understand why other people think and act the way they do.

The impact has been significant in im- proving my understanding of myself and several of the people I am closest to—my mother, my father, and my friends.

The students felt that the study of psychology was relevant in their lives in two principal ways—it increased self-understanding, and it increased understanding of others. As other responses from the class point out, students felt that such knowledge could help them better deal with life's problems.

Psychology is relevant to my life. In understanding psychology, I can understand myself better, it is easier to deal with my feelings and problems, and I find it easier to deal with others.

Psychology will help me learn how to cope with life's problems and learn how to get along with others in my career.

We would agree that increased self-understanding and understanding of others are two very important possible gains that may come from the study of psychology. We would hope such knowledge could lead to better self-management, and to personal growth and more rewarding relationships with others.

In addition to these very personal benefits, there are many other ways that the study of psychology may be useful to you. For example, a knowledge of the psychology of learning and memory may help you in forming better study habits. A knowledge of the purposes and limitations of psychological tests should help you understand what standardized tests are all about when you are asked to take them. An understanding of psychological studies of influence and persuasion may help you recognize techniques that may be used to influence your opinions and behavior.

So psychology can be quite relevant to you. More than that, we hope your curiosity will be aroused by the many fascinating problems in the field. Have you ever wondered what a Rorschach test is or how a polygraph works? If you have, read on!

Some Questions for You

What is your own interest in psychology?

Below are listed some topics in psychology. Decide whether you are "very interested," "somewhat interested," or "not at all interested" in each topic. **Write your responses on a separate sheet of paper.**

	Very interested	Somewhat interested	Not at all interested
1. Dreams	( )	( )	( )
2. ESP (extrasensory perception)	( )	( )	( )
3. Psychoanalysis	( )	( )	( )
4. The functions of the brain	( )	( )	( )
5. Abnormal psychology	( )	( )	( )
6. Problems of the aged	( )	( )	( )
7. Dating and marriage	( )	( )	( )
8. Theories of learning	( )	( )	( )
9. Theories of personality	( )	( )	( )
10. Problems of adolescence	( )	( )	( )
11. Psychological tests	( )	( )	( )
12. Hypnosis	( )	( )	( )
13. Aggression	( )	( )	( )
14. Psychotherapy	( )	( )	( )
15. Effects of divorce	( )	( )	( )
16. The influence of groups on individuals	( )	( )	( )
17. Children's play	( )	( )	( )
18. Other _____	( )	( )	( )

Test Your Knowledge

Read each statement and decide whether it is TRUE or FALSE. **Write your answers on a separate sheet of paper.**

1. Aristotle's approach to psychology was the same as that of the modern scientist who tests ideas with carefully controlled experiments.

2. The first psychology laboratory was founded in Germany by Wilhelm Wundt.

3. The conditioned reflex was discovered by Pavlov.

4. Some of the symptoms of hysteria are paralysis and insensitivity to pain.

5. The focus of both psychology and sociology is on group behavior.

6. Sigmund Freud was the founder of psychoanalysis.

7. Psychologists may prescribe medicine in their treatment of patients.

8. Psychotherapy is only done with individual patients, never with groups of patients.

9. Hysterical symptoms can be produced in some people by hypnosis.

10. Most psychologists who graduate today are involved in clinical work or teaching.

11. One of the functions of school psychologists is to diagnose students with learning disabilities.

12. Mental age is always the same as actual age.

13. Freud's approach to developing his theories involved careful observation of small, often-overlooked details.

14. One of the prescientific theories about abnormal behavior was that possession by evil spirits caused it.

15. The term mesmerize has nothing to do with hypnosis.

16. Records from the ancient world fail to show any interest in the problems of psychology.

17. Some of the founding fathers of psychology in the United States had their training in Wundt's laboratory in Germany.

18. Introspection is looking within oneself.

CHAPTER 2

Methods of Psychology

The scientific method was a historical development, growing out of the Renaissance and blossoming in the following centuries. There are towering figures in the history of science, such as Kepler in astronomy, Lavoisier in chemistry, and Lyell in geology.

The scientific method has given us rockets which have landed vehicles on Mars and probed through the rings of Saturn. It has led to the discovery of vaccines against dread diseases such as polio. While the limits of the scientific method in expanding human knowledge are arguable, there is no doubt that the method has worked, and worked very well.

It should be stressed that the knowledge which a field of science presents as true at any given time is not necessarily fixed and certain. Even in a traditional science such as astronomy, the textbooks of 50 years ago are very different from those of today. Scientific understanding changes as new facts are uncovered and new methods are devised to aid discovery. When the telescope was invented, astronomers learned much about the planets of our solar system. When space travel finally became possible, astronomers obtained a tremendous amount of new information which led them to change many of their earlier ideas. Who would have thought from the crude telescopic pictures of the 1950's that the surface of Mars would turn out to be pocked with craters?

In psychology, which is a very young science, there are still large gaps in our understanding. Sometimes scientists carry on vigorous disputes over unresolved issues. These disputes are often healthy because they focus scientists' attention on research that is needed to gain a better understanding of the problem.

You will discover as you read this book that psychology has not yet reached the point where it can provide firm answers for all of your questions. Nonetheless, the use of the scientific method has enabled psychology to make great strides during this century. The scientific method has become the keystone of modern psychology.

When applied to psychology, the scientific method stresses such ideas as these:

Objectivity: Psychological data (e.g., behavior, verbal statements, responses to a psychological test) is objective if two or more researchers acting independently can describe and characterize it in the same way.

Accurate and valid methods of data gathering: The use of data-gathering techniques that produce reliable information and measure what they are claimed to measure.

Quantification: The use of numbers in the description of data. Numbers allow for more precise description and for statistical analyses.

Theory building and modification: The development of systematic explanations to account for observed events.

Experimentation: A method of research in which changes are introduced into a situation under carefully controlled conditions. The effects of these changes, if any, are carefully noted.

Replication of results: Repetition of a study under conditions similar to the original study to see if the same results are obtained.

Objectivity

Let's take a closer look at what some of the terms mean. Consider objectivity—agreement by independent observers in describing and defining what they are looking at. Have you ever seen a news report in the paper or on TV of a trial in which the defense lawyer pleaded insanity for her client? To support her case, the lawyer called an expert witness, a psychiatrist or psychologist who testified that the client had a mental illness and thus wasn't responsible for her actions.

Not to be outdone, the prosecution called another psychiatrist who had also examined the defendant. This witness testified that the defendant did not have a mental illness.

Leaving aside the question of who was right, what you see here are two trained people using the same kind of data (interviews with the defendant) and coming out with two different conclusions. These differing conclusions raise questions about how objective the evaluation procedures were.

Let's take another example. Imagine you are looking for a summer job. You enjoy working with young children and you notice an advertisement. The Red Robin Day Care Center is looking for someone to work with the children this summer. During your job interview, you are told that a professor from the university psychology department will be carrying out research on the children. You are asked whether you would like to take part in her research. The idea sounds interesting. You say, "Sure."

One of the things you are asked to do is observe the children. The professor talks to you and another student—his name is Ben. The professor explains that she is interested in studying aggressive and cooperative behaviors. She goes over carefully what she means by the two types of behaviors and asks Ben and you to follow a child for a certain period of time and then make the following rating about the child's level of aggressiveness.

not at all aggressive	( )
slightly aggressive	( )
moderately aggressive	( )
very aggressive	( )
extremely aggressive	( )

You and Ben keep an eye on the child, then made your ratings. Suppose Ben rates the child "not at all aggressive" and you rate the child "extremely aggressive." From a scientific standpoint the professor is nowhere. She hasn't even gotten to square one. It sounds as if you and Ben are talking about two different people.

Let's imagine a happier circumstance. Both Ben and you independently rate the child "extremely aggressive." The professor beams with delight. She has begun to pin something down. She has taken a step toward developing a way of observing that will permit objective description of behavior. Of course, she will have to prove out the system by comparing independent ratings of many children, not just one.

At the very basis of scientific investigation in psychology are methods that will allow two or more trained persons to look at data independently and describe it in a similar way. The degree of agreement is unlikely to be perfect, but it certainly should be substantial.

Accurate and Valid Methods of Data Gathering

In the beginning stages of scientific investigation, it is often a good idea to spend some time thinking before plunging into the day-to-day grind of research. You may want to look over a range of possibilities before zeroing in on your project. For example, if you were an archeologist exploring possible sites for an excavation, you wouldn't just stick a shovel in the ground anywhere, dig a trench, and hope to find something. You'd explore around first, looking for telltale signs that there might be something of interest buried below.

When you begin to study a new problem in psychology, it often pays to look over the possibilities with as open a mind as you can manage. This, of course, includes reading through the professional journals to see what other people may have done before you. As your hunches begin to jell, it will be time to think about precise, focused data-gathering methods. We are going to discuss some of these methods, or *instruments*, shortly: observation, the interview, questionnaires, and psychological tests. Before we do, however, we are going to discuss some terms which are used in discussing these data-gathering methods: **sampling, reliability,** and **validity**.

To introduce the idea of sampling, let's return to your summer job at the Red Robin Day Care Center. You have been given the task of observing certain children and making ratings on their behavior. Obviously you can't watch each child every moment. In the interest of careful observation, you may want to focus

on each child for a certain period of time. This period of time is a portion, or **sample**, of the child's overall behavior. For your observations to be meaningful, you should try to establish that your sample gives an accurate picture of how the child usually behaves at the center.

One way of checking on the accuracy of your observations is to make the observations on several different days. If you find a great deal of consistency in what you see, you can be more certain your observations give a picture of the person's typical behavior. Checks on consistency over time are one way of measuring the reliability of observations. **Reliability** refers to the dependability or consistency of your measuring instrument. Can you imagine taking your temperature with a thermometer which registered 98.6° one minute and 104° a few minutes later when you retested yourself? You'd be well advised to throw out that thermometer. Either you have some weird disease or the thermometer is quite unreliable.

Another test of your data's accuracy is the validity of your data-gathering instrument. **Validity** means that the measuring instrument actually measures what it is claimed to measure. Let's take an example. Suppose you're giving out a questionnaire on drug use to a group of high school students. Suppose, further, you ask your subjects to write their names on the questionnaire and tell them that the completed questionnaires will be made available to their teachers, their parents, and the school principal. Do you think there is a chance that many students might fudge their answers? To the extent that people would falsify their answers, the data loses validity, and you are no longer obtaining useful observations. The questionnaire is not measuring what it is supposed to measure—the extent of drug use.

Validity of data-gathering techniques is usually established by research. A person could make up a test and claim it was a measure of intelligence. But until research was carried out which provided evidence that the test actually measured intelligence, there would be little reason to believe it did.

Now that we understand sampling, reliability, and validity, let's look at the data-gathering methods we mentioned earlier.

OBSERVATION

Direct observation of behavior is an important method of data gathering in certain areas of psychology. The method has been used often in the study of young children, in the study of people who are living in institutions, such as mentally ill patients, and in the study of people in small groups. Usually, the observer is asked to rate specific behaviors of the subjects. Sometimes these behaviors involve ways of relating to others, such as cooperative play or aggression. Sometimes the observer's focus is on aspects of problem solving. For example, a group of people may be observed at a meeting trying to resolve a work-related problem. Here the observer may record behaviors such as "asks question," "presents information," "gives an analysis," and "interrupts."

In addition to listening to the spoken words, the observer usually looks for nonverbal clues (such as expressions or gestures). The observer notices actions, facial expressions, signs of restlessness, boredom, and so on.

Observation can be a rather clumsy and time-consuming procedure. Observers must be trained and checked out to determine the extent of agreement in their ratings. It may take time to gather a large enough sample of observations to be trustworthy. Finally, the data itself can sometimes be hard to work with and require a great deal of time to analyze.

INTERVIEWS

We have all seen interviews on television. Typically, the newsperson asks a public figure (for example, a senator) rather direct questions. Sometimes the public figure hedges and dodges, trying to evade the questions. When this happens, the interview is something like a fencing match.

The interviews carried out by psychologists are usually less pointed than those the newsperson does. The subjects are not on the spot in front of millions of TV viewers. The subjects are often interested in the questions, and the data that is obtained can be very useful.

Interviews use two basic types of questions—*open-ended* and *closed-ended*. An example of an open-ended question would be: "How are you feeling today?" The subject is free to respond in almost any way he or she wishes. A closed-ended question on the same topic would be something like this: "Do you feel sick today?" The question tries to limit the subject's response in this case to "yes" or "no."

Open-ended questions are useful in getting people to talk because such questions are less likely to put people on the spot and give them a chance to explain things in their own way. The answers to closed-ended questions are much easier to work with when you analyze the data. It's easy to tally the number of "yes" and "no" responses to a question. You can see how much more difficult it would be to summarize the responses to open-ended questions.

When making up questions for an interview, the researcher tries to keep the questions as unbiased (fair) as possible. If you were conducting political interviews, for example, you would not ask a loaded question like this: "I'm interested in your feelings about Mayor Jones. A lot of people feel he's made a mess of things. Do you think he ought to be reelected?" A poll using a question like this might lead to the conclusion that Mayor Jones's prospects for reelection are rather dismal, but if you're interested in valid data, it's not the way to go.

QUESTIONNAIRES

The questionnaire is sort of like a mass-produced interview. Instead of having an interviewer work one-on-one with a subject, questionnaires can be given to groups of people to fill out or mailed to large numbers of people. Of course, many of the people may not return the questionnaires. When this happens, the researcher has to figure out what kind of a sample he or she is working with. The people who return the questionnaires may be different in important ways from the people who do not. The researcher can only make conclusions about the kinds of people who are well represented in the sample.

As in the interview, it is important to try to use questions in your questionnaire which are not loaded. It's also useful to pretest your questionnaire in advance with a few respondents to make sure they understand the meaning of your questions.

PSYCHOLOGICAL TESTS

There are various kinds of psychological tests. You are probably familiar with tests which measure achievement. These tests are similar to examinations given in a course at school. You have probably taken standardized achievement tests in reading comprehension and mathematics. The questions in such tests were carefully chosen to provide a good sampling of the subject matter. Then the answers of a large number of students were collected. These answers provide a basis for scoring an individual's performance.

In addition to achievement tests, there are tests measuring such things as general intelligence, specific aptitudes, interests, and personality.

INTELLIGENCE TESTS

Intelligence (I.Q.) tests are probably the best-known psychological tests. The tests most widely used today are those developed by David Wechsler, such as the Wechsler Adult Intelligence Scale. This test presents a variety of tasks to the subject. The tasks are believed to test various aspects of intelligence. Included are verbal tasks such as quizzes on vocabulary and information, and performance tests such as putting puzzles together and arranging red and white blocks into certain patterns. While the subject carries out the latter tasks, the examiner often times the performance with a stopwatch. Generally speaking, the faster you can do these tests, the better you score.

The I.Q. tests have proven useful in predicting performance in school and college, so they appear to have some validity as a measure of intelligence. The tests, however, do have limitations. For example, people, such as foreign-born students who have language problems might have difficulty with the vocabulary quiz and certain other parts of the test. The scores may also underestimate the ability of people who come from disadvantaged backgrounds and who therefore have had less exposure to verbal materials.

TESTS FOR APTITUDES AND INTERESTS

Some of the tests for specific abilities (aptitudes) include those for mechanical reasoning, spatial relations, clerical skills, computer operation, music, and art. The United States Army has used a wide-ranging aptitude test to help select people for different kinds of training.

Among the most widely used tests of interests is the Vocational Interest Blank (VIB) developed originally by E.K. Strong in the 1920's. The test is usually given by guidance counselors to students interested in choosing careers. The test scores enable the counselor to tell students if their interests resemble the interests of people who are working in certain occupations (for example, lawyers, doctors, architects, army officers, veterinarians). If the student's interests are similar to those of the people working in a particular field, it is believed that the student will be comfortable working in that field.

Betty provides an example of the use of tests in vocational guidance. Betty always loved to work with animals and wanted to be a veterinarian. Her guidance counselor gave her aptitude tests which indicated she had the ability to do very well in college and the VIB which indicated her interests were very similar to those of practicing veterinarians. For Betty, the tests helped confirm that she was on the right track.

PERSONALITY TESTS

Many personality tests rely on the subject's "self-report." In this way they are much like questionnaires. Subjects may be asked whether they feel angry, depressed, or whatever. Such tests have been criticized on the grounds that some subjects may not give truthful answers. This would diminish the test's validity.

One of the most widely used self-report measures of personality is called the *Minnesota Multiphasic Personality Inventory*. (Most psychologists simply refer to the test as the MMPI.) Many of the questions on the MMPI deal with symptoms of emotional and mental problems such as feeling depressed or hearing voices. High scores on the test suggest that the person may be having psychological difficulties.

Another type of personality test uses what is called the projective technique. **Projective tests** do not usually ask the subject for yes or no answers. Instead, the examiner presents incomplete or ambiguous materials to the subject. This allows the subject to "project" parts of his or her own experience and personality onto the materials. One widely used projective test is called the **Thematic Apperception Test**. The test consists of a series of drawings. A drawing might show a boy with a violin or a young woman in a field. The subject is asked to make up a story about the drawing. Since the content of the story is only partially suggested by the picture and comes in part from the person's experience, the story reveals information about the person's personality.

Probably the best-known projective test is the **Rorschach test**. The Rorschach test consists of a series of cards, each one showing a different picture of an inkblot. Subjects are asked what they see as they look at each card in the series. People respond in different ways. For example, some people focus on a few big objects; other people report on many small details. Some people may pay attention to the shape or form of objects they see in the inkblot. Other people may pay more attention to color when it is present in the blot. Some psychologists feel they can learn a great deal about the way the subject views the world from the responses to the Rorschach. However, others believe that convincing data for the validity of the Rorschach is lacking. These psychologists think that the test should not be given great credence.

QUANTIFICATION

Let's return to our study at the Red Robin Day Care Center where you and your co-worker Ben are looking at a child at play. Let's say both you and Ben rate the child "very aggressive." We might ask at this point: Very aggressive compared to what? And how much is very aggressive? Can you put some number on it—some quantitative measure?

Let's answer the first question. When we say very aggressive, we usually are comparing the person with other people. In this case, we're comparing the child with other children who may be more aggressive or less aggressive. Imagine our observed child—we'll call him Johnny—going around the room tearing up paper, throwing crayons at the wall, grabbing toys from the other children, and pushing and shoving the smaller children. Compare him with Albert, who sits quietly in the corner and plays with his modeling clay. If an observer were asked to sort the children into two categories, "aggressive" and "nonaggressive," the observer would probably put Johnny in the first category and Albert in the second.

Putting people in categories or classes is the simplest, roughest type of measurement. It is usually referred to as a **nominal** measure. Such measurement, while not very exact, can still be very useful. For example, let's say Ben and you have classified every child in the playroom as aggressive or nonaggressive. Let's say, further, that the psychology professor wants to find out whether the boys or the girls in the room appeared to be more aggressive. The professor can make up a table like this. Let's assume that 22 children (10 boys, 12 girls) were observed together.

	Classified as Aggressive	Classified as Nonaggressive	Total
Boys	8	2	10
Girls	3	9	12

Looking at the table, you can see that there was some tendency for more of the boys (8 out of 10) to be classified as aggressive than the girls (3 out of 12).

Putting people into categories is useful for doing research, but is still a rough kind of measurement. It is something like saying the weather is hot or cold instead of saying that the temperature is 34° Fahrenheit or 2° Celsius. Psychologists, of course, also use more sensitive types of measurement. Ranking people, for example, is a more sensitive measurement than simply classifying them.

Suppose we looked at the children in the playroom and rated Johnny most aggressive. Then suppose we rated James second most aggressive, and then went through the list until we had ranked each child from most to least aggressive. (In some instances you might have a tie.) The list might look something like this:

Rank of Aggressiveness	Name of Child
1	Johnny
2	James
3	David
4	Mary
5	Al
6	Liz
7	Floyd

And so forth until we reached the bottom of the list.

Ranking is more sensitive than using categories. More sensitive still is the scoring of psychological tests. Here it is possible to assign numerical scores to people. It is then possible to compare a person's score with the scores of many other people and say with some precision how the person did.

THEORY BUILDING AND HYPOTHESES

In any science, there is a time for careful observation. After you have made a number of observations, however, you will reach a point where you will try to make sense of them. You will try to figure out what is going on. If you are inspired enough, you may come up with an explanation that can account for your observations. Your explanation may be the beginning of an interesting theory.

In a mystery story, the detective often develops a theory to explain the facts of the case. The detective may then set out to obtain proof for the theory.

Science operates in a somewhat similar way. The theories of science, however, are stated in precise, formal language. Sometimes the theories are stated in mathematical form. An example is Einstein's famous theory stating the equivalence of energy and mass, $E = mc^2$. And scientific theories usually apply to a wide range of events rather than to a single case.

In psychology, there are theories offering explanations for observations about learning, human development, personality, and mental illness.

When you have a theory, you can "reason from" it. That is, you can make deductions. As Columbus might have said, "If the world is indeed round as I theorize, then if I sail due west, I shall eventually return to my starting point." When a deduction takes the form of a prediction that a certain thing will happen under a given set of conditions, it is called a **hypothesis**.

For an example of a hypothesis, let's return to our playroom. The professor observes that many of the children seem unusually aggressive. She wonders why this is so. She recalls a theory which we shall encounter later, in our chapter on motivation, that frustration may be a cause of aggression. She may decide to do a study to explore the sources of the children's frustration. She may even test a specific hypothesis: that reducing the amount of frustration the children feel will reduce the level of aggression in the playroom.

The Experiment

The experiment is the method that will most clearly point out cause-and-effect relationships. The basic idea of the experiment is to introduce a change (something new) into a situation and observe the effects. Let us call this change an experimental manipulation. Suppose the professor wanted to manipulate the situation in the playroom. She would introduce specific changes that would be likely to reduce the amount of frustration the children feel. For example, the professor might decide to start a program in which each child would spend a large amount of time working one-on-one with an adult on pleasant activities. The child would have the undivided attention of the adult.

In order to see whether this manipulation has any effect, you and Ben must observe whether there are changes in the children. In this case, you want particularly to focus on any changes in the level of aggressive behavior.

Suppose we want to calculate whether there is a change in aggressiveness. It will be very useful to obtain a measure of aggressiveness before we perform our experimental manipulation. We'll call this measure our pre-experimental or baseline measure. Sometime after the changes are introduced, we will take a second measure. This will be called our post-experimental or final measure. We can calculate the difference between the two measures to see how much change there is in observed aggressiveness.

CONTROL GROUP

When we perform an experimental manipulation, we would like to think that the change we make is the only thing that's new in the situation, and therefore any changes that occur in the children's aggressiveness are caused by our manipulation. But we can't really be sure of that. Who knows what else is happening to the children? A child might be sick or having a very bad time at home this week. To guard against the unforeseen, the unexpected, and the unknown, we use a *control group* of subjects.

The control group should have the same kinds of subjects in it as the experimental group. Insofar as possible, the control group should get the same treatment the experimental group receives. There is one exception: The control group does not receive the experimental manipulation. Measures of the behavior you are looking for (in this case, aggressiveness) should be taken at the same intervals in both groups. The amount of change measured in the control group can be compared with the amount measured in the experimental group. If the professor's hypothesis is correct, you and Ben should notice a greater change (decrease in aggressiveness) in the experimental group.

RANDOM ASSIGNMENT OF SUBJECTS INTO THE EXPERIMENTAL AND CONTROL GROUPS

In the experiment in the playroom, the subjects were already part of an ongoing group. We would have to find another similar group of children to serve as a control group. In the ideal experiment, the professor wouldn't want to use established groups. Instead, she would make up the groups herself by assigning subjects to the experimental or control group on a *random* (chance) basis. The assignment into one group or the other would be made on the basis of something like a coin flip. This procedure would help her guard against stacking one group or the other with particular types of people, which would influence the results. Using random assignment, each subject has an equal chance to be assigned to the experimental group.

Often, the researcher can't assign subjects randomly, but must use established groups. Then it is a good idea for him to try to show that the experimental and control subjects are similar. He can do this by showing that the groups match up well on such characteristics as age, sex, socioeconomic background and, in this particular experiment, the level of aggressiveness before the experiment.

OTHER CONTROLS AGAINST BIAS

Many forms of *bias* can creep into an experiment, causing distortions in the results. If a researcher uses teenage or adult subjects, the subjects may "catch on" to what the researcher is trying to do. The subject might say to himself, "Oh, she (the experimenter) wants me to do thus and so. O.K., I'll go along." For this reason, psychologists often take steps to disguise the nature of their experiments.

The appearance and behavior of the experimenter might also make a difference in the results. Then, too, if the experimenter is aware of the hypothesis being tested, he might unintentionally do things which would favor certain results.

In setting up an experiment, it is very important for the researcher to consider possible sources of bias in advance. Then he can take steps to try to reduce the bias.

Replication of Results

To **replicate** means to repeat or do again. Suppose you run your study a second time using new subjects and the results are similar. Then you can have increased confidence that you have really found something.

When the report of the study is written up and published in a scientific journal, scientists in other laboratories will be able to try the experiment. If most of the researchers who do the experiment confirm your finding, the finding becomes part of the body of dependable scientific knowledge.

The Use of Statistics

Statistics have two main uses in psychology. The first is to present a more precise description of what the researcher is doing and what she has found. The second is to help evaluate the results of studies—that is, to see whether one has really found an effect or whether the results are best interpreted as simply "chance" events.

DESCRIPTIVE STATISTICS

Statistics used for description are helpful in summarizing data. They allow the researcher to say in a nutshell, "This is what I have found."

Let's say in our study of the children in the playroom that you have followed seven children for a total time of one hour each. During that time, you have clocked the amount of time each child was engaged in constructive social play. When you posted your data, it looked something like the following list.

Name of Child	Number of Minutes of Social Play
Floyd	15
Liz	10
Al	9
Mary	14
David	6
James	7
Johnny	0

Let's see if we can make some overall statements about what you found.

MEASURES OF AVERAGE

First, we might want to know the average amount of time the children spent in social play. One of the most widely used measures of average is the **mean**. To obtain this figure, simply add up all your scores (15 + 10 + 9 + 14 + 6 + 7 + 0 which equals 61). Then divide by the number of scores (7). The mean amount of time the children spent in social play was 8.7 minutes.

Another useful measure of average is the **median**. If you ranked the scores of a group of subjects, the median would be the numerical value that would cut this list of scores into halves. As a handy rule to remember, if there are an odd number of scores, say 7 or 9, the median, is the middle score. If there are an even number of scores, say 6 or 8, the median is the mean of the two middle scores.

As an example, let's find the median value for time spent in social play for our children at the day care center. First let's rank these times from lowest to highest, like this: 0, 6, 7, 9, 10, 14, 15. As there are an odd number of scores, 7, let's find the middle score. You can see the middle score is 9 (0, 6, 7 fall below this number; 10, 14, 15 are above it). The mean and median may differ somewhat, but both are measures of average.

A third, less often used measure of average is the **mode**. The mode is the score that occurs the most times in a group of scores. If you had the following scores 3, 4, 6, 6, 6, 9, 12, the mode would be 6.

MEASURES OF VARIABILITY

Now let us turn to the idea of variability. Let's compare the data you obtained on the seven children in the playroom with observations of a similar group of children.

Number of Minutes of Observed Social Play			
Children in Our Playroom		Children in Another Playroom	
Floyd	15	Janet	7
Liz	10	Betty	10
Al	9	Alice	8
Mary	14	Ken	10
David	6	Doris	8
James	7	Andy	11
Johnny	0	Jim	9

If you look at the data from the two groups of children, you will find that the median value for both groups is 9. However, the figures in the first group seem more spread out. The high and low points for the scores in the first group are 0 and 15, while the high and low points in the second group are 7 and 11. We say that the scores in the first group have a *range* of 15 (15 − 0 = 15), while the scores in the second group have a range of 4 (11 − 7 = 4). The range of scores in the first group is much greater than in the second group.

The range is one measure of **variability**. Variability has to do with how far a group of scores are spread apart. As we saw from the data, the range is a measure of the difference

between the highest and lowest scores. However, a more often used measure of variability is the standard deviation. The standard deviation is based upon how far each score in the group is from the mean of the group. The more distant the scores are from the mean, the larger the standard deviation.

STATISTICS USED TO EVALUATE DIFFERENCES AND TEST HYPOTHESES

In the study of the children in the playroom, the professor was trying to find out whether introducing a program in which each child got the undivided attention of one adult for a period of time would reduce the amount of aggression in the children. As a researcher, she was interested in not only the children you were observing, but also interested in whether the findings could be applied (generalized) to other children. Could she expect the same results with other groups of children under similar circumstances? If she could, she would have made a meaningful contribution to the fields of psychology and preschool education.

Statistics help us answer such questions. Statistics help us decide whether the differences found by a study are clear enough that we can believe we would find the same results in similar samples.

In practice, the question boils down to whether the findings meet a test of statistical significance. The phrase "statistically significant" usually means that the odds that chance could produce your results are only 5 in 100— or, if you use a very tough standard, 1 in 100.

That sounds good, but you may be uncertain about the meaning of chance results. Just what are chance results?

Perhaps the most obvious illustration of chance results is the coin flip. If you flip a coin 10 times, you would expect to get 5 heads and 5 tails. But if you got 6 heads and 4 tails, would you think it very surprising? Not at all. It's a matter of chance to get a few more heads or a few more tails. But if you got 10 heads in a row, you'd think something was mighty funny. You'd say, "The chances are pretty slim that this could happen," and you'd be right. Better look at that coin. It may have two heads on it and no tails.

As we said, statistical tests tell us how likely it is that our results could arise by chance. These tests are not based on a few flips of the coin, as in our example, but on tables of probability based on much larger numbers. The tests can be run on a pocket calculator or a computer.

Suppose the professor tested the difference between the experimental and control groups using the data on aggression and found that the results could be caused by chance (like 6 heads and 4 tails on the coin flip). She would have to write off the difference as meaningless. However, if she found that the difference was statistically significant, she could conclude that the research team had probably uncovered a real effect. Then she would have to look closely at the finding and try to interpret it. She would consider such questions as: What does this finding mean? What alternative explanations might there be for the finding? What importance does the finding have?

CORRELATION

In psychological studies, you will often see a statistic called a *correlation coefficient*. **Correlation** measures the strength of the relationship between two other measures. Let's try to make this clear with an example.

At Northside High School, the psychology teacher wanted to find out whether there was any relationship between the number of hours students put in studying and their grades on an examination. For two weeks he asked students to keep a log of the number of hours they spent studying. Then he gave the students the examination. Let's imagine that the following numbers are a sample of his data.

Student	Total Number of Hours Student Reported Studying Psychology over a Two-Week Period	Score on Exam
Joe	5	75
Alice	3	70
Debbie	10	93
George	2	65
Ruth	0	60
Alex	15	97
Grady	6	80
Ian	4	82
Eve	18	95

As you look at these imaginary data, what trend do you see? The people who studied the least, like Ruth and George, got the lowest scores. The people who studied the most, like Alex, got the highest scores, and the people who studied a moderate amount got the in-between scores. According to these data, the number of hours studied was positively related to (correlated with) the grades obtained on the exam.

If you plotted the data on graph paper, the graph would look something like this:

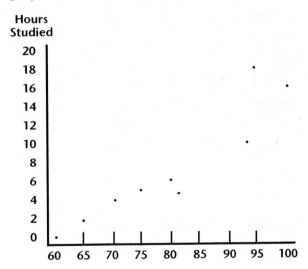

Notice the upward drift (from left to right) when correlations are positive. When correlations are negative, you notice a drift in the opposite direction, like this:

Can you think of a situation where two measures would have a negative relationship? How about the number of excess pounds a person is carrying and the time it takes the person to run a 400-meter race? Or how about alcohol intake and driving ability? In both examples, as one measure goes up, the other goes down.

When we find that two measures are correlated, it does not mean that we have found a cause-and-effect relationship. A correlation only means that two measures are related. Cause and effect is best established by very careful experiments in which possible causes are introduced and the effects observed.

Meta Analysis

Researchers routinely apply statistical procedures to their data to describe and evaluate what they have found. Over the years researchers have carried out many thousands of studies, reporting their findings in psychological journals. As a result, there is now a large amount of information available on many interesting problems. The question arises, Is there some way one can put all of the studies that bear on a particular problem together and summarize what has been found? Better yet, can we put this summary statement in a quantitative form for more precision? In recent years, a technique called **meta analysis** has been developed which allows one to consider the findings of a great number of different studies together, and to calculate what the overall effect seems to be.

In carrying out a meta analysis, the researcher first tries to locate every study—published or unpublished—that bears on the question he or she is interested in. For example, the researcher might be interested in the question, How effective is psychotherapy in treating depression? After locating as many research reports as possible, the researcher looks at each study individually. To obtain a measure of the effect size for a given study, the researcher notes the mean outcome reported for the group treated with psychotherapy and the mean outcome reported for the control group. Calculating the difference between these means and dividing by the standard deviation of the control group gives the researcher a measure of the effect size found in the study. The researcher then takes the effect size calculated for each study and computes a mean effect size for the entire body of studies.

Researchers have differed somewhat in the way they carry out meta analysis, but it has become a widely used tool in psychology. Meta analysis has been carried out on topics ranging from the effects of smoking cessation programs to the effects of computer-based instruction on achievement.

Some Questions and Activities

1. Can you think of some theories in fields other than psychology, such as physics, chemistry, astronomy, or biology?

2. Would you like to get an idea of what it is like being an interviewer? If so, interview one of your classmates about his or her use of leisure time. Make up ten questions about sports, hobbies, recreation. Put the questions into an order that has a good, conversational flow to it. Then try out your interview, keeping notes on the responses.

3. Here is a way to get a better feel for some of the statistical terms we mentioned. Temperature readings change from day to day. The high and low temperatures for the day are often posted in the daily newspaper. Keep a record of the daily *high* temperature for a week. Then calculate the mean and median high temperature readings for the week. Also calculate the range of these readings.

4. We mentioned projective techniques. One projective technique is to present the subject with beginnings of sentences and ask the subject to complete them. For example:

    I like _____ .

    I dislike _____ .

    My mother and I _____ .

    Try completing the above sentences. Then make up five sentence-beginnings of your own. Try them out on yourself and then on a classmate. What similarities and differences do you find?

5. Another projective technique involves making up stories after looking at a picture. Look at the picture at the right and try making up a story. Ask yourself: What is happening now? What has gone on before? How is the story going to come out?

Test Your Knowledge

Read each statement and decide whether it is TRUE or FALSE. **Write your answers on a separate sheet of paper.**

1. One way of checking the reliability of a psychological instrument is to see whether the instrument gives consistent readings over time.

2. When making observations in psychology, it is usually unimportant to obtain a representative sampling of the subject's behavior.

3. Intelligence tests do not have any ability to predict performance in school.

4. Intelligence test scores may be misleading in the case of people who come from disadvantaged backgrounds.

5. The Thematic Apperception Test is an example of a test which uses the projective technique.

6. Ranking people is a less sensitive type of measurement than grouping them into two or three categories.

7. The mean and the median are both measures of average.

8. Variability refers to the scattering of scores.

9. The standard deviation is a measure of variability.

10. An example of a negative correlation is the relationship between amount of cigarette smoking and life expectancy.

11. The MMPI is a well-known aptitude test.

12. The answers to open-ended questions are much easier to analyze than the responses to closed-ended questions.

13. A hypothesis is a prediction that something specific will occur under certain conditions.

14. The observer in psychology only pays attention to what is said—never to non-verbal behaviors such as gestures and expressions.

15. The researcher using questionnaires must be concerned about having a representative sample if only certain kinds of people return the questionnaire.

16. A standardized achievement test permits the comparison of an individual's score with those of a large number of other people.

17. Psychologists use only one method of data gathering, the controlled experiment.

18. Reviewing the research efforts of others in professional journals is part of the early research process.

19. The statistical technique that allows researchers to examine the results of many studies together is called meta analysis.

CHAPTER 3

Biology and Behavior:

Some Thumbnail Sketches

A knowledge of the workings of the human body can help us develop a deeper understanding of human behavior. The nervous system, the sensory receptors, and the brain play crucial roles in determining what we perceive in the world and how we react. In this book, where we are taking a broad look at the field of psychology, we can only introduce the subject of the biological foundations of behavior. What we will try to do is provide thumbnail sketches of some of these biological processes. We hope that you will become interested in the subject, and will increase your knowledge by reading further in *physiology* (the study of the functions and processes of the body).

The plan of this chapter is to discuss the nervous system and our most important sensory receptors, the eyes and ears. Then we shall look at the brain. There will then be a discussion of sleep and dreams. We shall close with a discussion of the *autonomic nervous system*, and of two interesting applications, the **polygraph** (or lie detector) test and **biofeedback**.

The Nervous System

The nervous system is the body's mechanism for processing information from the outside world and controlling our reactions to the world. The nervous system controls and coordinates our perceptions, our thinking, and our actions.

The nervous system is divided into different parts. The *central nervous system* consists of the brain and the spinal cord. The *peripheral nervous system* links the central nervous system to the other parts of the body. It functions somewhat like a feeder network of highways moving in and out of the central city. Sensory nerves run in from the eyes and ears and other sensory receptors to the central nervous system, bringing information. Motor nerves begin in the central nervous system and run to the muscles, dispatching signals for action. There are also nerves from the autonomic nervous system. These originate in the bundles of spinal nerves and travel to the internal organs of the body such as the heart and the stomach.

The nervous system is made up of billions of nerve cells called **neurons**. A neuron has a cell body with a long fiber called an **axon** extending outward. Extending from other points on the cell body are short fibers in the shape of branches called **dendrites**. Think of the dendrites as something like the branches of a bush or tree. An electrical-chemical signal (the nervous impulse) comes into the neuron through the dendrites and is passed along through the long axon to adjoining nerve cells. The area in which two nerve cells come into contact is called the **synapse**. There is a gap of about one millionth of an inch between the nerve cells.

The transmission of the nerve impulse across the synapse is accomplished with the release of certain chemicals called **neurotransmitters**. The impulse then moves through the cell to the next synapse. In this way the impulse moves across a network of nerve cells. The process is somewhat like an electrical current passing through a wire, but is much slower. This is because the nerve cells themselves are involved in producing the flow of current; an electric wire just conducts the current.

A certain amount of energy is needed to activate (fire) a neuron. Once this level of energy is applied to the cell, the neuron responds at maximum levels. Applying higher levels of energy would not change the neuron's performance. This is the "all or none" law. If the neuron is activated at all, it is activated fully.

When we use the term *nerve*, we are talking about a group of nerve fibers bound together, often protected by a sheath made of a white, fatty substance called **myelin**. For example, two of the peripheral nerves are the optic nerve, which links the brain and the eye, and the auditory nerve, which links the brain and the ear.

The Sensory Receptors

The *eye*, one of our most important sense organs, is the sensory receptor that processes light. The eye is a multilayered structure. Some of its parts are a tough outer coating ("the white of the eye"); the *cornea*, which transmits light to the inside; the *pupil* of the iris, which adjusts in size to regulate the amount of light coming in. The lens focuses the light on the *retina*, which contains the receptor cells. In the retina, a thin sheet at the back of the eye, are two kinds of receptor cells, *rods* and *cones*.

The rods and the cones have different roles in vision. When the light is bright, as it is on a sunny afternoon, the cones do the work. The cones are also responsible for color vision. At night, as light dims, the rods take over. The rods do not distinguish among colors, so what you see at night appears to be like the picture on an old black and white TV set.

When you walk into a dimly lit room like a movie theater, you will notice that there is a period of time during which you can hardly see anything. During this period, the eye is switching from one system of cells to the other. This process is called adaptation to the dark.

The retina contains millions of receptor cells. It also contains layers of nerve cells. The optic nerve begins with these cells in the retina. From the eye, the optic nerve transmits the information processed by the receptor cells to the brain.

The ear is the receptor that registers sound waves. Sound waves travel into the ear and pass through the *auditory canal* to a membrane called the *tympanic membrane*. The sound waves cause the membrane to vibrate. The vibrations flow across three small bones in the middle ear and then are transmitted to the inner ear. The inner ear contains several canals filled with fluid. One of these canals, the *cochlear canal*, contains the organ of hearing. Rows of hair cells are stimulated by vibrations in the canal fluid. The hair cells (receptor cells) are connected to the auditory nerve, which transmits the signals to the brain.

The sense of smell depends on receptors located high in the nasal cavity. The sense of taste is based on receptors on the surface of the tongue. These receptors enable us to distinguish salty, sweet, sour, and bitter tastes. Various other sensations come from receptors located in the skin. The sense of touch is the most obvious. But think of the sensation when you accidentally burn yourself, or when you plunge into cold water when you take that first swim in the summer. Then there are those more vague sensations that come from our muscles. Close your eyes; try stretching your right arm as hard as you can and then relaxing it by your side. Can you feel the difference? The information you are registering comes from what is called the **kinesthetic sense**.

The Brain

The brain has been described as extending out of the spinal cord like a large bulb. The adult brain weighs about three pounds and consists of nerve cells, supporting cells, and the blood vessels which supply them.

You may have heard the phrase *gray matter* when someone referred to the brain. Actually, a portion of the material of the spinal cord and brain is called gray matter—nerve fiber that is not covered by a sheath. There is also *white matter*—nerve fiber covered by a sheath of myelin.

The brain itself is divided into a number of parts. The largest of these parts, accounting for about 85 percent of brain weight, is called the **cerebrum**. Some of the smaller parts of the brain are the *pons*, the *cerebellum* and the *medulla oblongata*.

A Sketch of the Brain

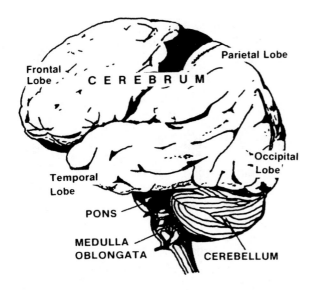

The largest section of the brain, the cerebrum, consists of two hemispheres. Think of cutting a globe in half. The outer layer of these hemispheres, called the *cerebral cortex*, is not smooth like a crystal ball, but is wrinkled and folded. The cerebrum has been described as resembling the inside of a shelled walnut. Like an accordion, the brain squeezes a lot of material into a small space.

Each of the hemispheres of the brain is divided into areas called lobes. The lobes are separated by deep cracks, or fissures, at the surface. These fissures are somewhat like the canyons or crevices you might encounter when you are hiking in rocky terrain. The lobe in the front of the brain is called, appropriately, the *frontal lobe*. Below the *frontal lobe* is the *temporal lobe*. As you move from the frontal lobe toward the back of the cerebrum you encounter the *parietal* and *occipital lobes*. A fifth lobe, the *insula*, is located in the part of the brain called the cerebellum.

By stimulating the different areas of the cerebrum electrically, and through studies of brain-injured patients, it is possible to learn something about what these areas are doing for you. Researchers have given psychological and neurological tests to patients with lesions (damage) in certain areas of the brain to see how their performance has been affected by the particular type of brain injury. Let's use as an example a study of patients who have lesions in the frontal lobe.

The study looked at the effects of the lesion on memory. The test for memory, as described by Ethan Gorenstein, went like this: "The materials are 35 cards bearing either a plus or a minus sign. The examiner shows the cards one by one while the subject must state the sign that appeared two cards previous to the one currently being shown." To give a correct answer, the subject must remember the sign that is two cards removed. The researchers found that patients with frontal lobe lesions made more errors on the task than control groups. It appears that these patients had difficulty holding such information in their memories when exposed to the intervening cards.

As a second illustration, let's consider damage to the parietal lobe. Research suggests that such damage may cause loss of the sensation of touch. Bette Erwin and Gerald Rosenbaum gave some blindfolded patients with parietal lobe damage a standard neurological test. They spoke to the patients as follows: "I want you to give me your right hand palm up. Now, I'm going to give each of your fingers a number. This will be (1) [touches thumb], and this will be (2), (3), (4) and (5) [moving from index finger to little finger]. When I touch your finger, I want you to tell me which one I'm touching. Ready?"

The patients made significantly more errors than control groups, demonstrating loss of the sensation of touch.

We mentioned the relatively small area of the brain called the cerebellum. It is located in the lower part of the brain, behind the brain stem. One of its important functions is to coordinate muscular movements.

The medula oblongata is an extension of the spinal cord into the back of the head. There are nerve centers here which control such functions as breathing, swallowing, and heart rate.

In a section of the brain called the *diencephalon* (the upper part of the brain stem), there are two interesting structures called the *thalamus* and the *hypothalamus*. The hypothalamus exerts control over hunger and thirst and is involved in such emotions as rage and fear. It is also one of the brain structures that plays a role in the control of sleep. When you find yourself too tired to get up for school in the morning and need an excuse (your usual one about the car breaking down is running thin), try blaming your hypothalamus.

The Split Brain

One of the most fascinating recent developments in the field of psychology has been the discovery that the two hemispheres of the brain seem to control different aspects of thinking. This discovery has led to the notion of the *split brain*. As we discuss this idea, we should remember that the two halves of the brain are connected by a bridge called the *corpus callosum*, and that thus all parts of the brain are connected by the nerve network to all other parts. This bridge makes it possible for the two parts of the brain to function in a coordinated fashion.

Language abilities and analytical thought are among the functions which scientists now believe belong to the left side of the brain. The right side of the brain seems to be the focus of perceptual skills, and less thought-out, more emotional reactions. Perhaps it is the left side of the brain that dominates the work of the scholar or diplomat, and the right side that plays a greater role for the creative artist.

When one side of the brain is damaged, it appears possible for the other side of the brain to take over some functions that it normally does not perform. For example, language is normally a function of the left side of the brain. Some researchers have reported that the right hemisphere was able to compensate for left hemisphere damage in children learning language.

When the connection between the two sides of the brain has been severed, the two sides will function as separate brains within the same person. Some epileptic patients underwent such a severing operation to stop severely disabling symptoms that could not be con-trolled by medicine, and were left in this rather strange multiple-brain condition. Roger Sperry, who has been a pioneer in the exploration of the split brain, summarized some of the effects of the operation this way:

> *One of the more striking features of this syndrome [condition] may be summarized as an apparent doubling in most of the realms of conscious awareness. Instead of the normally unified stream of consciousness, these patients behave in many ways as if they have two independent streams of conscious awareness, one in each hemisphere, each of which is cut off from and out of contact with the mental experiences of the other.*

Each hemisphere ends up with its own perceptions, its own impulses to act, and its own memory. One hemisphere appears to be unaware of what the other hemisphere is doing.

Sleep and Dreams

We have stated that the nervous impulse is an electrical-chemical signal transmitted through systems of nerve cells. One can take measurements of the electrical activity of the brain using a device called an *electroencephalograph* (EEG). Small electrodes are pasted onto the scalp. Signals from the brain (changes in electrical polarity) are transmitted from the electrodes, amplified by the machine, and recorded by a pen on moving chart paper. The up and down pen motions look like waves. These electrical changes recorded from the brain are called brain waves.

The EEG is one of the recording devices that is used in the sleep laboratory. As the name implies, the sleep laboratory is a laboratory devoted to the scientific study of sleep.

Let's imagine for a moment that you have volunteered to be a subject in a sleep laboratory. You are comfortably dressed in sleepwear and are about to depart for the Land of Nod. However, there are a few gadgets attached to you. First there are the electrodes that are attached to an EEG machine to record your brain waves. Then there are some electrodes pasted around your eyes to record eye movements. Finally, there are devices to measure your breathing and heart rate. They've wired you up, but you're a good sleeper and you can sleep anywhere.

As you drift into sleep, you pass into what sleep researchers call Stage One sleep. Your body muscles relax, breathing becomes more even, your heart rate slows. At this point, the brain waves recorded by the EEG are relatively small, and the waves are uneven.

Soon you drift into Stage Two sleep. The brain waves grow larger. There are sometimes rapid bursts of activity called spindles.

Now you are drifting into a deeper sleep called Stage Three. There are still spindles recording on the chart paper, but there are also large, slow waves. Your muscles relax further, breathing is even, your heart rate continues to fall.

Now you lapse into Stage Four, the deepest stage of sleep. When your sleep reaches this point, a burglar might be roaming around your bedroom carting off your stereo set and you might not hear anything. You look very still. The EEG recordings show a steady pattern of slow, curvy waves.

You will not stay in this stage of deep sleep very long. Instead, you will return to other stages of sleep, moving from one stage to the other in cycles. This happens throughout the night.

During the light stage of sleep, a very interesting thing happens. The chart paper that has been dutifully monitoring the movements of your eyes suddenly begins to record *rapid eye movements* (REMs for short). The suggestion is that you are watching something. After a few minutes of these rapid eye movements, someone awakens you.

"I was dreaming," you say, yawning. You recount a dream about being late for class. You were trying to climb a hill. You were running as fast as you could. You mention some other characters in the dream—your mother and a stranger you didn't recognize then you drift off to sleep again.

During the night you will experience additional periods of rapid eye movements. If you are awakened during one of these periods, chances are you will report you are having a dream. At this point your memory for the dream will be much clearer than it would be the following morning, and you are more likely to report that the dream was in color.

During periods of sleep in which you are not experiencing rapid eye movements, you may do some dreaming, but the quality of the dream is likely to be less vivid and more like ordinary thought.

You will probably experience about five REM periods during a night, each one up to twenty minutes or so in length. You may experience a dream during each of these periods. Your memory for these events the next morning, however, may be very poor. Some people seldom remember their dreams.

There has been a great deal of theory and speculation about the meaning of dreams. Many psychologists believe that the content of dreams and a person's associations with these dreams offer valuable clues about problems that the person has not fully resolved in waking life. The analysis of dreams is often a very interesting part of psychotherapy.

INSOMNIA

Do you know a person who suffers from insomnia? Insomnia is not being able to sleep well at night. Judging from the billions of barbiturates and sedatives manufactured by drug companies every year, a very large number of people have this problem.

Researchers talk about three types of insomnia. The first is difficulty in falling asleep (sleep-onset insomnia). The second is trouble staying asleep. The third is waking up too early.

Chris is a good example of a person who suffers from sleep-onset insomnia. Chris worries a good deal about what's going on in her life. She worries about her grades at school, about her boyfriend Kevin, and about what the future holds in store for her. When she goes to bed at night these problems seem to go round and round in her mind like a broken record. She just can't seem to fall asleep. The harder she tries to fall asleep, the less success she seems to have. In the morning she wakes up feeling tired and doesn't seem to have much energy for school. Her mother wants Chris to see the family doctor and try some sleeping pills.

There have been a number of studies of sleep-onset insomniacs in the sleep laboratory. Before people who have this problem fall asleep, their level of physiological activity appears to be higher than that of people in control groups. Measures of muscle tension taken from the scalp are higher and heart rate may be faster until the onset of sleep. Then the differences between the insomniacs and the people in the control groups appear to fade out.

When given psychological tests, insomniacs usually report higher levels of distress. They often worry a great deal. Their distress is made worse by the insomnia, and the two conditions, psychological distress and insomnia, make each other worse. Insomnia is very often associated with depression.

One interesting finding from sleep laboratories is that people suffering from insomnia may actually be sleeping a good deal more than they think they are. The condition often seems worse to the insomniac than it is.

The Autonomic Nervous System

When we discussed the nervous system, we focused on signals coming in from the sensory receptors to the brain. In the brain, the signals were processed, and appropriate signals were sent to the muscles of the body, causing them to react. We also mentioned briefly that signals may also be sent to the internal organs of the body through the autonomic nervous system.

The autonomic nervous system consists of two parts, the **sympathetic division** and the **parasympathetic division**. These systems tend to act in opposite ways. The sympathetic division responds when you are faced with a stress-provoking situation. Imagine you are in a situation of physical danger or are about to give a report in class for which you are unprepared. Or imagine you are in the middle of a heated argument.

In situations like these, the sympathetic nervous system passes signals to the body putting it on an emergency footing. These signals are something like the warning sirens that the crew of a warship hears when there is an imminent danger of attack.

In response to the signals of the sympathetic nervous system, the heart beats faster (sometimes you can feel your heart pounding), breathing is faster, blood supply to the muscles is increased, digestion is inhibited, and the pupils of the eyes dilate. The adrenal glands start releasing substances, including epinephrine, into the bloodstream, which speed up these reactions. Have you ever heard the phrase, "get the adrenalin flowing"? Adrenalin is another name for epinephrine. The action of the sympathetic nervous system, then, puts the person into a heightened readiness posture, sometimes referred to as the "fight or flight" reaction.

When the emergency is over, the parasympathetic branch responds, sending out signals to these organs to resume business as usual. The heart returns to its normal rate, breathing eases, the pupils shrink, and the stomach goes back to the business of digesting one's lunch. The function of the parasympathetic division is to maintain these normal body functions.

THE POLYGRAPH

We know that stress-provoking situations will cause the sympathetic nervous system to send signals to the internal organs of the body. We can measure some of the changes in the action of these organs with a machine called the polygraph. The polygraph measures blood pressure on a continuous basis. In addition, it records two measures of breathing, one from the stomach and one from the chest. Finally, it records the **galvanic skin response** (GSR), a measure of changes in the electrical conductivity of the skin.

When a polygraph is attached to a person, it makes continuous recordings of these physiological measures on chart paper. If there are sudden shifts in the pattern of these recordings, it is assumed that something that the person is thinking or feeling is stress provoking.

The lie detector test (*lie detector* is a popular name for the polygraph) is based on this idea. The basic procedure of the lie detector test is to first obtain baseline recordings of a persons physiological responses while the person is answering neutral questions. Then the person is asked to answer a series of perhaps a dozen yes or no questions. Some of the questions may be neutral. For example, the examiner might ask questions like these: "Your name is Richard Johnson?" "You live at 75 Hastings Lane?"

Other questions may be emotionally loaded but not related to the case. For example, the examiner might ask, "Mr. Johnson, have you ever told a lie to anyone?" Such loaded questions serve as a control; they gauge the person's levels of emotional response to potentially stress-provoking questions. Finally, there are the critical questions related to the case: "Did you open Mrs. Alderman's desk on Thursday afternoon and look through her papers?"

Experimental studies indicate that the polygraph will show greater physiological changes when one tells a lie than when one responds to control questions. However, the machine is not 100 percent accurate. For example, in one study it was found that the best combination of physiological indicators identified stealers and nonstealers with an 80 percent accuracy rate. This means that 20 percent of the people in the study were incorrectly classified. Defenders of the test claim higher rates of accuracy than the above while opponents claim that the test is even less accurate. Because there is a margin of error in the lie detector test, the results are usually not allowed as evidence in court. However, some U.S. government agencies and some businesses have gone ahead and used the polygraph in questioning their employees.

BIOFEEDBACK

It was once thought that the autonomic nervous system operated completely outside of conscious control. The system was thought of as totally automatic: the person could not consciously alter the workings of these internal organs. The discovery of biofeedback showed that this idea was incorrect. Within certain biological limits, it is possible to exert some deliberate control over indicators such as heart rate and blood pressure.

Machines which are used in biofeedback research or therapy communicate to the subject what certain physiological indicators are doing over a period of time. These indicators might be heart rate, blood pressure, or a measure of muscular tension. The machine puts out continuous signals which tell the person whether a particular measure is going up or down.

Let's look at two examples of biofeedback therapy, the first attempting to modify heart rate; the second, muscle tension. Imagine for the moment that you are sitting in a comfortable chair. A technician has pasted electrodes to your lower ribs. These electrodes are attached to a machine which continuously records your heart rate. A display panel in front of you contains a row of unlit white lights. Every time your heart beats, the lights begin to light up one at a time. They light up one after the other, very rapidly, as if they are sweeping across the screen. After each heartbeat, the lights vanish and start again. The sweep of lights across the screen tells you how fast your heart is beating. If your heartbeat slows down, the sweep of lights gets longer. The technician tells you to try to increase the length of the sweep of the lights; the technician sets a target and tells you to make the light sweep past it. After a while, you find that you are able to do this—the light sweeps past the target. You continue to try to do whatever it is that keeps the signal sweeping farther. In doing this, you are exercising some control over your heart rate, though you may not be precisely sure how.

Let's now consider muscle tension. Many people have problems relating to muscle tension. Biofeedback is one means of teaching people how to relax their muscles. The biofeedback procedure we're going to look at now uses a machine called an electromyograph, which records the level of muscle tension.

Imagine that once again you are the subject. This time you are resting on a couch in a dimly lit room. Electrodes pasted on your forehead are attached to the electromyograph. The machine continuously records tiny muscle movements in your forehead.

The technician may give you instructions like those used by Robert Coursey in one biofeedback study: "You have been connected to a machine which measures muscle tension. The machine then transforms your muscle tension into a tone, so that the more relaxed you are, the lower the tone. Your job, then, is to lower the tone you hear as much as possible by relaxing. The more you relax, the lower the tone will be . . . ."

You will probably find that you are able to begin relaxing and that the tone indeed gets lower. You continue to do more of what you are doing and the lower tones signal that your muscles are becoming more and more relaxed.

In both of the situations we've just described, you learn to control your own physiological responses using information sent back to you from your body. You are getting *feedback* from your biology hence the term biofeedback.

At this point, we do not fully understand how biofeedback works. One theory is that during and following biofeedback training, the subject becomes more aware of or sensitive to internal sensations of the body. He learns to tell the difference between those sensations which are associated with the desired response (for example, less muscle tension) and those which are not. Paying careful attention to sensations from the body that you would normally ignore may be an important part of the process involved in biofeedback.

A Polygraph Problem

Mr. Jamison was the manager of a small polygraph testing business. He did most of his work for retail stores, testing new employees. One day a high school senior, Jim Hamilton, came into his office asking to take a lie detector test, hoping to establish his innocence on an accusation of drug possession. In brief, the facts of the case were as follows.

On the first of March, Mrs. Andrews, a biology teacher, noticed some students on the edge of the school grounds smoking. As she walked by the students, she became convinced that they were using marijuana. She called the school principal, Mr. Jackson, who ordered a drug sweep through the school. Desks and lockers were searched. Many of the students and some parents became very angry, saying such searches were illegal. Among the drugs uncovered were two joints of marijuana in Jim Hamilton's desk in his homeroom. Jim, an honor student and a member of the track team, said he never used drugs. He said that other students using the desk during the day must have left the joints there.

One key piece of information had not been revealed to Jim. The drugs had been found stashed in a small box of Bandaids. This information had been given to Mr. Jamison, the manager of the polygraph testing firm.

Imagine for a moment that you are Mr. Jamison: (1) What would you tell Jim about the validity of the polygraph test for detecting lies? (2) What would you tell him about the test's usefulness as evidence in court? (3) Let's say that Jim was determined to go ahead with the test. Make up seven questions with yes or no answers that you would ask Jim while his physiological responses were being monitored by the polygraph.

Some Questions and Activities

1. Do you want to learn more about the structure of the brain or nervous system? Go to the library and look through an encyclopedia or a book on anatomy. Try making some sketches of the nervous system. Perhaps you might want to try your hand at making a model of the brain using modeling materials. It might be the first step in your career as a surgeon.

2. Now that you have shown your artistic skill, how about making sketches of the eye and the ear?

3. Many insomniacs take sleeping pills to help them get a night's rest. What do you know about these pills? Ask your pharmacist what the active ingredients are in over-the-counter sleeping aids. Ask your pharmacist or doctor what, if any, problems there are with taking prescription sleeping pills.

4. Many people are interested in their dreams. If you are curious about your own dreams, try writing them down as soon as you wake up in the morning. Do this for a few days. When you have recorded two or three dreams, try answering these questions.

   a. Did you have this experience: You knew you had had a dream, but by the time the morning came, the dream had almost entirely faded from your memory?

   b. Were any of your dreams in color or were they all in black and white?

   c. Did your dreams take you to any unusual settings (desert islands, beaches, airplanes in flight, etc.) or did they all happen in your usual surroundings?

   d. Were all the people in your dreams people you know, or were there strangers present?

   e. Did you recognize any of these dreams as being dreams you've had before? (These are called recurrent dreams.)

Test Your Knowledge

Read each statement and decide whether it is TRUE or FALSE. **Write your answers on a separate sheet of paper.**

1. One of the ways scientists learn about the functions of different parts of the brain is to study people with brain damage.

2. The two hemispheres of the brain are not connected and therefore operate as two totally independent units.

3. The machine used to measure brain waves is called an electroencephalograph.

4. Periods of rapid eye movement during sleep are usually accompanied by dreams.

5. The autonomic nervous system is the system that brings information in from the sensory receptors to the brain.

6. Signals from the sympathetic division of the autonomic nervous system will cause an increase in heart rate and faster breathing.

7. Studies indicate that lie detector tests are about 99 percent accurate.

8. Using biofeedback training, it is possible to learn to modify one's own blood pressure within certain limits.

9. Nerve cells are known as neurons.

10. Color vision is due entirely to receptor cells called rods.

11. The largest part of the brain is called the cerebrum.

12. The left side of the brain is believed to be concerned with logical thinking.

13. People suffering from sleep-onset insomnia are frequently tense and depressed.

14. Studies in the sleep laboratory show that sleep is uniform throughout the night.

15. The outer covering of the cerebrum is smooth like a billiard ball.

16. The nervous system is a passive conductor of electricity, just like a wire.

17. The part of the eye which contains the receptor cells is called the retina.

18. Psychologists believe dreams have no meaning and ignore them in therapy.

19. The nerve connecting the ear and the brain is called the optic nerve.

20. Biofeedback can be used as a means of teaching muscle relaxation.

The Basic Mental Processes:

Perception, Memory, and Learning

A person's ability to cope with the demands of everyday life depends on his or her ability to take in information from the environment, interpret it, recall it when needed, and use it constructively. Growth and development, success in activities, even survival itself, depend on these basic processes.

Perception, memory, and learning are closely related. It's difficult to conceive of memory without perception, or learning without memory. We will consider these three topics separately in this chapter. However, you should always keep in mind that these are not isolated processes.

Perception

In psychology books and journals you may find different definitions of the term **perception**. In this book, we will define perception as the process by which our brains give meaning to the **stimuli** registered by our senses. According to this view, perception is the process of recognizing, identifying, and interpreting the input from the senses.

That may sound like an unnecessarily elaborate definition. The reader may be wondering: "Don't we just see what's out there? Isn't what we see for real?"

Perhaps, but consider these examples.

A person who suffers from disorders of the inner ear sometimes experiences the sensations of vertigo. The room looks as if it's spinning around; the walls and ceilings are turning over and over. This is what the eyes say, but the person knows that it is not really happening.

Imagine that you wake up in the early morning, shortly after sunrise, and you see the sun low in the eastern sky. Later in the day, you see the sun in the western sky. Your eyes tell you that the sun has moved while the earth has stood quite still. Once again your eyes have suggested something that seems to be true but isn't true.

Have you ever had this experience? You are in a train or subway car. There is another train parked parallel to you. Your eyes are focused on this train as it suddenly begins to move. Did you have the sensation that the train you were in was actually moving, not the other train?

A movie consists of series of still pictures shown in rapid succession. Your brain interprets this series of pictures as one picture in continuous motion.

Imagine you and some of your friends are seated in a very dark room. There is a single light hanging from the ceiling. If you stare at the light, it will appear to move. Your friends might have somewhat different ideas about how far the light has moved, but in reality, the light hasn't moved at all. This misinformation provided by your eyes, called the *autokinetic effect*, was first reported by an astronomer at the end of the eighteenth century.

Try this: sit in a car on a straight road and watch a car approach and then go by, receding into the distance. If you just paid attention to the image in your eyes (retinal image), you would say the car is getting smaller and smaller. But your brain knows that the car isn't actually getting smaller—it's just moving further away. Your perception (interpretation of the sensory information) is that the car remains constant in size while the distance is changing.

From these examples, you can see something about how the input from your senses is processed by your brain and its memory systems. The resulting evaluation or interpretation of what is happening is your perception of the situation.

THRESHOLDS

We have talked about such basic aspects of perception as recognizing and identifying. One question psychologists have tackled is: How much of something has to be present before you are able to make it out and say what it is? Can you recall your last eye examination? Remember the chart with the big letters, the smaller letters, and the still smaller letters? It may have been easy for you to correctly identify the bigger letters, but as the letters got smaller and smaller, you probably reached a point where stating what the letters were became very difficult and then impossible.

Have you ever had your hearing checked? The person who tests you will play tones, some softer, some louder. She may ask you to raise your hand if you hear anything. Eventually, she will determine the loudness (decibel level) at which you can just hear something. Psychologists call this point the **threshold**. Threshold means the level at which something is *just noticeable*. A lower threshold means you note a stimulus of a weaker or lower intensity. Another way of saying you have a low threshold is to say that you are more *sensitive* to this particular kind of stimulus.

In practice, the threshold has usually been defined as the level at which a subject was able to recognize a stimulus 50 percent of the times it

was presented. That is to say, the person was able to make out something at this level about as often as not. Defined this way, the threshold has a now-you-see-it, now-you-don't flavor to it.

One problem in measuring thresholds is that people differ as to how clear evidence must be before they will take a stand. Some people are eager; they will say they recognize the stimulus at the faintest glimmer, perhaps even before something is really there. Other people will hold back, waiting for something definite before committing themselves.

Psychologists have worked out methods of measuring thresholds for sounds, sights, pain, tastes, and other stimuli. Such thresholds vary from one person to the next, and tend to change as a person ages. For example, studies have shown that older people had higher thresholds for (i.e., less sensitivity to) sweet, bitter, and sour tastes. This finding is important for nutritionists planning meals for older persons. The food may need more seasoning to give it the same taste that a younger person might experience with less seasoning.

So far we have been talking about what is called the *absolute threshold*, the point at which you can just make out a stimulus. Another type of threshold is the *just noticeable difference* or JND. If you were listening to a piano and someone sounded the note C, then the note D, you could easily tell they were different notes. If the notes sounded were C and D flat, you could still easily make out the difference. But if an electronic means of producing sound were used rather than a piano and the tones were squeezed closer and closer together, you would sooner or later have trouble telling which tone was higher. The point at which you could just make out which tone was higher than the other would be your JND. JND, then, is the threshold at which one stimulus is just noticeably different from another.

THE IMPORTANCE OF CONTEXT IN PERCEPTION

Look at the two sketches that follow:

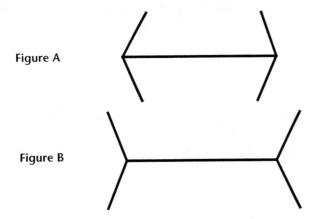

Figure A

Figure B

Which one of the horizontal lines seems longer to you? If you are like most people, you will say the line in Figure B looks longer than the line in Figure A. However, if you measure the lines with a ruler, you will discover that the lines are the same length. Your eyes have been tricked by a clever illusion called the *Müller-Lyer illusion.*

The point of the demonstration is not to show once again how your eye can deceive you, but to show one of the ways it does so. You usually don't look at something all alone; you generally look at something in a background or context. By context we mean that which surrounds what you are looking at. The context or background influences the way you evaluate the thing you are looking at. If you cover up all the lines in the Müller-Lyer illusion except the two horizontal lines, you will see that they now look alike.

A good illustration of the importance of context to perception is the perception of depth. Have you ever looked at a picture drawn by a young child? Everything looks as if it's in the foreground. You see little or no depth in the picture. But if you look at the paintings of, say, an eighteenth- or nineteenth-century master, you will see depth. The illusion of depth is created with such techniques as *linear perspective*, *atmospheric perspective*, *partial concealment*, and the use of *light and shadow.*

Linear perspective is created by having lines converge (come together) as they do in this photograph of a railway track.

Atmospheric perspective is created by the blurring and fuzzing of more distant objects. The artist might make the sky in the distance hazy.

In partial concealment, the object that is concealed is seen as further away.

Light and shadow help create the perception of distance; darker parts of the picture are seen as further away.

GESTALT PSYCHOLOGY AND THE ORGANIZATION OF PERCEPTION

The importance of considering a figure together with its context has been stressed by a school of psychology called **Gestalt psychology**. The founders of this movement were mainly from Germany and included Max Wertheimer, Kurt Koffka, and Wolfgang Köhler. The Gestalt psychologists developed a number of theories about the way people respond to stimuli and organize them into perceptions.

The Gestalt psychologists called the object a person was focusing on (paying attention to) the **figure**, and the background the **ground**. If you put this book on the rug and look at the book, the book is the figure, the rug is the ground. Sometimes figure and ground may be reversible, as they are in the drawing below. Do you see the drawing as a white vase and a dark background or as the faces of two people looking at one another?

The Gestalt psychologists believed that people tend to fill in details when forming their perceptions. Look at the following drawing. Do your eyes tend to ignore the breaks in the form and see the figure as a tortoise?

People also have a tendency to group things together into patterns. According to the Gestalt psychologists, if objects are close together, people will perceive the objects as a group. For example, look at the Xs that follow.

XXX   XXX   XXX   XXX

There are twelve Xs in all, but do you see them as four groups?

Similarity of color or shape will also act to produce the perception of a group. For example, in the next illustration, there are once again twelve letters, but you may perceive them as four groups, As, Os, Ps and Zs.

AAAOOOPPPZZZ

In general, the Gestalt psychologists believed that human beings have a tendency to organize their perceptions into meaningful patterns or wholes. One of the best illustrations of the Gestalt point of view is a melody. When you hear "Jingle Bells," do you hear it as a series of unrelated notes, or do you hear it as a single tune? Obviously, you hear the melody, not just a series of tones. This principle of the organized whole is important in Gestalt psychology.

An example of a Gestalt-oriented approach to perception is provided by studies of how people form impressions about other people. The experimenter provides the subject with various bits of information about a person and asks the subject for his impression of the person. The experimenter is interested in how these various bits of information are brought together into an overall impression of the person.

One interesting finding in some of these impression-formation studies relates to the importance of the earliest bits of information received. Initial information seems to have more weight in forming impressions than later information. This finding seems to confirm the popular wisdom regarding the importance of first impressions in dealing with people.

Sometimes in impression-formation studies, contradictory information is given to the subject. If you were told a person had all the traits listed on the next page, what kind of perception would you have of the person?

very friendly
extremely generous
ruthless
extremely dependable
overly conceited
very kind
scheming
very cold
highly loyal
insincere[1]

Arthur R. Cohen presented this list to his subjects, telling them that it described a fellow student. Then the subjects were asked to communicate their impression of the imaginary fellow student to others. They reacted by perceiving either the good or the bad traits. The subjects dropped or ignored the traits that didn't fit in with the pictures they had formed in their minds. Communicating to others seems to add to the need to form sensible perceptions from ambiguous material.

Experience and Perception

Before the invention of the telephone, the principal means of rapid long-distance communication was the telegraph. The telegraph operator heard a rapid series of longer and shorter sounds. To the untrained listener, such sounds had no meaning. To the trained operator, the sounds could be understood; they were a code for the letters of the alphabet.

Have you ever heard someone speak in an unfamiliar language? What did it sound like to you? You can see what it is like not being able to perceive meaning in the stimuli your senses register.

Experience can clearly make a difference in giving meaning to what you see. Think of an experienced quarterback ready to take the snap from the center. He looks over the alignment and recognizes the signs of an impending blitz.

The linebackers are about to vacate their positions and come after him. He signals a change in play to his teammates, instructing his receivers to run quick and deep on a fly pattern. An inexperienced quarterback might not have recognized the coming blitz and would have ended up on the seat of his trousers fifteen yards behind the line of scrimmage.

The physician has learned to recognize the meaning of the sounds of a heartbeat. A parent recognizes the meaning of a child's sounds and silence. A farmer has learned the meaning of certain kinds of black splotches on plants. A wine taster sniffs and tastes, then evaluates the wine. In all these instances, experience influences the ability to interpret stimuli and form meaningful perceptions.

The experience necessary to develop more "educated" perceptions or evaluations can sometimes be provided by direct training. One method is to provide immediate information (direct feedback) to judges after they make trial judgments. A possible application would be training a baseball umpire by using instant replay cameras behind the plate so he could see where he was making mistakes and learn to correct his errors.

A fascinating study of the teaching of perceptual skills was an attempt to train people to spot liars. One of the visual signs that was used in this training was the uneasy movements of the liar's hands and feet. Now you know the telltale signs.

Subliminal Perception

We have discussed the idea of a threshold, the point at which a person can just distinguish the appearance of a stimulus. You might be wondering what happens if stimuli are presented at an intensity at or just below this point. Will people show any evidence that they are reacting? Some psychologists think that people may react to stimuli at or below threshold levels. The term **subliminal perception** describes such reactions.

One method used in subliminal perception experiments is to present information in such

---

[1]Reprinted from "Cognitive Tuning as a Factor Affecting Impression Formation," by Arthur R. Cohen, pp. 235–245, in *Journal of Personality,* 29:2, Copyright 1961, by Duke University Press.

rapid exposures that people don't consciously register the information. One study reports that the messages "drink Coca-Cola" and "eat popcorn" were flashed at high speeds on a movie screen while theatergoers watched. It was reported that this subliminal presentation increased sales of both the soft drink and the popcorn.

A number of experiments on subliminal perception have also been conducted in psychological laboratories. Here are some examples of studies that reported some effect from subliminal stimulation.

In one study, the word *beef* was flashed over a classroom movie. The subjects who were exposed to this word reported they were hungrier than control subjects who saw the movie without the word *beef*.

In another study, high school students judging photographs of faces were influenced by word flashes of *good* or *bad* on the projection screen. Interestingly, these effects were only noticeable on students who reported they were aware of the flashing words.

In a third study, subjects were asked to make up stories in response to pictures. Pictures from the Thematic Apperception Test were projected on a screen. While the subjects were writing down their stories, subliminal messages were flashed on the screen stating "write more" or "don't write." "Write more" had no observable effect. "Don't write," however, was apparently effective. Compared to control subjects, the subjects getting this message wrote less.

Can you imagine having subliminal messages like this flashed on your TV screen?

Perhaps the most controversial experiments carried out on subliminal perception have been those on *perceptual defense*. In a typical experiment the subject viewed a series of words presented on a device called a tachistoscope. The tachistoscope can present words or pictures at very high speeds—so fast that the subject cannot make them out. The experimenter can slow the speed of exposure gradually until he finds the 50 percent recognition point or threshold. Using this procedure, the experimenter can determine the threshold for the various words. In the perceptual defense experiments, two types of words were presented: "loaded" words (usually sexual expressions) and neutral words. Typically, the subjects identified the neutral words more readily (at lower thresholds) than the loaded words. The researchers theorized that there is a screening process in perception. This screening process, they thought, interferes with the recognition of unacceptable stimuli.

Critics of the studies howled at this interpretation. The critics suggested, among other things, that it was more the "social" *report* which was delayed, not the perception. People didn't want to publicly state what they saw even when they saw it.

Undaunted, the experimenters went back to the drawing board. They decided to measure the subjects' galvanic skin response while the subjects were trying to figure out the meaning of the words. They did find an increase in the GSR during exposures to the loaded words. Somewhere in the recognition-report process, the subjects were being made uncomfortable by the loaded words.

Despite these findings, it seems clear that there are still many problems involved in interpreting the results of perceptual defense experiments. It is hard to judge how much of the effect was due to disturbances in perception, to unwillingness of subjects to report what they had seen, or to problems in the way the experiments were carried out. It remains difficult to separate the perceptual defense process from other perceptual processes.

EXTRASENSORY PERCEPTION

If the studies of subliminal perception brought on critical reactions, imagine what the response of psychologists was to the idea of extrasensory perception (ESP)! Surveys of psychologists indicate most of them are highly skeptical of ESP.

Extrasensory perception refers to the ability to perceive something (acquire information) without any observable evidence of sensory stimulation. None of the known senses (vision, hearing, touch, smell, taste, kinesthesia) are involved, yet the subject seemingly acquires the information.

The basic ESP experiment goes something like this. The experimenter has a deck of 25 cards. The 25 cards are divided into 5 different "suits": cross, star, circle, square, and wavy lines. The cards are shuffled. The order of the cards is unknown to both the experimenter and subject. A barrier shields the experimenter and the cards from the subject's view. The experimenter asks the subject to identify each card in order. The number of correct guesses ("hits") are tallied. If the subject consistently exceeds the number of hits one would obtain by chance, the subject is presumed to have ESP.

Try an informal version of the experiment yourself. Find a deck of playing cards. Then get some friends together. Have them sit in different parts of the room. Turn your back to your friends so they can't see you. Shuffle the deck of cards. Turn the cards over slowly, calling out the number of the cards, 1, 2, 3, etc., until you get to 52. As you look at each card and call it out, ask your friends to guess the suit of the card, writing down heart, diamond, club, or spade. See how many they get right. If anybody gets more than 13 right, shuffle the cards again and repeat the experiment. If he or she beats this figure again and again, you may have found something. May the force be with you all!

As we indicated, most psychologists who have responded to surveys about ESP have been very skeptical about the existence of ESP. They point out that many of the experiments designed to show ESP have not been well con-trolled and that the results have not been all that reliable. ESP has the reputation of having a now-you-see-it, now-you-don't character.

The challenge of traditional psychology to those who believe in ESP to do more convincing research has led to improved techniques to study ESP. One of the techniques that has been developed is to reduce to a minimum other sources of competing sensory stimulation. The idea is that the chances of receiving ESP signals, if in fact they exist, would be higher if all other sources of stimulation are blotted out. In these new experiments, two people, a sender and a receiver, sit in two separate isolated chambers. The eyes of the receiver are partially masked and a red flood light is directed toward the eyes. Headphones placed over the ears produce a steady humming sound called white noise. After the receiver goes through a series of relaxation exercises, the sender concentrates on a randomly selected visual target, such as a picture or brief video sequence. When the sending period of 30 minutes is over, the receiver looks at a computer screen which shows the correct target and three others. The receiver is asked to select the one which is closest to what he or she was thinking about during the experiment. Researchers have reported that the receiver's selection of the correct video clip (the one the sender was concentrating on) has been correct more often than one would expect by chance. These experiments pose a challenge to traditional psychologists to replicate them, to see if there is indeed something here which has to be explained.

Some people claim to have psychic powers, to know things by extrasensory means. It has been further claimed that psychic powers are particularly strong during dreams. Many years ago, Henry Murray and D. R. Wheeler ran a study which casts doubt on this idea. In the 1930's the United States was shocked by the kidnapping of the infant son of the famous aviator Charles Lindbergh. Murray put advertisements in the paper, asking if anyone had had dreams about the missing child which might provide clues as to where he was. A large number of people responded, sending their dream reports to Murray. When the whereabouts of the child's remains were finally discovered, it turned out that hardly any of the settings of the dream reports were even close to the truth.

Sensory Deprivation

Travelers who have been isolated in remote places (the arctic regions, deserts, at sea) have sometimes reported experiencing **hallucinations**. To hallucinate is to see or hear things that are not really there. In the 1950's psychologists began studying the effects of isolation and reduction of sensory stimulation in their laboratories. To restrain body motion, subjects were strapped in beds or placed in tanks like those used in the treatment of polio. One investigator went so far as to immerse himself in a tank of water, suspending himself motionlessly while breathing through a diving helmet.

To reduce visual input in these experiments, subjects were often kept in total darkness or under very low light. Sometimes the subjects wore special goggles that diffused light. The period of isolation might last a few hours or it might go on for as much as two weeks.

Like the isolated travelers, many of the subjects in these *sensory deprivation experiments* reported hallucinations. Sometimes these hallucinations were images with very little or no meaning: flashes of light, spots, geometric forms. Sometimes the hallucinations were perceptions of people, objects, or scenes. In a few cases, the hallucinations were frightening. In other cases, the hallucinations were amusing, like cartoons. One subject said he saw a line of squirrellike creatures with packs on their backs marching over a hill. In these initial studies on sensory deprivation, nearly half of the subjects reported seeing images such as flashes of light and geometric forms. About 20 percent of the subjects reported perceptions of people, objects, or scenes. In addition, some subjects reported auditory hallucinations as well. These subjects heard human voices or music.

Other perceptual distortions included difficulties in judging depth accurately. Not surprisingly, some of the subjects who took part in these experiments became uncomfortable and asked to be released early.

What Makes a Good Observer

There is a line attributed to the fictional detective Sherlock Holmes, "You see, Watson—but you do not observe." In concluding our remarks on perception, we would like to raise this question: Just what does make a good observer?

While people have drawn up lists of characteristics for the good observer, there are not too many facts. It does seem that a certain degree of age or maturity makes a difference. For example, a study was carried out with children to see how well they could interpret messages. The children were asked to judge whether the information in the message was adequate for understanding or ambiguous. The older children were able to recognize that a message was ambiguous, but the younger children were not.

If you were asked, "Generally speaking, who make better observers, men or women?", how would you answer? If you said men were better observers, you could well be wrong. Most studies, at least those dealing with *observation of other people*, suggest that women are better observers. Women seem better at picking up nonverbal communications (facial expressions, gestures, etc.). According to one review of the literature, in 84 percent of the studies in which the task assigned was to decode interpersonal communications, women outperformed men. These findings may reflect the traditional concern of women with other people and with human relations.

While we have as yet few conclusive findings about what makes a good observer, the following behaviors might be helpful.

1. Skill in asking questions. The ability to ask questions in a way that brings out information but does not make people defensive may help a person

obtain the kind of information needed for accurate assessments.

2. An open-minded approach. Having a mindset that is open and receptive will allow a person to pay attention to what is being said rather than interpret events in terms of his own biases.

3. Scanning before fixing one's attention. The idea is to look around at the whole scene before zeroing in. This will help prevent missing what may be important.

4. Avoidance of fatigue. As observational tasks are prolonged, the observers tend to become less able and less motivated.

Memory

Psychologists have long been interested in the processes of remembering and forgetting. They have been searching for an explanation of how our perceptions of our environment are turned into memories. They have also been curious about the rate at which we forget things and about the conditions under which forgetting is likely to take place. Some researchers have raised the fascinating question of whether information, once learned, is permanently stored in our memories. Does forgetting mean we lack the means to retrieve certain information, but that it's stored there somewhere in our memories all the same?

We are now going to discuss some of these issues. Along the way, we shall present some ideas that may help you improve your own ability to remember things, particularly when you study.

A THREE-STAGE MODEL OF MEMORY

Psychologists are not in complete agreement about the process of remembering. However, many researchers lean toward a three-stage process model of memory. The three stages have been called **sensory-information storage**, **short-term memory**, and **long-term memory**.

Perhaps we can understand this model better if we begin by thinking about a computer. A computer has memory systems in which a great deal of information can be stored on magnetic tapes or disks. The proper signal to the computer can call up any of that information very rapidly. When you think about it, the human brain works something like that. We have an enormous amount of information stored in our memories. Let us refer to this stored information filed away in our brains as our long-term memory. If we need this information, we can often (but not always) pull it out, just like that. When you take your history exam and are asked when the Declaration of Independence was signed, you may respond without hesitating, "July 4, 1776."

While this fact was stored in your long-term memory, not every bit of information that comes your way gets stored there. Imagine remembering every object that you have ever looked at or every sound you ever heard! What a lot of excess baggage that would be!

When you perceive something, there is clearly some kind of selective mechanism which decides whether to keep this information. Some information gets stored for long-term use, some does not. The first two stages of memory, sensory-information storage and short-term memory, have a brief, sifting quality to them. The processes work very quickly. Information can be lost here, never getting turned into one of the relatively long-lasting fixtures of long-term memory. You can see a dramatic example of this failure to remember in people with brain diseases. Such people may watch a television program, and if you ask them to describe what they saw, they may not remember anything. The program content never got processed into long-term storage.

We have suggested that the first two stages in the memory process have a brief duration. How brief? Here are the views of one researcher, Joseph Greeno, who has worked for many years on studies of learning. He describes the first two stages this way:

> *We are now aware of at least three memory systems: short-term sensory storage, short-term memory, and something less transient. . . . The general picture that has become common is that information is received by a sensory system with a very large capacity but a holding time on the order of a fraction of a second. Information selected from this system is held in short-term memory, which has a much smaller capacity, but ordinarily holds items for a few seconds. . . .*

In this view of human information processing, there is large but fleeting input from the senses which has a very brief existence in sensory storage. We are talking about a fraction of a second. Then there is a kind of funnel. This funnel (short-term memory) holds only a small amount of information at a time. Some of this information gets sent on to long-term, more permanent memory.

How much information is held in this funnel (short-term memory)? Not much, as you can see if you try the following experiment.

Have someone read the following group of letters slowly to you and see if you can repeat them without error.

L B R C O

Were you accurate? O.K. Try a larger group of letters.

D S A P M G I

Were you right again? Try this.

E U W G Z F T H N S V K

If you get that right, you should get a job replacing home computers when they break down and are being repaired in the shop.

You will probably find that if the letters are read to you in groups or chunks (such as EUW GZF THN SVK), they are much easier to recall. In any event, human short-term memory has a

rather small, defined limit on how many "bits" of information it can consider at any point in time. For many people, remembering seven bits of information at a time is about the limit.

LABORATORY STUDIES OF RETENTION

Even when information makes it through this sifting process and ends up stored in long-term memory, we are not always able to recall it on demand. At times, we have for the moment, or perhaps permanently, forgotten what we have learned.

The scientific study of retention or its failure, forgetting, dates in large part to the pioneering work of Hermann Ebbinghaus, a German psychologist who lived in the later part of the nineteenth century. Ebbinghaus conducted his research on himself, a remarkable feat. To carry out his research, Ebbinghaus invented some special materials for memory studies. These materials, three-letter syllables like HEF, KIR, RUL, MOS, he called nonsense syllables. Ebbinghaus made up around 2,300 of these meaningless syllables for his experiments.

In an experiment, Ebbinghaus might make up a list of say, 13 of these nonsense syllables. He would then set out to memorize the list, seeing how much time it took him. He would go about his task in a very methodical way, reading the syllables out loud while a metronome or watch ticked in the background, keeping a steady beat.

In one set of experiments, he first learned a list, then allowed some time to pass. As some forgetting had taken place, he set about relearning the list, once again noting the amount of time it took. He discovered that it took him less time to learn the list the second time. He used this "savings" in time of relearning as the basis for a measure of memory.

Over the years, psychologists have used nonsense syllables, as well as a variety of other materials with more meaning, to study memory. Such materials have included prose, pictures of people, names, and numbers. In these studies, researchers have sometimes used Ebbinghaus' savings method as a measure of retention. They have also used two other rather straightforward measures of retention called **recall** and **recognition.**

Recall tests how much you can remember when you are flat out asked to provide information. You are normally given no help, hints, or aids when recall is measured. For example, suppose someone asked you who the fourth president of the United States was. You might or might not be able to pull the answer out of your memory. If you could answer the question correctly, this would be an example of outright recall. Now, suppose the question were worded this way: "Which of the following people was the fourth president of the United States: John Adams, Andrew Jackson, Grover Cleveland, or James Madison?" If the name Madison rang a bell, you would be showing your ability to recognize the correct answer when it was presented to you. We call this ability recognition memory. You can see that recognition is easier than outright free recall.

At times, even recognition memory may only be partial. Have you ever heard a tune that you recognize but can't remember the name of? Or how about a person: You recognize the face, but can't recall the name?

In some experiments, measuring recall and recognition yields different results. For example, in studying the effects of the drug marijuana on memory, researchers have found that the effect on recall is more noticeable than the effect on recognition. One study reported that marijuana had little effect on recognition measures of memory, but greatly decreased the ability to recall materials outright.

In such experiments, subjects would read materials after smoking marijuana. Then they would be asked to recall the material. Not only would the subjects make more errors after using the drug, they would even recall things that were not in the material.

Time and Forgetting. In his experiments, Ebbinghaus found that a large amount of forgetting took place within an hour of the time he first memorized a list of nonsense syllables. When one hour had passed, it took him half as much time to relearn the list as it had taken him to learn it originally. After that, the rate of forgetting was not as great. When a full day had elapsed, his savings in time was still one third. A month later, the savings was still one fifth.

Ebbinghaus concluded that after learning there is a period of rapid forgetting. After this period the rate of forgetting slows down.

Meaningfulness of Material. Ebbinghaus compared his ability to remember nonsense syllables and lines of poetry from Byron's long poem, "Don Juan." Using his savings method, he found that he was able to relearn the poetry much faster than the nonsense syllables. It seemed clear from these brief experiments that meaning makes a difference in memory. Meaningful material is much easier to recall.

Massed vs. Distributed Learning. Experiments have suggested that breaking up learning activities into smaller time periods (distributed learning) leads to better retention than trying to learn everything in one large block of time (massed learning). As an example, let's look at a study carried out by Kristine Bloom and Thomas Shuell, using high school students enrolled in a French course. The students were asked to learn 20 new pairs of words. The pairs were English-French equivalents such as *lawyer/ l'avocat.* One group of students studied the words during a single 30-minute classroom period. Another group of students spent 10 minutes a day on the task on three successive days. Both groups learned the word pairs equally well. However, on a retest four days later, the group which had learned the word pairs in the spaced 10-minute sessions did 35 percent better.

Interference and Forgetting. Psychologists have run experiments that suggest that one of the times people forget is when one set of materials "interferes" with another. To make this idea clearer, imagine that you have memorized a list of five telephone numbers. Shortly afterwards, you are asked to learn a second set of five telephone numbers. Your memory for the first list of numbers might introduce some confusion, interfering with your ability to remember the second list. Psychologists call this type of interference **proactive inhibition**. What you have learned previously may interfere with the new learning.

Let's assume you are able to learn the second list. Now imagine that you are retested on your ability to remember the first list. You will probably find that your ability to recite the original list has been diminished. Learning the new list has interfered with your recall for the old list. Psychologists call this type of interference **retroactive inhibition**. What is newly learned may interfere with the memory of what has been learned before.

You will often encounter such interference when you study, particularly when you are trying to learn things that sound alike. Psychologists have found in experiments that the more similar two sets of materials are, the more likely interference will take place.

Imagine you have the task of memorizing a fairly long list, say a list of names or dates, or perhaps a lengthy shopping list. Researchers have found that items at the beginning and end of such a list are likely to be remembered better than items in the middle. This makes sense because as you move through the task, interference in the form of proactive inhibition builds up. Since there is little proactive inhibition as you start the list, these items are likely to stick with you. At the end of the list, there is little interference from retroactive inhibition, so these items may also stick with you. In the middle of the list, you will get interference from both types of inhibition; these items tend to be forgotten.

Let's try to translate some of these research findings into some practical guidelines for better retention of information.

1. Break up your learning activities into fairly short periods. Avoid working in long, uninterrupted blocks of time.

2. Sometime during a long study period, try changing the type of material that you are working with. Instead of spending all your time working with one type of material, try switching to a very different topic. This may help prevent the buildup of proactive inhibition. A good time to do this may be when you are feeling a sense of fatigue or resistance to the original task.

3. From time to time, try to integrate what you are learning with what you already know. This may make the material more meaningful. It should provide some context for your new learning and an anchor for it.

4. From time to time, rehearse what you have covered in your own words, either out loud or silently. This will serve as a check on your recall and should increase the chances of the material being stored in long-term memory.

5. Choose periods for studying which are followed by times of minimum interference (times when you will be exposed to little new information). For example, a good time to study may be during the hour before you go to sleep. Who knows, your book may even help you fall asleep.

EXPLICIT VS. IMPLICIT MEMORY

Psychologists have made a distinction between **explicit memory**, conscious recall of facts and events, the kind of thing you do when you try to answer the questions on a history exam, and **implicit memory**, various forms of nonconscious memory such as the skills involved when you walk down the street or ride a bicycle or when ideas suddenly pop into your head that you thought you had forgotten. Researchers studying brain-injured patients suffering from amnesia report that such patients may have severe impairments of explicit memory but still have intact implicit memory. One example reported in the scientific journals was an amnesiac patient who practiced a mirror-drawing task over a period of time, showing day-to-day improvement but no memory of actually practicing the task. Researchers are now trying to identify the areas and connections within the brain that seem to be involved in these types of memories.

THE PERMANENCE OF MEMORY

Psychological research has taught us much about the conditions under which forgetting is most likely to occur. What, you may be wondering, really happened to the information that had been stored in the memory? Has this information actually been lost? Has it faded or eroded away? Or is this information still there, but somehow we just can't pull it back?

Wilder Penfield, a neurosurgeon, has reported some dramatic observations suggesting that once information is stored in the brain, it remains there. Penfield electrically stimulated the brains of epileptic patients, trying to pinpoint damaged areas of the brain for possible surgery. During this procedure, the patients remained conscious. While their brains were being stimulated, some of the patients reported experiencing what seemed to be memories of sounds and sights. The patients later identified some of these memories as having been part of their previous experience.

For example, a man reported hearing a song that he had heard a long time ago. A woman said she heard a mother in her neighborhood call for a child, something that also happened years ago.

Penfield was impressed enough by these accounts to conclude that memories were permanently imprinted in the brain. He further believed that imprints could be traced again years later without loss of detail by using an electric current, almost as if one were playing a tape recorder.

If Penfield's speculations were correct, they would open up all kinds of possibilities for the scientific study of human experience.

Other researchers have taken a skeptical view of Penfield's observations. They point out

that the great majority of Penfield's patients did not report such experiences. They also point out that the memories "brought up" by Penfield's patients might not be pure memories fished out by electrical stimulation from long-forgotten chambers. Rather, these memories could well be current inventions of an active mind (like daydreams) that occurred during the stimulation.

There are other lines of evidence which lend support to Penfield's belief that memory is permanent. For example, sometimes people under hypnosis are apparently able to remember events they have forgotten. One use of this technique has been in criminal investigations. It has been reported that when witnesses to crimes have been hypnotized, memory for details of the crime has been improved, producing valuable leads for the police.

One striking example of such improved memory was described by Kroger and Douce. The case involved the kidnapping of two San Francisco girls. The kidnapper terrified the girls, telling them that the car was wired with explosives that he would set off if the car were stopped by police. He drove the girls to Mexico where he sexually assaulted one of them. When he released the girls, he told them that if they mentioned what had happened, it would put their parents' lives into jeopardy.

The girls could remember little when they were later questioned by the police. Then hypnosis was tried with the older girl to improve her recall. Quoting from the authors' description, what happened was as follows:

> At the hypnotic level, the girl recalled unique rust spots on the car body. Also, she remembered articles inside the car such as the specific color and brand names of a box of tissues and peanut butter cookies on the rear seat. She recollected that the gearshift knob of the car was held in place with a piece of tissue paper and that the right front passenger window made a noise when it was rolled up the last few inches. The only information available at the non-hypnotic level was the color and general description of the car. The brand name of the tissues

*and type of cookies were not recalled prior
to induction.*

*Even more interesting was the almost
total recall covering a transaction at a San
Diego gas station located on a hilltop where
the suspect had his car repaired. The hilltop
location was instrumental in readily locating
the gas station. In hypnosis, the girl remembered conversation between the repairman
and the suspect, the nature of the repairs
required, and the fact that the transaction
was paid for by the use of a red, white, and
blue credit card. . . . Although she was
totally unfamiliar with the type of repairs,
she specifically remembered that the repairman said to the suspect, "You need Freon."
The latter word, which she had never heard
before, was uttered by the girl almost as a
question, although she now remembered it
with a pinpoint specificity.*

*The FBI agents located the gas station
and the repairman. The credit card transaction was quickly identified and the suspect
was arrested at his home in northern California. Examination of the car confirmed
every single detail supplied by the girl while
she was in hypnosis.*

*In news releases made following the
arrest, the suspect's photograph was recognized by other young girls who had
been sexually assaulted. The suspect
was convicted and is serving an indefi-
nite sentence in a state hospital for the
criminally insane.*[2]

While case reports like the above seem
remarkable, many scientists are not convinced
that information obtained under hypnosis is
really accurate. They ask: How can we be sure
that the subject under hypnosis is not construct-
ing a story out of bits and pieces of information
and filling in the details from other experiences?
Perhaps the hypnosis is merely reducing inhibitions and not really enhancing truth. And indeed, a number of controlled studies in psychological laboratories have failed to show that

hypnosis improves memory. Because testimony
based on hypnosis is now considered question-
able, some courts have decided not to accept it.

Still another type of evidence of the permanence of memory is the spontaneous recovery of previously lost memories. Have you ever
had the experience of suddenly remembering
something that you had apparently forgotten?
As we indicated, this is an example of your
implicit memory at work. Or do you sometimes
have tip-of-the-tongue experiences, a name, a
fact, a telephone number—some bit of information that you might have easily volunteered
yesterday or last week, but at the moment has
vanished from your conscious memory like a
puff of smoke that faded into the air? If you
have such experiences, you are not alone. Most
of us have these can't-quite-remember-it experiences fairly often. Researchers have asked
people to make a record of these incidents when
they occur. Judging from the results of these
studies, younger subjects report such experiences on the order of once or twice a week while
older subjects report them more often, about
two to four times a week. Once again there
appears to be more in one's memories than we
have immediate access to. Still, both these tip-
of-the-tongue experiences and the spontaneous
recovery of memories coming out of the blue are
a long way from proof that all information that
enters our long-term memories is permanently
stored there.

The question is surely a fascinating one.
At the present time, however, there is no clear-
cut answer.

Learning

We have described a model of information
processing in which the person briefly registers
information, funnels it through short-term
memory, then stores it in long-term memory.
If we test the person at this point and find the
person can recite the information, we can say
that learning has taken place.

Learning, of course, is much more than the

[2]Reprinted from the October 1979 *International Journal of Clinical and Experimental Hypnosis.* Copyrighted
by the Society for Clinical and Experimental Hypnosis,
October 1979, pp. 369–370.

mere acquisition of factual information. Consider the newborn child for a moment and imagine all the things she will learn as part of growing up. She must learn to identify the meaning of the various parts of her complex environment—all those strange faces and objects. She must also learn language and master the physical and motor skills needed in daily activities and games. She must learn how to relate to other people, and absorb the values and beliefs of the adults in the society. Understanding learning is a key to understanding and explaining how human beings develop. Because of this, learning has been a central concern of psychologists.

LEARNING AS ASSOCIATION

Philosophers theorized about how learning takes place long before psychologists began to study the problem in the laboratory. One theory was that learning occurred when ideas were associated in the mind. For example, if you always saw dark clouds before it rained, you would soon link the two ideas (clouds and rain) together. Learning was believed to take place when the mind linked events which occurred together in space and time.

The philosopher's approach to learning involved mentalistic terms—trying to describe what went on in a person's mind. In the early part of the twentieth century, many psychologists became convinced that psychology would never get anywhere as a science if it used mentalistic terms. They thought that what went on in the mind couldn't be accurately measured. They insisted that psychology could only study what could be observed directly: that is, behavior. They substituted the terms *stimulus* and *response* for the term *idea*. Learning was viewed as a series of connections between stimuli (sounds, sights, or smells) and responses. These psychologists, calling themselves behaviorists, were heavily influenced by the writings of John B. Watson.

The behaviorists looked for models of how a stimulus and a response became connected by learning. They found such models in the studies of Ivan Pavlov in Russia and E.L. Thorndike in the United States. Pavlov's work provided a model which has been called *classical conditioning*. Thorndike's work led to our current **reinforcement theories** of learning and behavior.

CLASSICAL CONDITIONING AS A MODEL FOR LEARNING

In our opening chapter, we described Pavlov's basic discovery. You will recall that he gave an animal a stimulus (food) that would bring on a natural response (salivation); then he paired the food with a neutral stimulus (a musical tone). The tone would soon bring on salivation even when the food was *not* presented. The process usually involved a half dozen or so pairings of the tone and the food. The tone had to be sounded just before the food was presented. If the lag time was more than a few seconds, the procedure wouldn't work properly.

The procedure was called **conditioning**. The old stimulus was called the *unconditioned stimulus* (UCS). The new stimulus that acquired the power to bring on the response was called the *conditioned stimulus* (CS).

Continuing his research, Pavlov found that the power of the new stimulus (CS) to bring on salivation would be short-lived if it were repeatedly presented alone and not followed by the food. The animal would stop salivating. When this happened, the response to the CS was said to be *extinguished*. Conditioning could easily be restored by pairing the tone with the food a second time. As Ebbinghaus found in his experiments on memory, there was a savings in learning time the second time around.

You may have wondered whether you could use the newly powered CS (the musical tone) to condition some new stimuli. Suppose you forgot about the food entirely, and just played the tone to the animal. Before you played the tone you would flash a light. Could you condition the dog to salivate to the light this way? Pavlov found that you could turn the light into a CS this way. The procedure was called *higher order conditioning*. The new reflex was quite weak, however, and could easily be extinguished.

The fact that conditioned reflexes could be fairly easily extinguished in the laboratory and that higher order reflexes could be very easily extinguished seemed to take some of the glow off Pavlov's findings as a general model for learning. Could conditioning explain the many types of behavior that we see in everyday life, behaviors that keep occurring in the absence of an unconditioned stimulus? Using Pavlov's model, we would expect such behaviors to extinguish easily. But we can all point to examples of behaviors which, once learned, are very hard to get rid of. Psychologists, therefore, began to look for other models for learning.

REINFORCEMENT THEORIES OF LEARNING

The basic idea of reinforcement theories of learning is that when behavior is followed by consequences, future behavior of that type is likely to be affected. If behavior is positively reinforced (rewarded), the behavior pattern is likely to be strengthened. Future behavior of that type is more likely to occur. When the behavior is not reinforced, the behavior pattern is likely to be weakened and will be less likely to reoccur.

The idea that the consequences of actions are important in the learning process was developed by Edward Thorndike. Thorndike ran a number of experiments using both animal and human subjects. He concluded that learning seemed to depend on the presentation of a reward after the behavior had been successfully completed.

In a typical experiment, a hungry cat was placed in a box with an escape latch. If the cat could release the latch, it could get out of the box and find food outside. In the early trials, the cat might claw, bite, and thrash about the box before working the latch. Gradually, the cat began to operate the latch more quickly and with less wasted motion. The cat thus appeared to gradually learn through *trial and error* the behavior that was required to escape from the

box and get the food.

Thorndike thought of learning as a connection or bond. The learning connected two things: a situation, and a response that got strengthened by the consequences of a behavior. He called this principle the *Law of Effect*. Based on his experiments, he concluded that positive consequences (rewards) were important in strengthening these learned connections, but that punishments were not very useful.

Studies in the Skinner Box.   Two psychologists who picked up on Thorndike's Law of Effect and developed it in their own ways were Clark Hull and B. F. Skinner. Hull worked out an elaborate model for explaining how reinforcement influenced behavior. Skinner's approach was much less theoretical than Hull's. Skinner's idea was to carefully record animal behavior in a very simple experimental situation. As an experimenter, he wanted to set up conditions that would lead to predictable behavior on the part of the animal. Skinner's intent was not only to predict behavior in this simple situation, but to be able to control it.

Skinner's simple experimental situation was dubbed the *Skinner box*. It was a box containing a small metal lever. If the lever were pressed by the laboratory animal (a white rat), a food pellet was delivered. The lever was connected to a mechanism which recorded every instance in which the animal pressed the lever.

Skinner was able to measure the number of responses the animals would make in a given period of time. He was also able to find out how many times the rat would continue to push the lever after the experimenter stopped reinforcing (rewarding) the lever press. Using Pavlov's term, the experimental procedure of not reinforcing the response was called **extinction**. The rat's continued response in the absence of reinforcement was called *resistance to extinction*.

Partial Reinforcement.   Studies by Skinner and psychologists who followed his lead produced reams of data about how rats would behave in this small, simplified world. One of the most interesting findings had to do with the effectiveness of **partial reinforcement**. Partial reinforcement is a procedure in which the experimenter does not reinforce the rat after each press of the bar. The experimenter might only reinforce the rat after, say 15, 20, 30, or more unrewarded responses. Would the rat quit? Would the lever-pressing behavior extinguish? Not at all. *If the rat learns lever pressing under conditions of partial reinforcement, the rat's resistance to the extinction of that behavior becomes greater.* The animal will press the bar many more times before giving up.

> *The effectiveness of partial reinforcement in sustaining behavior has many practical applications in teaching and training. One good example is animal training. In the Johnson family, young Mike received a cocker spaniel puppy at Christmas. He was teaching his pet to obey the command sit, by reinforcing her with a dog biscuit every time she responded to his command. Mike's older sister Sally was taking a psychology course. She suggested to Mike that he switch the reinforcement schedule to reward the dog every third time she sat on command, then every fifth time, and then to make reinforcement irregular.*

Learning to Make Discriminations Between Stimuli. Skinner also used his simple apparatus to carry out experiments on *discrimination learning.* Everything was as usual in the box, only now a light shone sometimes and sometimes it was dark. When the light was on, lever pressing was followed by food. When the light was off, lever pressing brought nothing. Did the rats learn to make this distinction? You bet. In Skinner's view, the light (stimulus) now determined when the response may be reinforced.

Skinner also experimented with the "shaping" of behavior. The experimenter might start by reinforcing any old response that resembled the one he wanted. Later, however, he would become more and more selective about what behavior would be reinforced, rewarding only those behaviors which were closer to the desired response. A real-life application of this procedure would be a teacher instructing a young child to play the piano. In the beginning, the teacher might praise the child for producing any sounds which were approximately right; later on he would reserve praise for musical sounds which were closer to those he wanted to hear.

Secondary Reinforcement. In the real world, it is clear that people are not always reinforced by food, water, or some other primary reinforcer that satisfies biological drives. People are often reinforced by money, praise, and encouragement. Reinforcement theorists have called such incentives *secondary reinforcers.* They believe these secondary reinforcers act as general reinforcers for the control of behavior. And they think the secondary reinforcers acquire their power by being paired in the learning experience with primary reinforcers.

As an example of how this might work, let us return to the rat in the Skinner box. The rat has learned that when the light shines, food will come its way if it presses the bar. Suppose you wait around until the animal, for lack of anything better to do presses the bar when the cage is still dark. Quickly you turn on the light. You don't feed the animal, you just turn on the light. Then you turn the light off again. The animal will probably start pressing the bar to bring on the light. If this happens, the light is now acting as a secondary reinforcer. While the animal may perceive the light as a kind of way station on the road to getting its food, the light is still exerting control over its behavior.

Skinner and his followers continued to run their experiments. Sometimes rats were used as subjects, pressing the lever in the box; sometimes pigeons were used, pecking away at a disk. Skinner's pigeons bring to mind one of the more intriguing tales of modern psychology. Skinner related the story at a meeting of the American Psychological Association.

During World War II, when great cities like Warsaw and London were being devastated by bombing raids, the problem of air defense became critical. Scientists began to experiment with defensive ballistic missiles. However, the missiles were primitive at best; there was little in the way of effective guidance systems to ensure that they would come close to hitting their targets.

Skinner and some of his associates hit upon what he himself referred to as the "crackpot idea" of having the missiles steered toward their targets by pigeons. With the civilized world facing the prospect of living through another period like the Dark Ages if the Nazis won the war, no one gave much thought to the ethical question involved in turning the pigeons into unwittingly doomed pilots.

Suffice it to say that the idea of shooting down enemy bombers this way never got very far. However, the idea of destroying enemy warships with pigeon-guided missiles almost got off the ground. Skinner found that he could train pigeons strapped in a harness to peck at an image of a ship. The pigeons were reinforced for pecking at the image by receiving a supply of grain. The apparatus was so engineered that by pecking at the moving image the pigeons could guide the missile, effectively holding it on target. The idea was that if the pigeons pecked at the image long enough, the missile loaded with explosives would engage the ship and destroy it.

The idea seemed wild, but Skinner was able to train pigeons in a simulator to peck away at the images in a methodical and dependable fashion. Finally, a demonstration was arranged with a committee of top scientists. The pigeons performed perfectly, "pecking steadily and energetically at the image of the target as it moved about on the plate." However, its very success proved the project's undoing. As Skinner put it, "the spectacle of a living pigeon carrying out its assignment, no matter how beautifully, simply reminded the committee of how utterly fantastic our proposal was." The project was turned down.

When mechanical guidance systems were finally developed for missiles, Skinner went on to train pigeons for more peaceful pursuits like playing Ping Pong.

Punishment, The Aversive Control of Behavior. So far, we have been talking about the effects of positive reinforcement on the learning of new behavior patterns. What happens if we use punishment as a motivator rather than positive reinforcement? Psychologists sometimes refer to this as using an *aversive* stimulus or **aversive control**. Thorndike and some of the other reinforcement theorists believed that a punishment was not as effective a teaching tool as was a reward. However, there is little doubt that severe punishment may create an avoidance reaction.

One of the classic experiments on avoidance reactions was carried out by Neal Miller. Miller placed rats in a box that was divided into two compartments separated by an open door. One of the compartments was white, with a metal grid as a floor. The grid could be electrified. The other compartment was black and had a normal floor. At the start of the experiment, the animals showed no clear preference for either of the compartments.

Now the experimenter began to give electric shocks to the rats while they were in the white compartment. The rats reacted by moving through the door into the black compartment, where they did not receive shocks. After a number of trials in which they received shocks in the white compartment, the rats would run rapidly through the open door into the black compartment. They continued to do this even when no more shocks were given in the white compartment. The rats had learned to fear the white compartment.

Then, with the shock apparatus turned off, Miller shut the door, forcing the rats to remain in the white compartment. They could only open the door if they nudged a small wheel. Many of the rats learned to do this and moved into the black compartment. The punishing experience had set up an avoidance reaction. The escape behavior from the white compartment persisted for many trials after the shocks had been stopped.

THE NATURE OF REINFORCEMENT

Reinforcement theorists believe that reinforcement is at the core of the learning experience and is necessary to activate behavior. They believe reinforcement strengthens learned tendencies, increasing the chances that such behaviors will occur when appropriate drives are aroused. Suppose we ask the question: Just exactly what is a reinforcer? The reinforcement theorist might say something like this: "A reinforcer is anything that can get the subject to do something . . . anything that has meaning to the individual and can produce changes in the individual's behavior." Reinforcement theorist William Schoenfeld wrote that *any* stimulus could act as a reinforcer, that there were no special characteristics that set reinforcers apart from other stimuli.

Using this framework, it seems reasonable to look at reinforcers as stimuli (words, tokens, actions) that acquire their power to modify behavior either as satisfiers of biological drives or as part of the social learning process.

A final word about reinforcement theory, and particularly Skinner's position. The behaviorists' emphasis on the deliberate control of behavior has caused some uncomfortable reactions among critics. They see it as possibly creating techniques for behavioral control, techniques which could be misused. It would not take us too far into science fiction to imagine what a dictatorial regime or organization could do with an efficient set of behavioral controls. But the potential for misuse extends to other areas of the field as well; it is not limited to Skinner's work. Indeed, it extends to many areas of science. The issue raised—the use or misuse of scientific knowledge—is a very important one, and will become increasingly important in an age of advancing technology.

COGNITIVE APPROACHES TO LEARNING

When the behaviorists stepped forward in the early decades of the twentieth century, they insisted that the only reliable, scientific approach to psychology was to study observable behavior. This view led to studies of what animals and humans did in situations which the experimenter controlled. The experimenter observed the subjects, recorded their behavior, and then tried to make some sense out of his findings. From the behaviorist's point of view, it was considered bad taste, if not heresy, to ask his human subjects what they were thinking—

what was going on in their minds.

Many people found the behaviorist position too restrictive. They found not being able to use the human subject's ability to communicate his or her thoughts a tremendous waste of important data. It seemed like throwing out the baby with the bath water. The cognitive theorists decided to put the baby back in the tub.

The cognitively oriented psychologist tries to look at the world from inside the person. He or she is not so much interested in describing behavior as viewed by an outside observer, as in trying to understand the subject's view of reality. From this point of view, reinforcement theory does not seem like the best model to describe learning. It seems like an approximately correct model that works well only under certain narrowly defined conditions. The cognitive theorist would argue that a Skinner box is too simple an environment to provide an adequate sample of the real world. The theorist would also say that the capabilities of rats and humans are very different.

But the biggest reaction against behavioral theory came from the Gestalt psychologists. The Gestalt psychologists liked to view psychological reality in terms of the present and perception. Instead of saying that a person has learned to solve a certain problem because she has been reinforced 40 times, the Gestalt psychologist would say the person sees (has figured out) the solution to the problem. Seeing the solution is called an *aha experiment* or **insight**. It is like your reaction when you suddenly see the solution to the murder in a paperback mystery or figure out that difficult math problem.

The interest in insight as an alternative model to the trial and error model of the behaviorists was stimulated by the publication of Wolfgang Köhler's experiments with chimpanzees. Köhler conducted his experiments during the years 1913–1917 on an island off the coast of Africa. He set up problems for his chimpanzees that would permit them to work out insightful solutions. For example, he attached a banana to the top of the chimpanzees' cage, out of the animals' reach. In another part of the cage he placed a box. If a chimp moved the box under the banana, climbed on top of the box, and jumped, it could reach the banana.

Only one of the animals, a very intelligent chimp named Sultan, solved the problem without assistance. Sultan's problem solving, as described by Köhler, seemed like a remarkable feat.

> *The six young animals of the station colony were enclosed in a room with perfectly smooth walls, whose roof—about two metres in height—they could not reach. A wooden box (dimensions fifty centimetres by forty by thirty), open on one side, was standing about in the middle of the room, the one open side vertical, and in plain sight. The objective was nailed to the roof in a corner, about two and a half metres distant from the box. All six apes vainly endeavoured to reach the fruit by leaping up from the ground. Sultan soon relinquished this attempt, paced restlessly up and down, suddenly stood still in front of the box, seized it, tipped it hastily straight towards the objective, but began to climb upon it at a (horizontal) distance of half a metre, and springing upwards with all his force, tore down the banana. About five minutes had elapsed since the fastening of the fruit; from the momentary pause before the box to the first bite into the banana, only a few seconds elapsed—a perfectly continuous action after the first hesitation. Up to that instant none of the animals had taken any notice of the box; they were all far too intent on the objective; none of the other five took any part in carrying the box; Sultan performed this feat single-handed in a few seconds. The observer watched this experiment through the grating from the outside of the cage . . . .*
>
> *On the following day the test was repeated, the box being placed as far from the objective as the available space per- mitted, i.e., at a distance of five metres. As soon as Sultan had grasped the situation, he took the box, pulled it along till it was almost directly beneath the banana, and jumped. . . .*

Köhler's other chimps required help in solving the problem, such as having the box placed under the food. After the chimps had learned the solution to the problem, they would walk over to the box, move it under the banana, and get the banana. At this point, it looked as if the chimps could see what was needed to solve the problem. They had achieved insight.

Since Köhler's apes often fumbled around before achieving insight, it may be that their behavior wasn't all that much different from that of Thorndike's cats or Skinner's pigeons. Nonetheless, a considerable controversy arose, with one side waving the banner of learning as essentially a matter of trial and error, while the battle cry on the other side was insight.

In his book *Theories of Learning*, Ernest Hilgard argued that whether learning resembles trial and error or insight depends on a number of factors. One factor, Hilgard said, is the capacity of the learner. Older children, for example, are more successful at solving problems than younger children. A second factor is previous experience. If you have relevant experience that can be applied to a new problem, you may be able to solve the problem with less trial and error. A third factor is the way the problem is arranged. If the problem is set up so that you can see what to do, you may be able to "see" the solution within the problem instead of using trial and error.

EXPECTANCIES, OR THE HYPOTHESIS THEORY

One approach to learning theory, which is somewhere between reinforcement theory and the theory of insightful learning, uses the idea of expectations or *expectancies*. Edward C. Tolman was a pioneer of this approach. The basic idea is that when individuals are put into a learning situation, they develop a hypothesis about what is going on. Reinforcement may act to confirm the hypothesis. If confirmation fails to come, the learner changes the hypothesis.

This approach, which stresses expectations and hypotheses, lends itself to an information processing view of learning. The learner behaves and notes the consequences of his or her actions. Noting the consequences of behavior is another way of saying the learner is receiving feedback from the environment. The learner may form a new hypothesis about the situation, or may modify or confirm a previous hypothesis. The learner may then change his or her behavior accordingly.

Let's apply this kind of approach to what happens in an experimental situation using partial reinforcement. (Remember that partial reinforcement makes behavior very resistant to extinction.) Let's imagine for a moment that we are inside the animal's mind. We might imagine that the animal is thinking something like this: If I press this bar, they feed me. However, I've noted that this doesn't happen every time I press the bar. Since I should not expect to receive food each time, there is no reason to be discouraged by the failure of food to come. My experience has led me to believe that if I keep at it, I will, in time, get food.

Let's summarize. It is possible to look at learning in strictly behavioral terms. If the environment can be controlled, then behavior can often be predicted by following the principles of reinforcement theory. If the environment is set up to allow means-and-ends relationships to be perceived more clearly, you will more likely see examples of insightful learning. If you shift from only observing behavior to considering the learning situation from the point of view of the learner, you can observe changing expectations or hypotheses which reflect the learner's experience.

Some Questions and Activities

1. Imagine you are an astronaut alone in a spacecraft. Everything is dark around you. Your body is weightless. You float about the spacecraft. The sound system of your spacecraft is shut off in order to save energy. What is one of the psychological effects you might anticipate from being in this situation?

2. Have you ever tried to train an animal to perform a trick? If so, what did you try to do and how successful were you?

3. Try creating your own illusion. Draw two lines of equal length. Then add other features to the lines which will mislead a viewer about the length of the lines.

4. Try this experiment to demonstrate the autokinetic effect. Get a flashlight. Tape a piece of cardboard to the lens of the flashlight so no light will shine through. Punch a pinhole into the cardboard so that a small amount of light can be seen. Now attach the flashlight to your ceiling, say with string and tape, so that the light is visible. Come back when it is night. Turn the flashlight on. Close the drapes or blinds and darken your room. Now look at the light and keep looking at it. Does it appear to move? If the light does appear to move, estimate how far it moved. Try the experiment with someone else.

5. In a book on art or the history of art, look for illustrations of linear perspective, atmospheric perspective, the use of light and shadow, and partial concealment. See how these techniques are used to create the illusions of depth

6. You might find it interesting to recreate Ebbinghaus' experiment. Make up a list of thirteen nonsense syllables. Each syllable should have three letters (for example, KIR or JAC). See how long it takes you to learn the list. Wait an hour and repeat the procedure. See how long it takes you to learn the list the second time. What was your savings in time?

7. Imagine you are a writer and you have been asked to write a movie script about the misuse of scientific information in psychology. Can you think of a plot using any of the ideas in this chapter?

8. Some people who say they have psychic powers claim these powers can work over a great distance. While the evidence for this has not convinced many scientists, you may want to try the following experiment, just out of curiosity. Pair off with one of your classmates. One of you will play the part of the psychic, the other will be the target. Agree on a given time of day when both of you haven't much to do. The target will go somewhere, not giving the psychic any hints of the destination. At the agreed time, the target will concentrate on his or her surroundings and try to send a "thought message" to the psychic. At this time, the psychic will think of the target and draw a sketch of the surroundings that come into his or her mind. If your picture happens to turn out to be close to the truth, by all means repeat the experiment. If you are close again, you may be ready to open for business.

Test Your Knowledge:
PERCEPTION

Read each statement and decide whether it is TRUE or FALSE. **Write your answers on a separate sheet of paper.**

1. Extrasensory perception is accepted as a fact by the great majority of psychologists.

2. People experiencing sensory deprivation have reported visual hallucinations.

3. Subliminal perception refers to reactions to stimuli at or below threshold levels.

4. In Gestalt psychology, **figure** is the background in which an object is perceived.

5. Linear perspective as used by artists creates the perception of distance by making lines converge.

6. The absolute threshold is usually defined as the point at which everybody in the group can identify a hard-to-make-out stimulus.

7. According to the Gestalt psychologists, when you hear a melody, you hear it as a series of individual sounds, not as an organized whole.

8. Most of the evidence to date suggests that women tend to be better observers of other people than men.

9. Perceptual defense experiments have reported different thresholds of report for loaded words and neutral words.

Test Your Knowledge:
MEMORY

Read each statement and decide whether it is TRUE or FALSE. **Write your answers on a separate sheet of paper.**

1. Ebbinghaus' nonsense syllables were combinations of three letters with little meaning.

2. Ebbinghaus found that the highest rate of forgetting of nonsense syllables occurred during the first hour after memorization.

3. Ebbinghaus found that meaningful and meaningless material were forgotten at the same rate.

4. Retroactive inhibition is what happens when one learns two sets of materials and the learning of the second set interferes with the memory for the first.

5. When one learns a series of items, the middle items of the series are usually remembered better than the beginning or final items.

6. Experiments suggest that distributed learning often leads to better retention than massed learning.

7. In the three-stage theory of memory, sensory-information storage is thought of as a process lasting several minutes.

8. People can hold hundreds of bits of information at a time in short-term memory.

9. People usually remember more in recognition tests than in recall tests.

10. The procedure of hypnotizing witnesses in criminal investigations has won unqualified acceptance from the scientific community as a method of obtaining accurate information.

11. Brain-injured patients show excellent explicit memory and poor implicit memory.

12. Tip-of-the-tongue experiences are rare events.

Test Your Knowledge:
LEARNING

Read each statement and decide whether it is TRUE or FALSE. **Write your answers on a separate sheet of paper.**

1. The behaviorist believed the best way to study the learning process was for subjects to report their introspections (to say what was taking place in their minds).

2. Pavlov found that the best way to achieve a conditioned response was to show the animal the unconditioned (natural) stimulus first and then present the conditioned stimulus afterwards.

3. Higher order conditioning is easily extinguished.

4. Partial reinforcement produces greater resistance to extinction than reinforcing responses on every occasion.

5. A secondary reinforcer is a stimulus that is paired with a primary reinforcer in the learning process and acquires the power to reinforce behavior on its own.

6. Money is an example of a primary reinforcer, not a secondary reinforcer.

7. Electric shocks may produce long-term avoidance reactions in laboratory animals.

8. The Gestalt psychologists believed learning was more a matter of perception and insight than the results of reinforcement.

9. The Skinner box is a complex learning environment which provides many different response possibilities for the animal.

10. Discrimination learning can be achieved in the Skinner box by reinforcing the animal when a stimulus is present and not reinforcing the animal when the stimulus is not present.

CHAPTER 5

Motivation

The famous mountain climber George Leigh Mallory was asked why he had attempted to climb Mount Everest. He answered, "Because it is there." Mallory's answer implied that there was something about human beings that made them strive to do new things, to reach out and attempt the unknown.

Most of the time our motivations are more commonplace than this. Take Richard and Jeff, for example. Both are students in an eleventh-grade English class at Jefferson High School. Their teacher has assigned the class the task of writing a theme. Richard spent many hours in the library, reading and gathering material. Then he made up an outline, organizing what he wanted to say. He wrote and rewrote the theme. In contrast, Jeff watched TV industriously, went to a party, and put off writing the theme until an hour before class. Richard was motivated to achieve good grades. Jeff acted as if he didn't care about his grades.

Let's get even more commonplace. Take two white rats, Max and Mo. They've been trained by a psychology professor to press a bar in a Skinner box. The professor hasn't fed Max in a long time, while Mo has eaten until he is stuffed. When Max was given a chance to press the bar to earn food pellets, he went at it as fast as he could. Mo just went to sleep.

The words **motivation** and **motive** can take us in many directions. Here are two more examples. Have you ever seen a courtroom drama on

TV where the district attorney sums up the case against the accused? The district attorney points a finger at the defendant and says, "She had the opportunity, the weapon, and the motive."

An actress, while rehearsing a play, may speak to the director. She wants to better understand the character she is playing. She asks the director about the character's lines and actions. She inquires, "What is her motivation for doing this?"

From these examples, you can see that motivation has to do with the reasons for our actions, with the forces that make us behave certain ways. In our examples, the mountain climber wanted to experience adventure and challenge. Richard wanted to achieve good grades in school. Max wanted to satisfy hunger pangs. The district attorney was trying to point out reasons for a criminal act. The actress was trying to portray her part convincingly for the audience, so she wanted to know why the character was doing what she was doing.

One may think of the word *motive* as a reason for what a person wants to do or does not want to do. If you were asked, "Would you like to go to a party?", you might say, "Sure." You feel positively motivated or drawn to the idea. We sometimes call this an *approach motive*. If you were asked if you would like to take an hour-long psychology test tomorrow, you might say, "No." The thought might be an uncomfortable one and give rise to an urge to avoid the test if you could. We call such a desire an *avoidance motive*. Is there a way to develop a viral infection by tomorrow?

When looking at different types of motives, psychologists usually distinguish between biological drives and social motives. The biological drives, like hunger and thirst, are thought of as largely instinctive. The social motives are acquired as part of growing up in a society.

Another important distinction psychologists like to make is between **extrinsic motivation** and **intrinsic motivation**. When the source of the motivation comes from somewhere else, it's extrinsic. When it comes from within, it's intrinsic. If Sally only practices the piano when her mother nags her, the motivation is extrinsic. If she practices because playing the piano brings her pleasure, the motivation is intrinsic.

Motivation involves goals or objectives. When you want to do something or want to avoid something, you have some more or less specific goal in mind. People differ in the level of the goals they set for themselves and this in turn influences what they do.

Motives may be *frustrated*. You want to go to that party, but you hear a familiar voice in the background saying, "No way!" What happens then? And sometimes motives may be in conflict with one another. How are these conflicts resolved?

Let us take a closer look at some of the issues we have brought up here.

The Biological Drives

The biological drives are basic, relating both to the survival of the person and the species. One thinks of hunger and thirst, the sex drive, and some aspects of the maternal drive. Learning theorists such as Clark Hull believed that such drives, along with social motives, activate behavior and that reinforcement lowers the level of these drives. As a simple example, imagine a hungry person. He will do things to obtain food. The food will lessen the hunger pains.

To study the relationship of biological drives and behavior, researchers have invented ways of varying the level of drive in their subjects. To do this, the researchers deprive the subjects (usually laboratory animals) of reinforcement for different lengths of time. For example, one could study the effect of different levels of hunger on rats by not feeding them for certain amounts of time (6 hours, 12 hours, 18 hours, 24 hours, etc.). One could then see how the animals perform on some task, such as pressing the bar on a Skinner box or learning to run through a maze. As you might suspect, hungrier animals will do more to get food. However, if the animal is deprived for too long, it may react with apathy.

The sex drive has been the topic of much research, not only with human subjects, but with many other species as well. Scientists have studied the mating behaviors of species ranging from swallows to monkeys. Researchers have looked at the sex drive both from the standpoint of biology and social behavior.

Researchers in the 1920's carried out some interesting experiments in which they tried to find out which of several biological drives (thirst, hunger, sex, maternal) seemed to be strongest. The experiment went something like this. The subjects, laboratory rats, were placed on one side of an electrified grid. Something they wanted (food, water, a sexual partner) was placed on the other side of the grid. To obtain satisfaction, the rats had to cross the grid. The experimenters noted how many times the animals would cross the barrier to satisfy a specific type of drive.

Would you care to hazard a guess as to which drive proved strongest? In this study, it was the maternal drive. Mother rats were willing to sustain more electric shocks to get to their young than for any other type of reinforcement provided in the study. While these results don't necessarily apply to all mothers of all species, naturalists can point to numerous examples of the strength of the maternal drive of animals in the wild. Such examples include the sacrifice of the mother's own life to protect her young.

Social Motives

Social motives develop as part of the learning process. Social motives are acquired in childhood, taking form and shape as we move through the age-related niches the society has created for us.

There are many social motives. Henry Murray, in his book *Explorations in Personality*, worked out a long list of them. For people who are in their teens or early twenties, motives related to *achievement, affiliation, autonomy,* and *love* are usually of great importance.

Achievement motives have to do with the desire to accomplish something, and to win recognition for one's efforts. Affiliation is the desire to be with other people, to share experiences rather than be alone. Autonomy is the need for independence, the need to do things one's own way rather than follow the directions of others. Romantic love has been viewed as a fusion of the biological sex drive and the social affiliation motive.

Psychologists have been particularly interested in studying achievement motivation. To measure achievement motivation, psychologists sometimes use tests with direct questions. Such a test might ask: "Would you like to write an important book?" "How important is it for you to obtain high grades in school?" "Do you enjoy challenges such as solving difficult problems?" Psychologists have also used projective methods, asking subjects to make up stories in response to pictures from the Thematic Apperception Test. If the stories contained ideas relating to achievement, it was assumed that the subjects had higher needs for achievement. This was because the ideas came in part from the person's mind and were only partly suggested by the contents of the picture.

One of the conclusions from research on achievement motivation was that we cannot necessarily make good predictions about achievement behavior from simply knowing a person's achievement motivation. In one study, for example, it was found that people with high achievement motivation tried harder on some laboratory tests but didn't perform any better than people with low achievement motivation. Another study found only a weak relationship between achievement motivation and the kinds of jobs students aspired to. Clearly, other things intervene between what one wants to achieve and what one can actually do.

Social Influence

Affiliation, or the desire to be with others, to share experiences, is an important social motive. Being a member of a family, group, or social organization provides much of the meaning in our lives. There is, however, another side to the coin. Groups exert pressure on individuals to conform to their values. The pressure exerted by the group on individual members to share the views of the group and conform to its values is an important form of social motivation. One finds this kind of pressure operating in both organized social settings (for instance, in school or at work) and informal social relationships. What we call peer pressure is mostly found in informal relationships.

A classic experiment demonstrating the power of group pressure was performed by Solomon Asch. Picture a situation in which a number of people are seated around a table. You are one of these seated. The experimenter shows drawings of lines to the group and asks each person to estimate the length of the lines. One by one, the people around you make their estimates. You are surprised by how out of line the estimates are. You have no way of knowing that all these other people are working with the experimenter and the procedure is rigged. There you are alone. You can't believe what people are saying, but now everyone has finished and it's your turn. Do you report what your eyes tell you, or do you go along with the group? Asch found that when there was a unanimous majority against a single person, about one third of the lone subjects agreed with the group's opinion even when it was wrong.

Ordering Motives in Terms of Priority

In addition to the motives we have already mentioned (achievement, affiliation, autonomy, etc.), we could offer a list of many more. For example, have you ever watched a baby crawling around the kitchen opening up cabinets? We might call this motive curiosity or an exploratory motive. Or have you watched a mother tenderly cuddling her baby? Murray would call the need expressed here nurturance. We could easily extend our list by carefully watching human beings as they went about their daily activities. Our list, however, might become unwieldy and disorganized, something like a shopping list.

Abraham Maslow suggested an interesting way to organize our thinking about motives. He felt some needs or motives were more basic than others; they had a higher priority and had to be satisfied first. Maslow believed that once people satisfy their more basic needs, they can turn their attention to the motives waiting "on the back burner." Maslow ranked a number of basic needs in terms of the order in which they required attention. He called this ranking a *hierarchy of needs*.

In Maslow's scheme, the most basic needs are physiological needs, such as hunger and thirst. All else waits upon the satisfaction of these basic needs.

The next step is *safety needs*. The individual requires protection, security, stability, and freedom from too much anxiety.

When physiological needs have been satisfied and safety needs met, the individual seeks satisfaction on the next level. The next set of needs, according to Maslow, relate to love, affection, and a feeling of belonging.

At the fourth level in Maslow's scheme are motives relating to self-respect and self-esteem. These needs include a sense of mastery, achievement, and recognition by others of one's achievements.

The fifth level, in Maslow's view, is self-actualization. Maslow describes self-actualiza-tion as "man's desire for self-fulfillment, namely, . . .the tendency for him to become actualized in what he is potentially."

Beyond this Maslow speaks of needs to learn and to satisfy one's intellectual curiosity, and needs for beauty and order.

In Maslow's theory, more basic motivations take priority over less basic motivations. One can see from observations in everyday life that this is not always the case. For example, Maslow theorized that safety motivations had a very high priority. But how many times have you seen people ignore health and safety in favor of other considerations? Think of the behavior of some people behind the wheel of an automobile. If Maslow were correct, why would a soldier perform heroic acts in war? He is risking his life for values and social needs which have a lower priority on Maslow's scheme. Counterexamples such as these raise questions about the usefulness of Maslow's scheme.

Extrinsic vs. Intrinsic Motivation

Intrinsic motivation refers to doing something because you like the activity. Good examples would be hobbies that bring you pleasure, sports that you enjoy, being with people that you like. Extrinsic motivation refers to doing something because of external demands on or rewards for your efforts. A good example would be working at a job you dislike because you need the salary check to pay your bills.

Common extrinsic motivators or incentives are praise for a good performance, disapproval for a bad performance, and, of course, money. Money has long been used as an incentive for improving performance. The basic idea is to link pay to performance; the better one produces, the more one gets paid. A review of 20 studies looked at the effectiveness of financial incentives in improving worker output in industry. The review found evidence in 18 of the 20 studies that financial incentives improved a worker's output. Plant-wide or department-wide incentive plans are now being used as well as incentive plans for individual workers.

Extrinsic and intrinsic motivations can occur in combination. A good example would be a professional athlete who is well paid for her performance but also plays for pride. Her athletic skills are important to her and she wants to do her best.

Jay Efron and his colleagues provided a neat demonstration of the power of combining intrinsic motivations, personal pride, and acceptance of a challenge, with an extrinsic motivation, living up to a commitment to another person. Efron's subjects were asked to take part in an endurance test; they held a 5-pound dumbbell with one hand, palm down, straight out to the side at shoulder level. They were told to hold the dumbbell in this position for as long as they could. After an initial trial, the subjects in one group were asked if they would make a verbal commitment to *better* their endurance score. If the subjects accepted this verbal contract, they were to make it their job to hold the weight "much longer." A number of comparison groups were used, including one in which the subjects were offered a chance at winning a $25 prize. These subjects were told that the longer they held the dumbbell, the more chances they would have to win the prize.

The results? The subjects who accepted the verbal commitment increased their endurance more than the subjects in the comparison groups. The combination of pride and commitment was the most effective form of motivation used in the study.

Goal Setting

No matter what the kind of motivation, it is usually possible to set higher or lower goals. The level of the goal a person sets is sometimes called the person's **level of aspiration**. Take Maureen and Andrea as examples. Both young women are joggers. If you ask Maureen how many miles she wants to jog, she might say, "Four." If you ask Andrea, she might say, "Ten." Andrea's level of aspiration for running is higher. She's even thinking of training to run a marathon.

Or look at Jim and Bruce. Jim is trying for A's in school, hoping for a scholarship; Bruce is content with C's.

Psychologists have carried out a great deal of research on goal setting. In reviewing this research, Edwin Locke and his colleagues reported that the goal set makes a difference in performance. *Higher goals usually bring higher levels of performance.* They found this to be true in studies in which subjects were given tasks like addition, card sorting, perceptual speed tasks, and learning prose. They found it was also true in real-life field tests with outdoor workers (logging crews) and indoor workers (typists). Higher goals were associated with a higher level of performance in a large majority of the studies. So it seems a pretty good bet that if you want to do more, you should set your goals *high*. Not so high that you set yourself up for failure, but high enough to push yourself some.

Locke and his colleagues came up with another interesting conclusion in their review of research. If you set a goal, make it clear-cut and specific. People who are given clear-cut goals tend to outperform people who are simply told to "do their best."

Combining these two ideas suggests that setting challenging, clear-cut goals will lead to a higher level of performance.

Frustration

We may be motivated to do something, but we may find obstacles in our path which prevent us from reaching our goal. We are hoping to attain some kind of satisfaction, but we may be delayed or stopped outright. We refer to what we feel in this kind of situation as **frustration**.

Think of a child who wants to go out and play but is told by his mother he can't. Or imagine a student who is eager to take the driver training course at school but is told she has to wait six months until there is an opening. Have you ever seen cars stuck in a traffic jam, inching along the highway like so many turtles? Imagine what some of these drivers are muttering under their breaths.

One frequent effect of frustration is anger, sometimes accompanied by aggressive acts. In 1939, a group of psychologists working at Yale University developed a theory about the conditions under which frustration would lead to aggression. They believed the chances of frustration producing aggression would increase when the motivation to perform the frustrated activity was strong, the interference was great, and there were other frustrations in the person's life adding to the overall level of frustration. They believed that whether an aggressive act would occur depended on whether the person expected retaliation for the aggression.

It is clear that frustration does not *always* lead to aggression. If a frustration is perceived as a reasonable or understandable one, the person may accept it gracefully. For example, if there is no money available to go on a vacation at the seashore, one might accept this and plan for a less expensive vacation. Or one might try to overcome the frustrating condition by trying to solve the problem. For instance, one might look for a part-time job to earn additional money. Nonetheless, it often happens that anger is preceded by frustrating incidents.

If you ask people who are angry or annoyed why they are feeling that way, you will often find clear-cut examples of frustration in their answers.

My colleague, Roland Tanck, and I asked college students to keep a diary over a ten-day period. We asked the students to write in the diary the answer to the question: "Did you feel angry or annoyed today? If yes, what was it that made you feel angry?"

Some examples of frustrating incidents that preceded their anger are:

"The teacher refused to give me the exam today, and she said to come in and do it tomorrow morning."

"I got waked up by my roommate's alarm clock at 7:15 in the morning."

"The fact that I had to stay in Johnstown longer than I wanted to."

"A person came along on our picnic that I and others didn't want there."

Sometimes frustration can come from one source and aggression can be vented on another—an innocent party. Have you ever seen a situation like this? George had a bad day. He received a failing grade on an algebra exam. His father was so upset that he took away George's privileges to use the family car for a week. That evening when George had a date with his girlfriend Marsha, he was feeling frustrated and irritable. He got into a big fight with Marsha. She never really understood what was going on and was bewildered by the whole thing.

Psychologists have run many studies on the effects of frustration. Here is an example of such an experiment. It was conducted by Arnold Buss.

Imagine you enter a room where there is an apparatus with buttons to push, lights that may flash on, and electrodes to attach to people. You are told that the buttons numbered from 1 to 10 will deliver increasing intensities of electric shocks to anyone attached to the electrodes. The electrodes are attached to you. Some of the buttons are pushed so you can get an idea how the shock feels at different levels.

There is another student in the room with you. The two of you have been told you are going to serve as subjects in an experiment on learning. One of you is going to be the teacher (experimenter) and the other the learner (subject). You each draw a card. Yours says *experimenter*. He says he drew *subject*. Actually, the draw is rigged. As in the Asch experiment, your fellow student is really an accomplice of the experimenter and everything he does is part of an act. But you don't know this.

You begin the phony learning experiment. You have already been told by the instructor that how fast you are able to "teach" your subject will influence the grade you will receive in the psychology course. The faster he learns, the better will be your chances for a higher grade. Your instructions are to give your subject an electric shock every time he makes an incorrect response in the learning test. You are to decide the intensity of the shock. The subject starts making mistakes. You think that if he doesn't learn in a hurry, you may get a lower grade in the course. You hit the shock button. If it is a high intensity button, he groans. Actually, the shock device has been secretly turned off, but once again, you don't know that. The subject continues to make errors and you continue to give the electric shocks. You wonder how high a shock you should give him.

There is a control group of students who go through the same procedure, except that the "experimenters" are not told anything about their performance affecting their grades. There is much less reason for them to experience frustration when the subject makes an error.

The study showed that in the frustration condition the students gave higher levels of electric shock than in the control condition. The experiment provided further support for the theory that frustration may bring on aggression.

As a footnote to the study, we should mention that the students were told about the deception after the study was completed. The ethics of psychological research with human subjects require that the investigator discuss deceptive procedures with the subjects and attempt to dispel any negative reactions created by the experiment.

Conflict

In psychological terms, a **conflict** between goals is usually described in terms of *approach* and *avoidance*. Sometimes a person may be torn between two positive goals. This is called an *approach-approach conflict*. As an illustration, let's consider Ellen's problem. Ellen, a high school senior, has been accepted by two excellent universities. Ellen is attracted to both schools. Which one does she pick?

Compared to the difficulties posed by other types of conflicts, an approach-approach conflict is not much of a problem. Since both universities are excellent, Ellen can't really lose much no matter which she chooses. And take Joe; he hasn't been accepted by any school. He'd love to have Ellen's problem.

APPROACH-AVOIDANCE CONFLICTS

Have you heard this tale from the *Odyssey*? The hero Ulysses' ship approached the lair of the sirens. Their song was so enticing that sailors who heard it were mesmerized into crashing their ships on the rocks. Ulysses wanted very badly to hear the song, but did not want to risk the destruction of his ship. He managed to resolve this classic *approach-avoidance conflict* by having himself bound to the mast of his ship so he could hear the song of the sirens. Meanwhile his men, their ears filled with wax, continued to row the ship safely through.

Approach-avoidance conflict involves a situation that has both positive and negative meanings for a person. Terms like "love-hate relationship" or "ambivalence" are used to describe it. A person may have both positive and negative feelings about another person, about a school, about a work situation, or even about a car.

What happens when a person begins to move toward a goal that has both approach and avoidance aspects? If the push from the avoidance is stronger than the pull from the approach, something like this may happen. The person approaches the goal at a distance, begins to get closer, then begins to feel the avoidance elements. Anxiety mounts. She stops when the approach and the avoidance forces are about equal. She hesitates and perhaps retreats slightly. For a time, she may become stuck, neither attaining nor giving up the goal.

Imagine yourself in this typical approach-avoidance situation. You'd like to call someone up on the phone for a date. The person seems very attractive to you, but you have a strong feeling you're going to be turned down. You don't like the idea of being rejected. You approach the phone. Your anxiety mounts. You lift the phone. You hear the buzz. You begin to dial and stop. That's it. You put the phone down and move away. The avoidance push was too strong and took control.

What happens if the approach is stronger than the avoidance? This shouldn't be a problem if the goal in question is basically desirable. But suppose it's undesirable. Say the goal is obtaining an addictive substance like alcohol or heroin. Have you ever known a person who is an alcoholic or a drug addict? For many people the lure of the drug seems stronger than the knowledge that the use of the drug could have disastrous consequences.

AVOIDANCE-AVOIDANCE CONFLICTS

Have you ever heard such phrases as "damned if you do and damned if you don't" or "caught between a rock and a hard place"? Such expressions are about *avoidance-avoidance conflicts*. Both situations appear negative. Both push you away and you're in between, having to make a choice between undesirable alternatives.

Here's an example. A young woman is living at home. Her father is an angry man; he's dictatorial and he drinks a lot. Her mother is passive and puts up with her husband's abuse. The young woman finds the situation very unpleasant. But the outside world doesn't look too good to her either. She has no money, and no job skills. She has little experience in coping with the world, and has never been away from home. Faced with the choice between a known quantity which is bad and an unknown one which in her own mind may be worse, she may feel her situation is hopeless.

How are avoidance-avoidance conflicts resolved? Several possibilities come to mind. Perhaps there are actually more than two options available. When people are filled with a sense of despair, they may not consider all the possibilities that are open to them. If one of the options involves unknowns, as in the case of the young woman's fear of the outside world, it is

possible to set about carefully "testing the waters." Things out there may be better than she imagines them to be. If the negatives around one are real, then one may have to consider making changes in the situation, difficult as it may seem.

Avoidance-avoidance conflicts are difficult to deal with and can lead to a demoralized emotional state.

Anxiety

Anxiety is an uncomfortable feeling that is often brought on by the expectation of unpleasant events that may have to be faced. Anxiety is usually thought of as the anticipation of the unpleasant. The perception that something really unpleasant is about to occur is often accompanied by physiological reactions triggered by the sympathetic nervous system. These reactions include an increased heart rate, faster breathing, and sweating. Indications of severe anxiety are disturbances in speech and muscular tremors.

A situation in which there is uncertainty about something important is often accompanied by feelings of anxiety. You may be on the edge of your chair while watching your favorite team compete in the big game. But if you see the game on the following day on a television replay, it's unlikely to cause much tension.

Any situation that arouses anxiety may be called a *stressor*. The experiences of stress or anxiety are basically similar. We are occasionally exposed to physical stressors, situations which pose dangers to our health and safety. Combat and physical assault are clear-cut examples. More commonly, stressors are social-psychological in nature. Anxiety can be aroused by situations that threaten one's self-esteem, by the fear of being evaluated unfavorably by others, and by worries about performing poorly. For students, impending tests and exams are clear-cut examples of psychological stressors.

When Roland Tanck and I asked students to keep a diary, we included the question, "Did you feel tense or anxious today?" (and *if yes*)

"What do you think was causing these tense feelings?" We often got responses such as these:

"The exam for tomorrow."

"The thought of getting my test back."

"Worrying about the results of the history exam."

"Test anxiety."

Anxiety may serve as a mobilizer. You are keyed up for whatever it is that is anticipated. This may help your performance. Intense anxiety, however, can be a hindrance rather than a help. A good example of intense anxiety is the feelings that come with stage fright. You want to be mobilized to perform, not immobilized. Some laboratory studies have suggested that anxiety disrupts the performance of complex tasks more than the performance of simple tasks. Other studies suggest that people who tend to be anxious do not perform well when they expect failure. It has been suggested that when anxious people are required to perform, they may pay too much attention to themselves, their performance, and their own anxiety to do as well as they are capable of doing.

For an example of the negative impact of anxiety on performance, let's look at an athletic activity, scuba diving. In a study carried out by T. J. Griffiths and colleagues, beginning scuba-diving students were used as subjects. The subjects were first asked to take a psychological test assessing their current anxiety level. Then they were graded on their performance in a series of scuba-diving tasks, including skin diving skill, putting on and removing scuba-diving equipment under water, and making a deep-water quarry dive. The researchers found that higher anxiety levels before the performance were associated with poorer performance on the more difficult scuba-diving tasks.

Moods and Performance

We have seen that anxiety is an emotional state that may affect performance. In general, we would expect that a person's moods might affect her performance. If a person is in a depressed mood, for example, we might find that her concentration and motivation are reduced. She might attempt less and do less. What about a positive mood? Will such a mood have a positive impact on behavior? Does "feeling good" have a positive impact?

One rather neat experiment suggests that a positive mood may cause one to reach out toward others, resulting in increased helping behavior. This experimental demonstration of what has been called "the glow of good will" goes something like this. The setting is the student union of a university campus. Students walk up to use a pay telephone. One out of every two students who pick up the phone will discover a coin that has "accidentally" been left in the coin return compartment of the phone. Whether a student takes the coin is noted.

A female member of the research team sits a short distance from the phone booth. After the subjects finish their calls, they walk toward the woman. She "accidentally" spills a large folder of papers on the floor. Would you guess that the subjects who have received the mood-enhancing coin will more often help her pick up the papers than the subjects who didn't find the coin? Well, that's what happened in some, though not all, of the studies like this. In one experiment, for example, 65 percent of the subjects who received the coin helped the woman. Only 30 percent of the subjects who did not get a coin helped her.

Some Questions and Activities

1. What are the activities you like to do, activities that intrinsically motivate you?

2. What are some of the extrinsic motivations that you see in everyday life?

3. If you had to motivate yourself to a super-high performance level, what things would you tell yourself?

4. Sometimes a high level of anxiety can interfere with one's performance. This can happen while one is taking an examination. What are some things a person might do to reduce such "test anxiety"?

5. Can you think of an approach-approach conflict that occurs in the school situation?

6. Can you think of an approach-avoidance conflict that occurs in the school situation?

7. Can you think of an avoidance-avoidance conflict that occurs in the school situation?

8. Of the three conflicts you described above, which do you feel would be hardest to resolve?

9. If you knew someone who "blew up" every time he or she experienced a feeling of frustration, what things would you tell the person about other ways of handling the problem?

10. Try designing an experiment to find out what effect different levels of reward (for example, different amounts of money) would have on performance. Pick a type of performance that's easy to measure.

Test Your Knowledge

Read each statement and decide whether it is TRUE or FALSE. **Write your answers on a separate sheet of paper.**

1. Intrinsic motivation is motivation that comes from within oneself.

2. According to Maslow, self-actualization is the most basic human motive and must be satisfied before attention can be paid to other motives.

3. Studies show that measures of achievement motivation are excellent predictors of a person's actual level of attainment.

4. Studies show that people who set low goals for themselves tend to perform at high levels.

5. Aggression always follows frustration.

6. A high level of anxiety tends to interfere with the performance of difficult tasks.

7. Ambivalence is a term referring to approach and avoidance tendencies toward the same person or situation.

8. The term *level of aspiration* refers to the level of the goals one sets for oneself.

9. Having to choose between two desirable jobs is an example of an approach-approach conflict.

10. The experiment by Asch showed that in a group setting, a unanimous majority may exert considerable influence on the stated opinions of people who find themselves alone in their position.

11. Studies suggest that urging a person to "do well" is more effective than setting a specific goal for the person.

12. Studies in industry indicate that using money as an incentive does not help to improve performance.

13. Anxiety is usually thought of as the anticipation of an unpleasant event.

14. The physiological reactions associated with anxiety reflect the action of the para-sympathetic nervous system.

CHAPTER 6

The Study of Personality

The study of **personality** deals with the enduring traits or characteristics of persons. Most everyone has their moments when they might feel angry, happy, or sad, but these are moods that come and go. The study of personality deals with characteristics that last. If a person acts in an aggressive way much of the time, one might speak of that person as having an aggressive personality. If a person rarely takes risks, one might speak of a cautious personality. The language of personality describes the more enduring ways a person behaves, perceives the world, and relates to other people.

In our exploration of personality, we will discuss three questions. These are: How do we describe or talk about personality? What are some of the major theories about personality? How do psychologists study personality?

The Language of Personality

There are many ways of describing people. To give you an idea of some of the possibilities, we will begin with a game. Browsing through the dictionary, we took out some descriptive words here and there, one or more for each letter of the alphabet. We put these words, and some phrases suggested by the words, in the following list.

Try rating yourself on each descriptive word or phrase on a separate sheet of paper. Use the following guidelines:

If the word or phrase hardly ever describes the way you are, check (√) hardly ever.

If the word or phrase describes the way you are once in a while, check (√) once in a while.

If the word or phrase describes the way you are fairly often, check (√) fairly often.

If the word or phrase describes the way you are very often, check (√) very often.

O.K.? Go ahead!

Descriptive Word or Phrase	Hardly Ever	Once in a While	Fairly Often	Very Often
adventurous	( )	( )	( )	( )
aggressive	( )	( )	( )	( )
ambitious	( )	( )	( )	( )
anxious	( )	( )	( )	( )
assertive	( )	( )	( )	( )
athletic	( )	( )	( )	( )
bold	( )	( )	( )	( )
cautious	( )	( )	( )	( )
careful	( )	( )	( )	( )
clownish	( )	( )	( )	( )

Descriptive Word or Phrase	Hardly Ever	Once in a While	Fairly Often	Very Often
considerate	( )	( )	( )	( )
creative	( )	( )	( )	( )
dependent on others	( )	( )	( )	( )
domineering	( )	( )	( )	( )
easygoing	( )	( )	( )	( )
energetic	( )	( )	( )	( )
fair-minded	( )	( )	( )	( )
fearful	( )	( )	( )	( )
friendly	( )	( )	( )	( )
fun loving	( )	( )	( )	( )
get along well	( )	( )	( )	( )
helpful	( )	( )	( )	( )
hot tempered	( )	( )	( )	( )
impulsive	( )	( )	( )	( )
independent	( )	( )	( )	( )
irritable	( )	( )	( )	( )
jovial	( )	( )	( )	( )
kindhearted	( )	( )	( )	( )
low-keyed	( )	( )	( )	( )
loyal	( )	( )	( )	( )
moody	( )	( )	( )	( )
nervous	( )	( )	( )	( )
noisy	( )	( )	( )	( )
obedient	( )	( )	( )	( )
open	( )	( )	( )	( )
passionate	( )	( )	( )	( )
passive	( )	( )	( )	( )
pessimistic	( )	( )	( )	( )
pleasure seeking	( )	( )	( )	( )
quick-witted	( )	( )	( )	( )
quiet	( )	( )	( )	( )
rebellious	( )	( )	( )	( )
reserved	( )	( )	( )	( )
romantic	( )	( )	( )	( )
self-controlled	( )	( )	( )	( )
shy	( )	( )	( )	( )
sociable	( )	( )	( )	( )
supportive	( )	( )	( )	( )
sympathetic	( )	( )	( )	( )
trusting	( )	( )	( )	( )
unlucky	( )	( )	( )	( )
uptight	( )	( )	( )	( )
vigorous	( )	( )	( )	( )
wise	( )	( )	( )	( )
xuberant (*Well, you find something that starts with* x.)	( )	( )	( )	( )
yielding	( )	( )	( )	( )
zestful	( )	( )	( )	( )

Remembering that what you have just done is not a personality test, just an informal exercise to get us started, look back at the words or phrases you marked "fairly often" or "very often." Do these words provide a fair description of the way you see yourself? Psychologists use the term **self-concept** to describe the way one perceives oneself. Just as one may perceive others, one may look at oneself as an object.

Other people may perceive you differently from the way you perceive yourself. Imagine that one of your best friends went through the preceding list of adjectives in an attempt to describe you. How would your friend's choices about you differ from your own self-concept?

As you can see from the list of words, there are many ways of describing people. Some of these words, for instance *domineering* and *supportive*, describe personality or character traits. Because it's difficult to keep in mind hundreds of possible personality traits, psychologists have looked for ways of organizing these traits into simpler working models.

Some psychologists have used a statistical technique called *factor analysis*. Done with the aid of computers, factor analysis is used to identify a small number of factors which underlie a large number of traits. For example, imagine you had given out a personality questionnaire to your fellow students. The questionnaire contained many items, including the following three questions: "Do you like to go to parties?" "Do you enjoy the company of friends?" "Would you generally rather be alone than with people?" A factor analysis would probably show that the responses to these three questions hung together (correlated), and that the questions were assessing a common factor. We might name such a factor friendliness, affiliation, or extroversion.

A number of studies have been carried out using factor analysis. The findings from these studies have led researchers to conclude that much of the way we describe personality can be boiled down to five broad factors. These factors have been called by different names by different investigators but are usually referred to as "the big five." These five general personality factors have been called *extraversion* or *surgency* (think of people who are active and outgoing); *agreeableness* (think of people who are likeable); *conscientiousness* (think of behaviors like prudence, dependability, and self-control); *emotionality* or *emotional stability* (think of people who are often upset or distressed); and *intellect*.

Another, more intuitive, approach to organizing personality traits was developed by Timothy Leary. Leary worked out a model of the way personality traits related to each other, using a geometric form, the circle. In simplified form, Leary's idea is something like this.

First, we'll draw a circle.

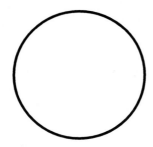

Now, let's put a label at the top of the circle, which we'll call *dominant*. Think of strong, assertive, active behavior. Let's go to the bottom of the circle and label it *submissive*. Think of weak or passive behavior. On the right side of the circle, we'll affix the label *affiliative*. Think of friendly or affectionate behavior. On the left side of the circle, we'll put the label *oppositional*. Think of behavior which is unfriendly or hostile.

Now let's divide the circle into four equal parts (quadrants).

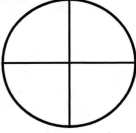

Think of some behavior patterns that might fall into the upper right part of the circle. You'll want to think of behavior patterns which have an assertive thrust and are positively oriented toward other people. How about a teacher who has good relationships with her students, or a father playing with his child, or a physician taking a case history of a patient.

Sally provides a good example of behavior which usually falls into this quadrant of the circle. Sally is a confident, outgoing person who often takes a leadership role at school and with her friends. She frequently makes suggestions and organizes activities.

Now let's think of some behavior patterns which might fall into the quadrant below: behavior patterns which are friendly, but more passive. How about the actions of people who tend to be followers or just like to get along?

For example, most people describe Brian as a quiet, likeable person who gets along well with others. Brian fits in as part of the group. Brian is usually agreeable to the suggestions of others and goes along with what the group does.

Let's try to imagine some behavior which is oppositional, but in a passive way. Have you heard the phrase *passive-aggressive behavior*?

Ellen is a good example. Ellen is very angry with her parents, but doesn't feel free to express her anger at home because she is afraid of the consequences. In trying to deal with the situation, she has begun to behave in passive-aggressive ways. At home, she has been avoiding responsibilities and doesn't tell the truth to her parents. Lately, this behavior pattern has extended to school, where she has been cutting classes.

What pictures come to mind when you think of dominant, oppositional behaviors? How about someone who is bossy and pushes other people around?

Mary is a good example. Mary has several younger brothers and sisters. When she is with her brothers and sisters, Mary is very bossy. She tells the kids what to do and yells at them if they don't pay attention. When she is around her brothers and sisters, she looks tough, sounds tough, and rules by intimidation.

SOCIAL ROLES AND BEHAVIOR

We do not wish to leave the impression that all people can easily be pigeonholed. Some people may show a very wide range of behaviors. Also, a person may behave differently from time to time, and from situation to situation. Take Mary, who is very bossy with her younger sisters and brothers. At school, she is quite cooperative with her teachers. In her biology teacher's words, she is "a very good pupil." And Brian, who is a very pleasant guy most of the time, can be a very tough competitor on the basketball court. He is a physical player around the backboards.

Behavior may change somewhat from situation to situation, depending on the **role** you happen to be in. By role, we mean patterns of behavior that are expected under certain defined social conditions. Think for a moment about your typical behavior when you're:

> having dinner with your family;
> attending a class in mathematics;
> going for a ride with your friends
>   in a car;
> playing in a softball game;
> attending a church or synagogue;
> out on a date;
> working at a summer job.

The expectations for your behavior differ somewhat in these different situations. You are likely to modify your behavior as you move into different roles in society. The roles of student, teacher, parent, employee, etc., are different, and carry different expectations with them. While you are obviously the same person in all the social roles you play, certain of your behaviors are more likely to come out in some situations, while other behaviors are restrained.

Although social roles have an effect on behavior, they may only partially mask the individual's basic personality. If you look at two people in the same social role (say, two of your teachers, two policemen, two doctors, or two mothers in your neighborhood), you may see great differences in their daily behaviors. These differences in part reflect differences in personality.

Personality as a Way of Looking at the World

We have been looking at personality in terms of personality traits: descriptions of typical behavior. Psychologists have also looked at personality in terms of characteristic ways in which the individual views his or her world.

One theory which has aroused a great deal of interest was developed by Julian Rotter. Rotter wanted to learn more about the reinforcement that is a part of peoples' lives. Rotter asked: in the person's view, who controls this reinforcement? Is it viewed as mainly under the control of forces in the outside world? Or does the person believe that he or she has a large degree of control over the likelihood of reinforcement coming in? The characteristic Rotter defined was called **locus of control of reinforcement**. Rotter talked about the degree to which people perceived control of reinforcement as *external* (coming from the outside) or *internal* (coming from the inside).

A good example of different views of the locus of control is provided by the Miklovic sisters. Denise believes that she is in control of her life. She feels that if she works hard in school, gets a college degree, and is assertive in seeking employment, she can have a successful career. In contrast, her sister Betty thinks that how you do in life is pretty much a matter of luck, or who you know, or how the economy is doing. She feels her own efforts wouldn't make much difference. Denise believes that the possibility of getting the things she wants is largely under her own (internal) control, while Betty views external events as being mainly in control.

One of the best-known examples of a personality characteristic based directly upon perception is the concept of *field dependence* developed by Herman Witkin and his colleagues. Have you ever seen a puzzle in which a figure (an object) is hidden or embedded in a background of other objects so that it's hard to pick out from the background? Witkin and his coworkers believed that the ability to break up a background and separate out a figure is an important aspect of personality. The less capable a person is at sifting out figures from the field in which they are located, the more field dependent the person is considered to be. An example of a field-dependent person would be a person who tries to solve a problem, gets lost in details, and has a hard time picking out what's important.

We would like to mention one more characteristic of personality, *tolerance for ambiguity*. Tolerance for ambiguity refers to a person's ability to comfortably exist in a situation in which things are unclear or the outcome is uncertain. George is a good example of a person with a high tolerance for ambiguity. George has been waiting for a letter of acceptance or nonacceptance from a leading university. While he waits, he seems as cool as a cucumber. His friend Alfie is also waiting for a letter. Alfie has little tolerance for ambiguity. He feels threatened by unclear situations. When last seen, he was climbing the walls, feeling irritable, and driving his family nuts.

Theories of Personality

Personality is more than a list of traits or characteristic ways of looking at the world. We are organized, problem-solving creatures who feel things deeply. We sometimes do some remarkable things, and sometimes some very strange things. How does this all work? Do we have a model of personality with which to explain ourselves? While we don't yet have a generally accepted theory of the way personality develops and is organized, there are some very interesting ideas. We are going to look first at

some of the psychoanalytic theories of personality. Then, we will consider a different view of personality which owes much to the studies of anthropologists working in different societies around the globe.

The Psychoanalytic Approach to Personality

The psychoanalysts were the first group of psychologists to undertake a serious study of human personality. The ideas of the psychoanalysts are sometimes complex, and their language can be rather technical. We will attempt to offer a translation, beginning with a glimpse at the theories of Sigmund Freud, the founder of psychoanalysis.

SIGMUND FREUD

Once when Sigmund Freud's father was annoyed at his young son, he was said to have remarked that his boy would never amount to anything. Talk about misjudgments! That had to be one of the all-time examples.

Young Freud went to the head of his class in high school, entered the University of Vienna, and studied medicine. For a while he engaged in scientific research, including studies of the brain and research on the drug cocaine. Eventually, he went into the private practice of medicine.

Freud's interest in the psychological aspects of medical practice was stimulated by his friend Josef Breuer, who was treating a patient he called Anna O.

Anna O. was an extremely intelligent young woman who had been given the task of nursing her sick father. She had little hope of doing anything with her own talents, and instead led a dull life in a puritanical family. Anna developed a host of physical complaints. These included weakness, anemia, distaste for food, inability to talk (for two weeks she was unable to say a syllable, despite making a great effort to speak), and paralysis in her limbs. Breuer noticed that when Anna began to talk under hypnosis about her symptoms and the circumstances under which they arose, the symptoms disappeared. Freud became very interested in the patient and in the possibilities of Breuer's "talking cure."

Later on Freud spent time in Paris. There he observed Charcot's ability to produce hysterical symptoms such as paralysis in normal people by means of hypnosis. Freud moved toward the conclusion that the physical symptoms of hysteria were produced by mental processes.

A few years later, Breuer and Freud published some of their observations and ideas in a work called *Studies on Hysteria*. The book was criticized by some of their medical colleagues, but Freud continued with his investigations.

In trying to understand Freud's theories, it is useful to reconstruct something of the atmosphere of nineteenth-century Vienna, particularly in regard to the attitude toward sexuality. In contrast to the current outlook, sex was a subject that was swept under the rug, kept in the closet. Sex was equated with the forbidden and seemed to be the source of a great deal of guilt.

When Freud worked with his hysterical patients, he often noticed conflicts about sexuality; he concluded that hysterical complaints had their origins in sexual disturbances. At first, Freud believed that his patients had been victims of seduction by members of their own families. At least that is what his patients reported to him. Later on, he suspected that most of these reports were probably not accurate, but were fantasies, things the patients concocted in their own minds.

Freud wondered why his patients reported such things. He did a great deal of self-analysis, and continued working with his patients. Eventually, he developed some theories which aroused a storm of controversy.

The Unconscious.   Freud theorized that there was a part of the mind that was unconscious. This unconscious mind, which Freud called simply **the unconscious**, contained ideas that were out of awareness, normally not accessible to the conscious mind. The ideas in the unconscious were thoughts that the person in

full consciousness would find very unacceptable. The ideas might be painful, disagreeable, even frightening. Freud believed that these thoughts often had to do with sexual impulses and desires.

Freud developed an important concept he called **repression**. Repression is a process by which unacceptable ideas are excluded from consciousness. The process of repression is not a conscious act in which a person says, "I am not going to think about this idea anymore." The process of repression takes place without awareness. Think of repression as a process that can remove uncomfortable ideas from memory and keep them out of awareness.

Freud did not conceive of the unconscious as a quiet place where these unacceptable ideas lay dormant, out of sight for all time. Rather, he believed that these ideas had a certain force or energy attached to them, and sought expression in consciousness or behavior.

The idea may become clearer if we use a rough analogy. Let's make up a computer game called Prisoners. Imagine that on our display screen there is a marked-off zone called the unconscious. This area has all the appearances of a jail. It isn't a totally secure jail, though; the lock is rusty. The prisoners (little blips on the screen) can pick the lock if they work at it. However, there is a guard posted nearby, and as long as he's alert, he isn't about to let anyone pass. Freud would call the guard a censor or a repressive force. In the game the guard has to watch the prisoners all day long, and at times he gets tired and needs rest. While he is relaxing, the prisoners try to escape. Now this guard can regain his alertness very quickly (become energized), and is a whiz at rounding up escaped prisoners. The last thing the prisoners want to do is to make too much noise or become too visible, so to escape, they will *disguise* themselves. In Freud's view, this is what unconscious thoughts do to gain expression. They adopt disguises.

Freud believed that unconscious desires emerged into consciousness in a number of disguised forms. One place they appear, he thought, was in dreams. He believed that at the root of dreams were unacceptable wishes, often sexual, that gained release in the dream. He believed these wishes were usually so disguised in the dream that the person would have trouble understanding their true significance.

Freud believed that another sign of the influence of unconscious thoughts was slips of the tongue. For example, Freud told a story about a sick man who went to his doctor to see if he should go on a special diet. His doctor replied that a special diet wasn't important. In relating the conversation between the man and his doctor, the man's wife misspoke. She said, "The doctor said that diet has nothing to do with his ailments, and that he can eat and drink what I want." In Freud's view the change from "he wants" to "I want" conveyed deeper meanings. Concealed or unconscious thoughts had surfaced, changing the speech process.

Freud believed that the inability to remember names could also be a clue to the action of unconscious thoughts. "Forgetting may be motivated by repression."

Perhaps most important for Freud's use of psychoanalysis as a method of treatment was his belief that unconscious thoughts played a crucial role in the formation of symptoms. Let's return for a moment to Freud's observations of his hysterical patients. Freud believed that, in hysteria, unconscious sexual drives were being held in check; a censoring agent in the personality would not permit these impulses normal expression. To provide a vent for the pressures exerted by the impulses, a kind of compromise was reached between the impulses striving for release and the inhibiting forces. This compromise took the form of a symptom. For example, when a patient experienced a hysterical paralysis, the pressure from the unconscious thoughts was released to some extent in the symptom, while sexual activities were still safely restricted. Meanwhile the patient received some "secondary gain" in the form of attention from his doctors and family. A neat package!

The Oedipus Complex.   Repressed sexuality played an important part in Freud's theory. He believed that sexual feelings developed at a very early age and that these early sexual feelings were for members of the child's family. Freud believed that young children developed such feelings toward their parents: boys toward their mothers and girls toward their fathers. In Freud's view, the boy saw his father as a rival for his mother's love and the girl saw her mother as a rival for her father's love. Freud gave a name to these feelings: the **Oedipus complex.**

The Oedipus complex was named after the tragic character in the ancient Greek play by Sophocles, *Oedipus the King*. In the play, Oedipus, a stranger, comes to the city of Thebes, having performed a great service for the city. He marries the widowed Queen Jocasta. Later on, it is discovered that Oedipus, who had been taken from the city as an infant, is really the son of Jocasta. These revelations bring disaster to the principal characters.

Freud believed that the child's sexual stirrings are a normal part of child development. He theorized that these feelings are turned aside during middle childhood. During adolescence, when sexual interests undergo a strong development, the Oedipus complex is usually resolved.

What happens, according to Freud, is that the adolescent discards the early parental fantasies and seeks mature attachments to peers of the opposite sex. Freud believed that a failure to resolve the Oedipal situation was a prime cause of later psychological disturbances.

The Structure of Personality: The Id, Ego, and Superego.   As Freud's thinking progressed, he began to think of the human personality in terms of three agencies or components. He called the first agency the **id.** The id contained buried and unconscious desires, passions, urges, and primitive impulses, held in check by repression. Freud saw the id as "the dark, inaccessible part of our personality." He called the second agency, which was the reasoning, executive part of the personality, the **ego.** The ego developed out of the primitive id. Its task was to deal with the real world. Freud saw the ego as the agency that perceives, thinks, and makes judgments. He looked upon the third agency as a kind of conscience, full of "should nots" and reproaches for misconduct. He called it the **superego.** The ego was seen as harassed, trying to deal with the demands of the real world plus those of the other two parts of the personality, the id and the superego.

Differences Within the Psychoanalytic Movement

Freud founded psychoanalysis, developing its theories and a set of techniques for therapy. Because his theories about sexuality were so shocking at the time when he introduced them, they aroused a great deal of opposition. The concept of the Oedipus complex, for instance, aroused anger and ridicule. Still, some people were very impressed by Freud's theories. He attracted a number of followers, who practiced psychoanalysis and spread his ideas. Some of these recruits eventually found that they differed with Freud on important issues, and the psychoanalytic movement split in various ways. Two of the best known of psychoanalysts who disagreed with Freud and went off on their own were Carl Jung and Alfred Adler.

CARL JUNG

Carl Gustav Jung was born in Switzerland, studied medicine, specialized in psychiatry, and then became a close associate of Freud. The two men wrote letters and exchanged ideas, and for a while Freud felt that Jung would be his successor as the leader of the psychoanalytic movement. As time went by, however, Jung began to question some of Freud's ideas, especially the importance Freud attached to sexuality and the Oedipus complex. Freud reacted by stating that Jung was in error; the two men finally ended their relationship. Jung then developed his own branch of psychoanalysis, which he called *analytical psychology.*

Jung's view of the unconscious was different from Freud's. Jung pointed out that the unconscious was an idea, a concept. You couldn't see, touch, or feel the unconscious. The nature of the unconscious had to be inferred from behavior. Based on his experience, Jung believed that the unconscious was not just a Pandora's box of unacceptable thoughts and impulses. Rather, he believed that the unconscious contained many potentially useful ideas as well, ideas that, when emerging into consciousness, could find their way into creative expressions. Jung noted that many artists and scientists had had inspirations that suddenly emerged from the unconscious. Jung also theorized that there was a part of the unconscious (he called it the **collective unconscious**) that was a storehouse of the ancestral memories of humankind. The collective unconscious, Jung believed, contained the wisdom and experience of countless centuries. Holding this different view of the unconscious, Jung and his followers became interested in such topics as creativity and mythology.

Jung also is known for his use of the *word association* technique. He did not invent the technique, but applied it to the study of personality. The basic idea of the technique is to present a stimulus word, such as *dog*, to a person and ask for the first word that enters the person's mind. You might expect to hear a response like *cat.* While the person is thinking of a word, one might monitor pulse, respiration,

or galvanic skin response. If the response to the word is unusual or takes a long time in coming, or if there are heightened physiological reactions, one might find some clues to the issues that are troubling the person. Jung believed his word association experiments provided experimental evidence for the theory of repression.

Incidentally, here are a few words from a well-known word-association list. What would your responses be?

sickness   _____

butterfly   _____

stove   _____

red   _____

sleep   _____

blue   _____

lion   _____

cheese   _____

Some popular associations for these words are health, moth, hot, white, bed, sky, tiger, and crackers.

We are also indebted to Jung for the concept of **introversion-extroversion**. This is a basic distinction in the way people relate to the world: inwardly or outwardly; toward the self or toward other people. One thinks of the shy person who is uncomfortable in social gatherings as introverted and the person who seeks out and enjoys social interactions as extroverted.

ALFRED ADLER

Freud's reaction to Jung's leaving the ranks of his followers seemed to be one more of sorrow than of anger. When Alfred Adler left, Freud's reaction seemed more contemptuous. He suggested that Adler had only a slight talent for recognizing unconscious materials and seemed overly concerned with promoting his own ambitions. When Freud and Adler parted company, Adler founded a school of psychology called *individual psychology*.

Adler turned his attention to the social aspects of human beings, rather than the sexual, and to consciousness rather than to the unconscious. Adler is probably best known for coming up with the idea of the **inferiority complex**.

Adler believed that all people experience feelings of inferiority. He felt that an effective way to deal with such feelings was to work hard to try to change the situation that was bringing on the feelings. For example, if you are learning to play the piano and you feel you're not very good at it, you might practice harder in order to improve. Indeed, some people may work so hard at it that they may develop great skill. This pattern, beginning in an inferior position and pushing oneself to overcome the inferiority, Adler called *compensation*. A well-known example of compensation is the behavior of Demosthenes, the ancient Greek who stuttered as a child and by great efforts became a famous orator.

Adler noted that when some people experienced feelings of inferiority, they could not realistically deal with the source of the problem, but often tried to cover up the feelings. Such a person might use various tricks to "reassure himself of his importance." He might deceive himself, try to deceive others, put excessive limits on what he is doing, act with bluster when he feels frightened, or become aggressive and strike out.

Adler believed that the striving for superiority is behind human advancement and creativity. In Adler's view, healthy people move ahead, and when they are blocked, seek new openings and directions. In contrast, unhealthy people are "turned away from the real problems of life and engage in shadow-fighting to reassure themselves of their strength."

The psychoanalytic movement continues to produce theorists who write about the nature and development of personality. Some writers continue to take a Freudian position, stressing instincts, repression, the unconscious, and sexuality. Other writers have turned their attention to the development of the ego and to interpersonal relations.

The Defense Mechanisms

One of the contributions of psychoanalysis to the study of personality is the idea of **defense mechanisms**. Freud pictured the ego (the executive part of the personality) as being buffeted by demands from instinctual drives and the conscience. Considerable anxiety can be raised by these conflicting demands. To deal with this anxiety, the ego uses defense mechanisms. These defenses are not conscious. Freud theorized that the defense mechanisms operate outside the person's awareness.

We have already mentioned the process of repression, which excludes unacceptable ideas from consciousness. Repression is usually viewed as defense mechanism. Another defense mechanism is **projection**. The idea here is that unacceptable impulses or behaviors are disowned and attributed to someone else. Think of a man who is interested in a romantic fling with a co-worker but, because he is married, cannot fully admit the idea. Instead, he begins to see romantic designs in the behavior of the co-worker. Another example is the projection of anger. Think of a woman who cannot admit to her own angry feelings. Instead, she believes other people are angry with her.

A very primitive kind of defense mechanism is **denial**. The person simply denies that what is clearly happening is happening. An illustration is the case of a person who experiences a huge weight loss such as occurs in *anorexia nervosa* and denies that anything is wrong.

One of the more complicated of the defenses is **reaction formation**. Through an unconscious process, an anxiety-provoking idea is turned into its opposite. In reaction formation, an unacceptable feeling of hate may be turned around 180 degrees, becoming a feeling of love. Talk about disguises!

A more superficial type of defense is the tendency to **rationalize** one's difficulties and failings. The human mind is adept at inventing excuses to help ward off feelings of self-reproach.

Try completing these sentences with the

first thought that comes to mind, and you may get an idea of the games we all can play with ourselves. Use a separate sheet of paper for your responses.

I didn't study much last night because . . . .
I am eating too much because . . . .
It doesn't matter that I got a poor grade on that test because . . . .
I didn't take care of that chore I was supposed to do today because . . . .
I was late because . . . .

Some rationalizations come under the heading of *sour grapes*. The rationalization is that what one previously desired wasn't worth much anyway. (For example, I didn't win the contest, but the prize really was so trivial, I wouldn't have wanted it anyway.) Another type of rationalization has been called *sweet lemons*. Here one makes a virtue out of a necessity. (For example, I didn't get the car I wanted, but walking will be much better for me.)

The Validity of Psychoanalytic Theory

Psychoanalytic theory remains both fascinating and controversial. The question arises when one reads about the unconscious mind, early sexual feelings, the Oedipus complex, and defense mechanisms: Is all of this really true? The fact that people have developed an intriguing theory and believe it to be true doesn't necessarily make it true.

Psychoanalytic theories were suggested by close observations of patients. Some psychoanalysts believe that the theories have been confirmed by more observation of patients. However, scientific proof requires more objective standards than an analyst's conviction that her clinical case material fits her theory. Science demands research which is objective and can be replicated.

Unfortunately, there is a scarcity of hard-nosed evidence for or against psychoanalytic theory. Part of the failure to carry out research on psychoanalytic concepts is due to the elusive

nature of what one must try to investigate. How do you study something that you can't see, like the unconscious?

To illustrate the difficulties of research in this area, let's take the defense mechanism of projection. Samuel Juni, who has reviewed the research in this area, suggests that an experiment on projection should include the following features:

a. An unacceptable impulse must arise within the subject.

b. This impulse must be unconscious.

c. The subject must be given the opportunity to project this impulse onto another person. This projection should be observed.

d. The anxiety level of the subject must be measured before and after the projection. (If the defense is successful, we would expect the anxiety level to drop.)

When Juni completed his review, he concluded that *no* studies had been carried out which met all of these standards.

Researchers have tried to develop approaches to studying psychoanalytic concepts, and from time to time, interesting findings are published. But it seems fair to say that there is at present little convincing evidence from the laboratory either verifying or disproving Freud's ideas.

Culture and Personality: A Wider View

The psychoanalytic movement started in nineteenth-century Vienna. Vienna was a splendid city of the old world, capital of the Hapsburg empire, celebrated for its musical tradition. In Freud's day it was also a place where sexuality was kept under wraps. Freud's patients grew up in this society, and Freud's theories were based on what he observed. It is possible that if Freud had lived in our more open society, he might have developed somewhat different theories. Can you imagine young Freud transplanted to our time, strolling along one of our ocean beaches filled with sun worshipers in bikinis? He might have decided that repression of sexuality wasn't the foundation to build his theory on after all.

American society in the l990's is very different from the Viennese society of the l890's. Indeed the planet has known a variety of human societies. Anthropologists think of societies which have different traditions or different ideas about how human beings are supposed to behave as different *cultures*. The people living within a cultural tradition have by and large accepted certain patterns of behavior. They transmit these patterns of behavior to their young. The culture, therefore, persists over time. These accepted patterns of behavior are called *cultural norms*.

Let's use a rough analogy and think of a culture as something like a mold in which infant human beings are placed. The society's intention is to create a particular system of values in the child, to promote certain types of behavior and exclude others. The task of rearing the child according to the cultural norms is left to the child's parents or other caretakers, and they will carry out this task in various ways. Of course, the person doesn't always turn out to be exactly what the society's elders have in mind; human beings are not all that easy to mold. All societies have probably had their share of escapists, resisters, discontented people, and revolutionaries.

Cultures have differed considerably in the kinds of molds they try to fit people into. In other words, different cultures have worked out different definitions of approved (valued) and disapproved behaviors. Anthropologist Clyde Kluckholhn referred to these expectations as **cultural cues**. Citing examples among North American Indian cultures, Kluckholhn pointed out that Crows learn to be habitually generous, while Yoruks learn to be habitually stingy.

Let's look at some more examples of differences in cultural expectations and role models. Let's begin by using aggression as an illustra-

tion. One might think of the ancient Greek city of Sparta, where male children were raised from infancy to be warriors. Warlike behavior has also been valued among more recent societies, such as those of the Plains Indians of North America. The Plains Indians fought hard against their foes. The battles led by chiefs like Sitting Bull and Crazy Horse have become part of the lore of the western frontier.

The culture of the Plains Indians emphasized rivalry and hostility between men. A man could raise his status by being a good hunter. Success in battle would raise it even more. Stealing a horse or a gun, or taking a scalp in combat gave a man prestige in the eyes of his peers. The victor in combat was given the honor of telling the story of his triumph during a special ceremony. The training of a young boy among the Plains Indians stressed hunting and fighting skills; the boy needed these to become an accepted adult member of the tribe. A Sioux boy started learning to use a bow and blunt arrows as early as five years of age.

In contrast, the Pueblo Indians of the southwest United States have been described by anthropologists as peaceful and cooperative, kind and unselfish. The people engaged in farming and crafts. This behavior provided a vastly different role model for young Pueblo boys from the one provided for the children of the Plains Indians.

In our own culture, boys and girls have been given different cultural cues on aggressive behavior. Traditionally, most boys have been encouraged to be physically aggressive under certain conditions (for example, when attacked, in athletic contests). Traditionally, most girls have been taught to restrain such aggression. They are taught that physical aggression is unbecoming and undesirable in girls. Thus, a number of studies have shown that girls tend to be less aggressive than boys.

Interestingly, researchers have reported that when girls are reinforced for imitating aggressive behavior, their behavior begins to resemble boys'. Another observation along these lines was a research finding that the more girls watch contact sports on television, the more aggressive they seem to be. These studies suggest that when cultural cues are altered, we may expect to find changes in personality.

As another example of cultural cues, let's think about competitive behavior. American children are raised in what is in many ways a competitive society. Achievement is applauded. A well-known football coach was said to have likened losing a football game to death. Certainly it is no joy to a child or his or her parents when report cards come home from school loaded with D's and F's.

While competition and individual achievement are values many of us take for granted, they are not the norm in all cultures. For example, the Pueblo Indians stress cooperative behaviors rather than competitive ones. Pueblo students might feel it would be wrong, even shameful, to attempt to outshine their peers.

Cultural explanations for personality development, of course, have their limits. For example, one cannot ignore the role that heredity plays on personality. The way one behaves is influenced in many ways by one's genes. Evidence for this point of view was provided in a study carried out at the University of Minnesota. Scientists studied identical twins (these are twins who share the same heredity) that had been separated early in life and were raised in different homes. The twins were given an array of personality tests and scored much more alike than one would expect by chance.

It should also be pointed out that there are some aspects of human behavior which seem to be pretty much the same regardless of the culture in which one is raised. A good example is the recognition of human emotions. Researchers have shown subjects pictures of faces with different expressions and asked the subjects to associate the pictures with words describing various emotions such as happiness, sadness, surprise, disgust, fear, and anger. Testing students from many lands, researchers have reported a large degree of agreement in the way people identify emotions. There was very high agreement for happiness and surprise. Almost everybody recognizes these emotions when they see them.

Keeping such limitations in mind, it is clear that culture influences many things about the way we behave, about what we recognize as important and about the kinds of restraints we will feel. Let's turn our attention to the question, How does the process of cultural learning take place?

We know from our studies on learning that behaviors which are reinforced tend to be repeated (they become part of the person's way of doing things), while behaviors which are not reinforced tend to be extinguished. Parents or other caretakers systematically reinforce some behavior patterns in their children and try to discourage others. Children who do not behave according to their parents' expectations may experience a loss of approval or love. This feeling of rejection can be quite painful and may make the child conform. In some cultures, shaming the child into conformity is a crucial technique. Threats of the wrath of supernatural powers or "evil spirits" are sometimes used.

When a child sees he is doing what pleases his parents and that he is behaving like everybody else, he is likely to experience reinforcement and likely not to feel rejection. A process takes place in which the child begins to model his behavior on that of parents, older siblings, and peers. The child views these models' behaviors as successful, and imitates them. When the child is exposed to little contradictory input, he is likely to come to believe that his role models' ways of doing things are the natural or correct ways.

The Objective Study of Personality

We have looked at some of the contributions of the psychoanalysts and anthropologists to the development of personality theory. We could also list a number of psychologists who have contributed to personality theory. Abraham Maslow and Gordon Alport are two of the most important. But perhaps the most important contributions of psychologists have been not so much in the development of theory as in devising more objective ways of gathering information about personality. They have done this using both personality tests and experimental studies. We will close this chapter with an example of how psychologists use personality tests to expand our objective knowledge in this area.

We could use as our example a test like the MMPI or the Thematic Apperception Test. However, since we have discussed the idea of locus of control of reinforcement in this chapter, let us use a test of locus of control as our textbook case.

Julian Rotter, who developed the idea of locus of control of reinforcement, also developed a self-report test to measure it. The subject is given a form on which are listed pairs of statements. The statements might look something like this:

    a. Success in business is a matter of luck.

    b. Success in business is a matter of hard work and skill.

The subject is asked to mark the statement she agrees with most. If she marks *b*, she is given a point for perceived internal control. The subject reads through additional pairs of statements each pair presenting an internal-external choice. The more internal choices the subject makes, the higher the score the subject will receive for perceived internal control of reinforcement.

After Rotter developed the scale, many researchers used it to investigate questions of internal versus external control of reinforcement. For example, some researchers wanted to find out whether scores on this test could be related to other measures of personality. They found that internal control was associated with self-reports of better adjustment and less anxiety.

Researchers also wanted to know whether people who scored higher as "internals" really tried to take more control of their own behavior. Many studies, for example, were carried out relating locus of control to health-related behaviors. Some researchers reported that internal locus of control was associated with stopping smoking. Among tuberculosis patients, internal locus of control was associated with learning more about the disease. In a study of high school girls from middle-class families, it was found that internal control was related to lower rates of pregnancy. Not all of the studies using locus of control measures have produced positive findings like these. Still, it does appear that the perception that one can control events may make a difference in one's behavior.

Researchers have gone on to ask what causes a person to develop a more internal or external view of the control of reinforcement. Some investigators believe that "externals" might have experienced more stress in their early years. There is some data indicating that this may be the case. If these findings are confirmed, it sounds as if heightened pressures during the early years may contribute to lessened confidence later on that the person can control his or her own life.

Locus of control measures have also been used to test hypotheses about the influence of culture on personality. For example, researchers have found that subjects from two Oriental cultures (China and Japan) were more external in their view of control of reinforcement than subjects from Anglo cultures. These differences on the view of locus of control were thought to reflect traditional differences in the cultures. Another example would be studies of Mexican students. It has been suggested that the Mexican students might have developed a more fatalistic (external) attitude toward life by virtue of their cultural experience. However researchers using the locus of control scale have found that this hypothesis was not borne out. The Mexican students tested were every bit as internal as comparison groups of students from other countries.

Some Questions

1. Can you think of any situation where psychological defenses (for example, rationalization, repression) might seem helpful to a person?

2. Can you think of any situations where psychological defenses might cause great difficulties for a person?

3. President Theodore Roosevelt was said to be a weak and frail person when he was young. He went out West, built himself up, and throughout his career was a man of vitality and energy. How do you think Alfred Adler would have explained this behavior?

4. Jung talked about writers who reported that ideas suddenly popped into their heads. Jung believed these ideas came from the unconscious. Have you ever had the experience of a good idea just popping into your head? Can you describe the circumstances?

5. Rotter originated the concept of locus of control of reinforcement. Some people seem to feel they have little control over the reinforcement that comes into their lives. What kinds of experiences do you think could change this view, make a person feel he had more control over the chances of reinforcement coming into his life?

6. Jung described people as introverted or extroverted. Think of some of the people you know well. Do most of them fit into one of these categories or do most of them fit somewhere in between?

7. In the last chapter we mentioned Penfeld's finding that memories could be brought up by electrical stimulation of the brain. Do you think this offers any support for Freud's theory of the unconscious? If so, how?

Test Your Knowledge

Read each statement and decide whether it is TRUE or FALSE. **Write your answers on a separate sheet of paper.**

1. Extroversion-introversion was an idea developed by Freud.
2. On the locus of control scale, a high score on the internal side means the person believes that fate and luck are controlling the amount of reinforcement in his or her life.
3. Personality traits are very changeable moods rather than stable characteristics.
4. Freud placed very little emphasis on sexuality in his theories.
5. The self-concept is the way other people perceive you.
6. Projection is a defense in which ideas unacceptable to the self are attributed to other people.
7. Adler believed that one of the important aspects of human behavior was the way a person dealt with feelings of inferiority.
8. Freud and Jung had identical views of the unconscious.
9. Anthropologists have found that all North American Indian cultures placed a high value on aggression in males.
10. Jung believed that unconscious ideas could be sources of inspiration for creative ideas.
11. The Oedipus complex was one of Freud's theories that was universally applauded and accepted.
12. Repression was thought of as a deliberate, conscious effort to banish unpleasant ideas from awareness.
13. Reaction formation was thought of as a defense mechanism in which unacceptable feelings are turned into their opposites.
14. Anthropologists have found that all human societies place a high value on competition and achievement.
15. Freud believed that unconscious ideas could gain access to consciousness in disguised forms in dreams.
16. A person's behavior may undergo changes when he or she is in different social roles.
17. Psychoanalytic theories have been definitely proven by thousands of laboratory experiments.
18. One of the major contributions of psychologists to the study of personality has been the development of personality tests.
19. A person who becomes uncomfortable in an unclear situation is said to have low tolerance for ambiguity.
20. One of the measures used in a word-association test is how long it takes the subject to respond to a stimulus word.
21. In the "big five" model of personality, the major factors are dominance and dependency.

CHAPTER 7

Human Development:
Infancy and Childhood

In his play *As You Like It*, Shakespeare sketched out the course of human life with an eloquence that is hard to match.

> All the world's a stage,
> And all the men and women merely players:
> They have their exits and their entrances,
> And one man in his time plays many parts,
> His acts being seven ages. At first the infant,
> Mewling and puking in the nurse's arms.
> Then the whining school-boy with his satchel
> And shining morning face, creeping like snail
> Unwillingly to school. And then the lover,
> Sighing like furnace, with a woeful ballad
> Made to his mistress' eyebrow. Then a soldier,
> Full of strange oaths, and bearded like the
> pard,[1]
> Jealous in honour, sudden, and quick in quarrel,
> Seeking the bubble reputation
> Even in the cannon's mouth. And then the
> justice,
> In fair round belly with good capon lin'd,
> With eyes severe and beard of formal cut,
> Full of wise saws and modern instances;
> And so he plays his part. The sixth age shifts
> Into the lean and slipper'd pantaloon,
> With spectacles on nose and pouch on side,
> His youthful hose, well sav'd, a world too wide
> For his shrunk shank; and his big manly voice,
> Turning again toward childish trebles, pipes
> And whistles in his sound. Last scene of all,
> That ends this strange eventful history,
> Is second childishness and mere oblivion,
> Sans[2] teeth, sans eyes, sans taste, sans
> everything.

---

[1] leopard
[2] French for "without"

This is a canvas painted by a master playwright who was an astute observer of the human condition.

One of the branches of psychology, called developmental psychology, has tried to take a close, detailed look at this canvas of human growth and change. Shakespeare paints with a broad brush. In contrast, the scientific approach seems almost microscopic. It is one of painstaking care and slow, steady progress. Among the basic questions posed are: What happens in the course of human development? When do these things happen? How and why do they happen?

Infant and Child Development

Observations and experiments have both helped give us an increasingly detailed picture of infant and child development. One of the pioneers in developmental psychology, Arnold Gesell, took motion pictures of infants, from the first month through the age of 56 weeks, and later at benchmarks of 18 months, 2, 3, 4, 5, and 6 years. Having these permanent records on the same child enabled Gesell and his co-workers to offer some objective descriptions of the changes that took place with age.

Gesell and his co-workers observed motor behaviors (for example, rolling over, sitting, creeping) and language behavior. They also looked at adaptive behaviors such as eye-hand coordination, and personal-social behaviors (such as play and smiling responses to a person).

Here are a few examples of their observations:

> The 4-week-old infant will look briefly at a face that bends over into his or her field of vision.
>
> The 16-week-old infant will make sounds, such as coos and gurgles and laughs.
>
> The 28-week-old infant will sit alone.
>
> The 40-week-old infant can pick up tiny objects.
>
> The 1-year-old infant may say dada and mama, plus one or two other words.

When Gesell published his findings, he gave some mothers an anxious moment. Such mothers were concerned about how their children's performance compared with the "typical performances" of the children described by Gesell. According to Gesell's data, the average child might be saying a few words by son Jimmy's age, while Jimmy was still babbling. Jimmy's mother might have felt better if she knew that Einstein was said not to have talked until the age of 4.

MATURATION

Looking at Gesell's observations, one can see that certain developments do not happen until the child reaches a certain age range. No matter how much you coax a 2-month-old infant, she is not going to walk. The level of the child's physical development has not yet reached the point that would allow her to do this. The process of physical development which begins at conception and continues into adulthood is called **maturation**. The degree of maturation puts limits on the kinds of learning that can take place in young children.

A neat demonstration relating to maturation was presented in an early study carried out by Wayne and Marsena Dennis. The Dennises were observing the child-rearing practices of the Hopi Indians. Many of the Indians kept their children in tightly bound cradles during much of the day. While the infants were not totally restrained, they had little chance to practice moving about. When the children were finally given an opportunity to walk, were they slower to learn this skill than other Hopi children who had not been cradled? According to the Dennises, the answer was no. Practice would have made little difference to these infants; when they were ready to walk, they walked.

The point here is not that stimulation of infants is unimportant. Stimulation of the child at the proper time can be very important. The point is that one cannot expect certain performances from a child until maturation permits.

HEREDITY AND ENVIRONMENT

Obviously, children are not born into the world equal in all things. With the exception of identical twins, each child has a unique heredity, which will predispose the child to become taller or shorter, more or less intelligent, and probably influence many other characteristics in ways which are still only dimly understood. From day one in the nursery, children act differently.

The child brings into the world a unique heredity and then finds himself or herself in a particular environment in which to grow and develop.

The question is often asked: Which is more important in shaping the child, heredity or environment? The answer probably differs for different characteristics. But the best general answer is that both heredity and environment play important roles.

We have already touched on this question in our discussion of personality. Let's take scores on intelligence tests as another example. If you look at the scores of identical twins who have exactly the same heredity, you will find the scores of the twins are very similar. If one twin has a high score, it is very likely the other one will. If one twin has a low score, it is very likely the other one will.

There have been some cases of identical

twins who have been raised in different environments. The I.Q. scores of these twins are still similar, but are not as similar as those of twins reared in the same environment.

These studies point to the very important role of heredity in determining intelligence. But other studies suggest that a reasonably stimulating environment is required if the potential of inherited intelligence is to be fulfilled. One of the best known of these studies was carried out by H.M. Skeels on very young children living in overcrowded orphanages. Skeels was able to have a number of these children, who were thought to be mentally subnormal, placed in a more stimulating environment where they received much more individual attention. The children who were shifted to the new environment showed rather dramatic increases in I.Q. scores.

The Child's Environment.   The Skeels study and others like it point to the importance of the child's environment in making possible the development of the child's hereditary potential. Cultural and economic factors will influence the type of environment in which the child will be raised.

One may pose many questions about the infant's environment. Who takes care of the child? Is it the mother, or is she out working? How much time do adults spend with the child? Are there brothers or sisters around? How much room is there in the home? Are there toys around? Does the child have his or her own toys? Is there adequate nutrition? How much freedom to explore does the child have? What role does the father play in caring for the child? Is there a father present at all?

The Importance of Early Affection.   Studies such as Skeels' point out the need for stimulation in the child's environment if the child is to realize his or her intellectual potential. Other studies suggest that a parallel requirement for normal *emotional* development is a close, affectionate relationship with a parent or parent substitute. Interestingly, it took some clever studies with monkeys to really make this point in a dramatic way.

The experiments were conducted by Harry Harlow and his coworkers. Harlow was studying the way monkeys learned and needed laboratory animals to use in his experiments. When raising young monkeys, Harlow sometimes separated the young babies from their mothers to prevent infection and increase the chances of the babies' survival. The infants were fed with the aid of mechanical devices they could cling to. The devices each contained a nipple and a milk supply. These artificial devices were called surrogate mothers. One of these surrogate mothers was made of wire mesh. Another of the surrogate mothers was "made from a block of wood, covered with sponge rubber, and sheathed in tan cotton terry cloth." The monkeys showed a very strong preference for the terry cloth mother, seeming to like the "contact comfort" the terry cloth provided.

Harlow observed that the baby monkeys became very attached to their terry cloth mothers. To demonstrate this attachment, the animal was put into a strange room sometimes with its surrogate mother, sometimes without it. When the mother was present, "the infants always rushed to the mother surrogate. . .and clutched her, rubbed their bodies against her, and frequently manipulated her body and face. After a few additional sessions, the infants began to use the mother surrogate as a source of security, a base of operations . . . ." They would explore and manipulate objects in the room and then return to the mother before venturing again into the strange, new world.

What happened when the monkeys were placed in the strange room without the terry cloth mother? "Frequently they would freeze in a crouch position . . . some experimental monkeys would rush to the center of the room where the mother was customarily placed and then run rapidly from object to object, screaming and crying all the while. Constant, frantic clutching of their bodies was very common...."

Harlow's experiments showed rather dramatically the importance of a comfortable contact relationship between the infant and his mother and the reassurance that the infant gets when he is close to his mother.

Harlow's experiments suggest that a strong

attachment between the child and his caretaker is an important part of normal development. What happens if this attachment is disrupted? Drawing on observations of children separated from their mothers during war and children who have been placed in institutions, John Bowlby, an influential British psychoanalyst, has concluded that the breaking of attachments can have very negative effects on the young child.

Bowlby conceived of *attachment* as a basic type of behavior. He believed its disruption or even the threat of disruption had serious consequences. Bowlby observed that the child who was separated from his mother (or other primary caretaker) for a prolonged period experienced what appeared to be a depressive reaction. The reaction included three stages: protest (angry response), despair, and finally detachment.

Bowlby's writings stressed that children need to receive uninterrupted mothering from a primary caretaker for some time if they are to develop in an emotionally healthy way. This idea caused a lot of concern, because many mothers find it essential to work outside the home and must leave their young children in some form of day care. Would this fragmenting of maternal care create emotional problems in the children?

Research was undertaken on this very important question. Studies were made comparing children receiving day care and children being cared for by their mothers. The tentative conclusion from such studies is that if the day care is *quality* day care, the children do not show evidence of negative effects. It seems that studies of the effects of separation in wartime or of children in institutions have only limited application to the far less unsettling practice of sending children for day care, now becoming routine in the United States.

Issues relating to attachment between child and caregiver continue to receive a good deal of attention from researchers. Mary Ainsworth and her colleagues have developed a procedure for studying the type of attachments infants have formed with their mothers. The procedure is called the *strange situation*. In the procedure,

the mother and her infant enter an unfamiliar room where they are joined by a stranger. The mother leaves the child with the stranger, then disappears from the room. The behavior of the infant is observed while her mother is gone and when her mother returns. Then, both mother and stranger depart leaving the child alone. Observers again note the behavior of the child when alone and when the mother returns. Variations of the procedures are repeated giving the observers enough information to classify the child's attachment style as secure (children who are quickly comforted by the return of the mother and return to normal activities) or insecure in various ways such as patterns of avoidant or anxious, ambivalent behavior. Secure and insecure attachment styles is an interesting idea and some researchers have applied the idea to describe the way adolescent and adult couples relate to each other romantically. Think of a couple where the partners are secure with one another. Then think of another couple in which one of the partners is anxious about being "dumped" and clings excessively. Do you see some parallels with the attachment style of young children and their mothers? Some researchers do and have carried out research which suggests links between the romantic attachment styles of young adults and their early parent-child relationships.

DEVELOPMENT OF MASTERY SKILLS

The newborn infant is born in a nearly helpless condition. When lying on his back, he cannot even lift his head. A pleasant musical tone will seldom bring a reaction from the newborn child, but the noise of a stick hitting a plastic block will produce a blink of the eye, a movement of the hands, or a startled reaction. The infant's principal avenue to the strange new world is a well-developed sucking reflex. Researchers have found that newborn infants given a pacifier might spend 30 minutes of each waking hour sucking it regardless of whether they have been fed.

In the weeks and months that follow birth,

the infant begins to develop some orientation to and mastery over his environment. Using his hands, eyes, and ears, the infant begins to gain familiarity with the objects around it. The infant recognizes his parents and smiles at them. His motor movements become increasingly coordinated. By the age of six months, psychologists can carry out research on the infant, observing his mastery skills.

Imagine a scene like this: The infant sits on her mother's lap at a feeding table. The examiner sits across from her. The examiner presents a task to the infant, first demonstrating it, then saying, "Can you do it?" These are some of the tasks:

A yellow plastic bucket containing three toy men is placed near the infant. The toy men are to be removed from the holes where they are placed.

A squeeze toy is placed beyond the child's reach on a blanket. To get the toy, the child must pull the blanket.

A rectangular board will produce sound and color if the child moves certain dials and levers.

The infant's responses are videotaped. Leon Yarrow and his associates, who conducted this research, later analyzed the child's performance. They measured such things as how long it took the child to become involved with the task and how long the child stayed with it.

The researchers studied the response to toys as an indicator of the development of mastery skills. If you watch infants at around nine months of age play with toys (for example, dolls, trucks, toy telephones), you will find that most of the time the toy is not used in the way it was designed to be used. The child will wave it, finger it, put it in her mouth, or bang it against another toy or the floor. Studies suggest that the nine-month-old child will seldom use the toys in an appropriate manner. You begin to see some "functional play" (that is, dialing the toy phone rather than waving it) at around 12 months. By 18 months, there is much less

mouthing and banging and much more adult-intended use.

SOCIAL PLAY

The early studies carried out on the social play of infants found that infants were not very sociable toward their peers. There was a great deal of squabbling. Critics of these studies pointed out that some of them were carried out in small playpens. When the children were removed from the playpens and could move around more freely, they got along better.

Research also suggests that the presence of the young child's mother will make a difference in the interest young children will show in each other. When the mother is present, say at a nursery school, the child will focus her attention on her mother, babbling or talking to her and bringing her the toys. When the mother is absent, the child will begin to pay more attention to the other children.

Observers of young children have noted that children's play seems to go through stages. The very young child will play alone with his toys. The two-year-old child may engage in what has been called *parallel activity* or *parallel play*. The child plays independently but he does it around other children. He plays beside but not with the other children. Mildred Parten, who described this behavior, watched a group of children playing in a sandbox, each "doing his own thing" rather than cooperating. There is more cooperative play as the child matures, say during years three to four.

THE DEVELOPMENT OF LANGUAGE

There are studies dating from at least as early as the 1920's attempting to show how fast children acquire vocabulary. Gesell observed that children varied greatly in the extent of their early vocabulary; he believed that normal children who spoke no words at all by 18 months were not rare, while some children at that age spoke from 150 to 200 words. The typical child in Gesell's own studies spoke about 10 words at 18 months.

The acquisition of vocabulary picks up speed as the child approaches two years. One study reported an average of 328 words at that point, with that number more than doubling in the next six months.

The child's sentence at 16 months may resemble the kind of communication used in the early Tarzan films: "Cheetah, come." By 24 months, the child's "Daddy, come" has given way to "I don't want to go to bed." Gesell's data showed that the average sentence length increases from one word to nearly five as age increases from 18 to 54 months.

INTELLECTUAL DEVELOPMENT

The use of language, of course, is related to increased understanding and to intellectual development. In adult tests of intelligence, vocabulary is a very useful measure. Scales have been devised which measure intellectual development in young children. While providing interesting data for research, these scales do not predict very well how normal children, much less adults, will perform later on. The very young child who does well on such tests may or may not do well on intelligence tests taken during the school years, and the same is true of the very young child who does poorly.

To illustrate how intellectual abilities increase with age, let's look at a study of Gesell's, in which he asked children to complete a partially finished drawing of a man. The child's task was to put in missing parts such as eyes, ears, and fingers. At the age of three, only eight percent of the children put in a missing leg. By age four, 61 percent of the children were doing this, and by age five the figure was 95 percent.

THE VIEWS OF PIAGET

Current views of the intellectual development of children have been heavily influenced by the work of the Swiss psychologist Jean Piaget. Piaget was not trained originally in psychology. His Ph.D. was in the natural sciences, and the early part of his career was spent studying mollusks in the Swiss lakes. He

later became deeply interested in psychology and took a job where he was concerned with intelligence testing with children. Piaget was fascinated with the kinds of responses children gave to the questions on the test. He wanted to learn more about the thought processes underlying their answers and developed a lifelong interest in children's thinking and logic.

Piaget's methods were much more informal than those American psychologists were used to. Piaget would ask children questions. Then he would probe their answers, trying to understand the logic behind their responses.

For example, Piaget was interested in the child's concept of night. He'd ask a child a question like "What is night?" The child would reply that night was when it's dark. Piaget would probe further, asking where darkness comes from. The child would answer, "From the sky." Piaget would continue by asking how night began. The child would reply that it began because the clouds were black.

In the child's mind, it appeared that the clouds produced the darkness and therefore the night.

Piaget studied children's intellectual development over time and concluded that it occurred in several stages. He called the first stage the *sensori-motor* period. It typically ran from birth to about two years. During this period the child develops the basic use of sight and touch and learns to manipulate his environment. He tests things out rather directly and sees what happens.

The second stage, typically running from ages two to seven, Piaget called the period of *preoperational thought*. The basic change was from manipulating the environment directly to thinking about it. The child no longer has to physically move the objects in his environment to see what happens. Now, he can represent them in his thoughts and consider them. His thinking, however, lacks important qualities of mature logic.

For one thing, according to Piaget the child's thinking during this stage tends to be egocentric (self-centered). The child does not take the viewpoint of others and may believe that everyone thinks the same thing as he does. It is also difficult for the child at this stage to move from the sensory perception of events to think abstract thought. A good illustration of this difficulty is the attempt to solve problems relating to conservation of matter.

As an example, imagine the following experiment. The child is presented with two jars of equal size and identical shape. The experimenter pours some water into the jars. The child is asked to compare the amount of water in the jars. The experimenter will pour a little water into one jar or the other until the child says they are equally filled. Now the experimenter pours the water from one jar into a tall, thin jar. She asks the child once more to compare the jars. During this preoperational stage of thinking, the child will probably say there is more water in the tall, thin jar. The child has failed to comprehend that there has really not been any change in the volume of the water.

The child's thinking becomes less bound to immediate perceptions in the third stage, the period of concrete operations. This period occurs from about ages 7 to 11. The child can now easily solve the conservation problem that would have thrown her a few years earlier and has better ideas about cause and effect, space and time. The child can now solve many concrete problems, but still has difficulty dealing with hypothetical and abstract ideas.

The fourth and final stage, occurring between the ages of 11 and 15, is the period of formal operations. The child now has her full capability of logical thought. The child may not have the training and experience to solve some types of problems, but now has the *potential* to learn to solve such problems. It's now time to buy the child that advanced computer and set of mathematics books.

Another feature of the young child's thought that interested Piaget was a tendency for the young child to think animistically, that is, to regard nonliving objects as living and having will. Piaget believed that in the beginning, the child views all objects which have some use as alive. Then the child's thought goes through several stages in which she first restricts the designation of life to what moves, then to what moves on its own, and finally to plants and animals.

Studies testing Piaget's ideas have found that young children (that is, four-, five-, and six-year-olds) do indeed respond animistically at times. For example, in one study about half of the children labeled a nonliving object (for example, the sun, a car) as alive. However, the children seldom responded that such objects could sleep, breathe, or grow, and drew the line completely at eating.

SOCIALIZATION

The young child learns what his culture considers appropriate behaviors during a lengthy socialization process. He is rewarded for certain behaviors and punished for others. He models his behavior on his parents, siblings, and peers, and develops attitudes and values based on theirs.

There are a number of basic social forces which mold the child in this socialization process. The cultural norms that his family identifies with provide a backdrop of values and beliefs. The school and church serve as institutions for social learning. There are also role expectations based on the child's sex and age.

The Development of Sex Roles.   Differences in sex roles have their roots in a long-standing historical tradition in the division of labor by sex. R.G. D'Andrade carried out a study looking at the way activities were divided between men and women in preliterate (primitive) societies that have been studied by anthropologists. He found that sex differences in assignment of tasks were marked. For example, in 168 of the societies studied, men *always* had the task of hunting, women *never* had it. In 158 such societies, women always had the task of cooking; in only five societies did men always have this responsibility. There were only a few activities, such as preparing and planting soil, in which men and women were equally involved.

In western societies, sharply distinct sex roles existed until rather recently. Fifty to one hundred years ago there were clear-cut and complementary roles for men and women. Essentially, the man's function was to work outside the home to act as provider. The woman's role was to look after the home and take care of the children. Along with this basic difference in responsibilities, men were expected to be more aggressive, women more nurturing.

For many men and women, this pattern has greatly changed in the past decades. Women now have a wide range of career options open to them. Families in which both parents work outside the home and families headed by a single parent are now commonplace. With these dramatic social changes, one might wonder whether traditional sex roles and different patterns of expected behavior for the sexes have entirely vanished. The answer is clearly no, and a number of psychological studies show that boys and girls are still raised quite differently.

The differences begin with parental expectations. Studies of college-age adults (prospective parents) show they have different ideas of how young boys and girls should play. The adults viewed roughhousing, playing with vehicles, and aggressive behavior as more appropriate for boys than girls. Doll play, dressing up, and looking in the mirror were seen as more appropriate for girls than boys.

When the child is born, the decorations of the nursery are often different for boys and girls. The colors are traditionally different: blue for boys, pink for girls, and the frills are for the girls. Toys for boys and girls may be different within a few months after birth.

Studies suggest that parents tend to handle infant boys more roughly than infant girls.

Parental touching remains pretty constant for the young girl, but drops off for the young boy. Parents seem to be more concerned about the physical well-being of girls than boys.

These studies indicate that the cultural pattern of raising boys in a tougher, traditionally masculine image and girls in a softer, traditionally feminine image is still very much alive.

The children absorb these messages. There are distinct sex preferences for certain toys at an early age. As they grow up, boys learn to prefer active play and manual arts; girls more often learn to enjoy music, art, and homemaking activities.

The differences in sex roles continue in adolescence where girls usually place more importance on their acceptance by peers, and are more concerned about personal attractiveness and acceptance by the opposite sex. Girls also report they feel less push from their parents to go to college.

When asked to pick out the turning points in their lives, women are more likely to mention marriage, the birth of a child, and the child's eventual marriage or leaving home. In contrast, men will name events relating to school, jobs, and retirement.

It seems likely that social forces will continue to produce some changes in these sex-linked roles in the coming years. There has been a strong effort by women's organizations to create more options for women, including careers previously dominated by men. Women are seeking careers in law and business in large numbers. There are new role models for women, including women astronauts and prime ministers. In addition, there has been a rapid growth in high-tech industry, in which the premium is no longer on strength and endurance but on mental abilities and education. All of these factors are blurring the sex-linked roles that have been accepted as historical traditions.

DEVELOPMENT OF THE SELF-CONCEPT

The proud mother remarks of the child in her lap, "She looked in the mirror. She knows who she is." What the parent is saying is that the child has developed a sense of identity. The child has begun a process of *individuation* in which she learns to understand herself as a unique individual with characteristic ways of thinking, reacting, and doing things.

The development of the child's self-concept (the perception of one's self) is considerably influenced by the reactions and evaluations of others. Sometimes the reactions are to the child's behavior. One may think of countless everyday examples: the parent who says the child is "bad" when she does something that displeases the parent; the teacher who praises the child for a good performance; the peer who says the child is a "baby" because she cries; the approval that comes when she makes a good play in a ball game.

Sometimes the reactions of others are based on very superficial characteristics. Physical appearance is a good example. Researchers studying fourth- and sixth-grade children found that the children whose photographs were judged as less attractive by a disinterested panel were in fact less popular among their peers and evaluated as less able by their teachers. The children whose physical appearance did not happen to meet the society's standards of what was good-looking were penalized.

To compound matters, what often happens is that less physically attractive people incorporate these reactions into their self-concepts and may have lower self-esteem.

There are other arbitrary evaluations as well. People often have mind-sets about other people, even before they meet or talk with them. Sometimes these mind-sets are based on the ethnic origin of the person. Many years ago researchers gave a list of characteristics to people and asked which of the characteristics they would say were typical of certain groups. People labeled Italians artistic, Irish pugnacious, Turks cruel, and Germans scientifically-minded. These beliefs about people from different groups are called *stereotypes*. The person coming from one or another ethnic group often has to deal with such prejudgments.

People may even have stereotypes about proper names. A study was carried out in which a list of names was presented to people. The subjects were asked what characteristics they associated with the names. The name Herman was associated with stupidity, Agatha with being old-fashioned. If you're looking for a name that people have a pleasant image of, try Richard.

The reactions of others, then, may be based both on how the child acts and on superficial characteristics such as appearance and ethnic background. The child must deal with all this feedback from others and integrate it with her other experiences. She begins to develop a sense of her own identity and worth.

Low self-esteem can be a serious problem. It may lead to lack of confidence or to unwillingness to try or take risks, and may interfere with the child's ability to realize her potential. Low self-esteem may be correlated with feelings of depression, and one of the goals of therapy is often to help the person develop a more positive view of herself.

STRESS AMONG CHILDREN

Childhood, a period of rapid intellectual and social development, is not without its sources of stress. Kaoru Yamamoto asked American fourth-, fifth-, and sixth-graders to look at a list of possible life events and rate them on a seven-point scale as to how upsetting they would be. "Losing a parent" was rated the most stressful event on the list and had been experienced by 20 percent of the children. "Parental fights" was also very high on the list and had been experienced by 64 percent of the children. Both of these items point to a fear of loss of security and stability (a break in attachment) as the worst fear for the child.

Personal embarrassment or loss of face was also high on the list of fears. Among the items that were rated high in this area were "being kept back, "a poor report card," "suspected of lying" (82 percent of the children had experienced this), and "being sent to the principal" (42 percent had made this forlorn journey).

Yamamoto presented the list of experiences to samples of Japanese and Filipino children and found very similar results. These fears of children are widespread, occurring in both eastern and western cultures.

THE EFFECTS OF PHYSICAL AND SEXUAL ABUSE ON CHILDREN

In an ideal world all parents would act toward their children in ways that are sensitive and nurturing. Unfortunately, some parents may not only neglect their children, but also physically or sexually abuse them. While it is difficult to estimate the number of children who are being abused, it is clear that the numbers are uncomfortably high. Reported cases of physical abuse are in the hundreds of thousands in a given year and the number of unreported cases make the actual total much higher. Judging from research on women college students, the incidence of sexual abuse during childhood is higher than many of us might suspect. In a study carried out at Memphis State University on over 1,000 women students, 13 percent reported having been abused by a family member and 10 percent by a nonfamily member.

The effects of physical abuse on children have been studied by observing the behavior of abused children, both in the home and in interacting with peers and by asking teachers and parents about the children. The studies suggest that physically abused children tend to be more aggressive toward adults and peers than children who were not abused. Some studies, though not all, find that abused children tend to be less socially skilled than nonabused children. They seem to have more difficulties relating to both family and peers. Abused children are also more likely to feel depressed and perform less well on cognitive tasks. It is noteworthy that men who are spouse batterers were often abused themselves as children.

The consequences of childhood sexual abuse range from effects which are barely noticeable to very serious problems. Studies suggest that about one-third of the children will experience symptoms of anxiety and depression. Nightmares are a common experience. Some children who have been sexually abused show inappropriate sexual behavior such as making advances towards other children. The chances of experiencing lasting psychological problems from incidents of childhood sexual abuse seem greater if the incidents happened when the child was older (approaching adolescence) and if the acts were repeated over an extended period of time. Damaging psychological effects from childhood sexual abuse can persist into adulthood.

Some Questions and Activities

1. Harlow found that infant monkeys seemed to need the contact comfort provided by the terry cloth mothers. From your own observations, can you give some examples of the need of young children for contact comfort?

2. Traditionally, men and women have had very different roles in society. This has been changing. Many women are now working outside the home. What ideas do you have that could help working parents with young children meet the needs of both family and jobs?

3. Early stimulation seems to be important for children to develop their full intellectual potential. What kinds of activities can you think of that would help stimulate a young child's intellectual curiosity?

4. Piaget has some interesting ideas about the child's intellectual development. You might find it interesting to try out some of his informal experiments. For example, if you can find two fairly wide jars of equal size and shape, and a tall, thin jar, you can try out his experiment on conservation of matter (see page 97). For your subjects, find children of about five years of age.

5. There has been some research which has supported Piaget's idea that young children often think animistically. You might want to check this for yourself. Make up a short list of things that are not alive, but have some lifelike qualities such as the ability to move. Two examples might be *truck* and *fire*. Add some objects to your list which are actually alive, like *bird* and *plant*. Read this list to your young subjects, asking them in each case, "Is it alive?"

Test Your Knowledge

Read each statement and decide whether it is TRUE or FALSE. **Write your answers on a separate sheet of paper.**

1. Gesell found large individual differences in the vocabulary of very young children.

2. Tests of infant intelligence are excellent predictors of measures of adult intelligence.

3. Studies of children's fears suggest that one of the greatest fears is losing a parent.

4. Harlow's studies point to the importance of contact comfort in the infant-mother relationship.

5. Studies of identical twins suggest that heredity plays only a minor role in the development of intelligence.

6. Studies indicate that people disregard physical appearance in their reactions to children.

7. Piaget is noted for identifying different stages in the thinking of children.

8. A child who believes a car or street light is alive is thinking animistically.

9. Bowlby believed that children who experience prolonged separations from their mother or other primary caretakers were prone to depression.

10. Parallel activity is a kind of play that often occurs before children engage in joint cooperative play.

11. The "strange situation" is a procedure for studying attachment styles between infants and their caregivers.

12. Physically abused children seem less likely to be depressed than children who have not been physically abused.

CHAPTER 8

Human Development:
Adolescence and Adulthood

Western society has never quite made up its mind about adolescence. Adolescence has been portrayed in literature, on radio, in movies, and on television. At times these portrayals have been sympathetic and sensitive, at others highly exaggerated almost to the point of ridicule. What can we say about adolescence that makes sense? The first and foremost fact of adolescence is that it is a period of great biological change. It is a time of rapid growth and physical development, including the development of adult sexual characteristics.

PHYSICAL CHANGES

Both boys and girls experience rapid physical growth. Boys show marked increases in growth of the heart, systolic blood pressure, the size of the lungs, and respiratory capacity. Their muscles greatly increase in both size and strength.

Both genders experience pronounced sexual development during this period, including maturation of the reproductive systems and the development of other sexual characteristics. These physical changes do not coincide with society's idea of when a child becomes an adult. Sexual readiness and social role, then, are not closely coordinated in time. Society has a dilemma. How does it reconcile sexual maturation and the long training necessary to equip people to do well in a complex society?

In considering this question, one might look at some of the ways adolescence has been handled in more primitive (preliterate) societies. Primitive societies usually require fewer years of training for adult responsibilities. In one society, the Tiriki of Africa, the problems posed by adolescence were solved by simply not recognizing adolescence as a fact. Following an initiation ceremony, the individuals moved directly from the role of children to the role of adults. Before the ceremony, the boy ate with the other children, was allowed to enter the women's section of the hut but was forbidden to have sexual relations. After the ceremony, he ate with the men, could no longer enter the women's section of the hut and was permitted to engage in sexual relations.

Margaret Mead described a very different kind of adolescence in Samoa in the 1920's. Mead did not observe abrupt transitions. Life for the young seemed something like a teenager's idyllic dream of endless beach parties. Recently, however, questions have been raised about the accuracy of Mead's observations.

Even in preliterate societies, there are instances where the society has sought to delay the movement of its young into adulthood. In these societies the adult community was none too anxious to share the privileges which were "age graded" with its young. Among the Kipsigis of Africa, the older warriors would beat up the young ones who wanted to replace them.

Among the African Samburu, young men were denied marriage until well in their twenties. The young men were said to have reacted with disobedience, theft of stock, and other aggressive acts.

In western culture, with its demands for education running for years past the development of sexual maturity, the question of adolescent behavior has been largely thrust back on the adolescents themselves. Adolescents receive a variety of messages on what to do and what not to do. The messages come from parents, teachers, other adults, and peers, and sometimes the messages conflict. The adolescent is left to make his or her own choices.

DEVELOPMENT OF INDEPENDENCE FROM PARENTS

The movement from dependence on parents toward independence is one of the developmental tasks of adolescence. While the young child must develop mastery skills to cope with the environment within the family setting, the adolescent must learn to cope with the environment outside the family setting. Some preliterate societies recognize this transition explicitly; the child participates in elaborate ceremonies after which he is gradually initiated into the customs and lore of the society.

Although western societies don't have such elaborate rituals, we do have a variety of benchmarks. Think of the first day of high school, the first date, the driver's license, the senior prom, and graduation from high school. All of these events provide a kind of social recognition that certain changes are taking place.

How much independence and when are defined within the culture and the family. In general, the pattern is one of diminished parental control, increased attention by the young adolescent to the standards of the peer group, then increased self-confidence and self-reliance.

An interesting study documented some of these changes. Children and adolescents were given a series of statements. The subjects were asked: If you aren't sure whether the statement is right or wrong, who would you have help you

make up your mind? If it were a question of fact, the fifth-grader would most often turn to the parents. In marked contrast, the ninth- or twelfth-grader would rarely do this, looking to some outside adult for expertise. The early view of the parent as "all-knowing" seems to be replaced by an equally extreme view of the parent as "know-nothing."

When the statement had to do with friendships and social relationships, the fifth-grader might turn about equally often to parents, outside adults, and peers. By the seventh grade, the peers became the source of advice and remained so throughout high school.

In our society, the high school is one of the important settings for this transition from dependence on parents to independence. High schools are often located a good distance from the home and they promote activities (football games, dances, clubs) that occupy the students' time away from home. Coeducational high schools also provide opportunities for daily interactions between boys and girls which promote the development of social skills.

Some studies suggest that students at coed high schools like the atmosphere of the school better than their counterparts at all-boy or all-girl high schools. The students say they prefer the friendlier climate of the coed schools and the peer-oriented nonacademic activities.

Future educational and career plans are often worked out during the high school years. One study found that about 90 percent of high school seniors who plan to go to college will enroll in one. Students who get better grades in high school are more likely to continue with school. The same is true for students who take part in high school extracurricular activities. Girls whose interest is in early marriage appear less likely to go to college.

THE PEER GROUP AND PEER PRESSURE

The movement of the preadolescent and the adolescent away from parental control is usually accompanied by increased reliance on the peer group for companionship and for setting standards. The influence of the peer group may be particularly strong in making social judgments such as who should be a friend and with whom one should associate.

Adolescents did not invent the peer group and peer pressure, although one hears so much about it in discussions of teenagers, one might think so. The influence of peers in shaping attitudes and behavior seems to start in early childhood. This influence was studied in an experiment with preschool children.

Preschool children tasted small samplings of different foods and were asked to list their preferences. On following days, a "target child" (for example, one who liked peas a lot but didn't like carrots) was seated at a table with a group of children who liked carrots and didn't like peas. The children were allowed to pick whatever they wanted to eat. After four days of lunching with carrot-eating peers, most of the target children shifted to choosing the carrots, too. Of 17 target children, 15 chose their initially preferred food at the first group lunch. Ten of these children shifted to the nonpreferred food by day four.

Some studies of conformity carried out with adolescents suggest that the tendency of the adolescent to defer to the judgment of his peers may reach a peak around the ninth grade. This would be about the time the adolescent is in the midst of major physical changes and has little experience in coping with the new world that is opening up. Perhaps the influence of the peer group is highest when personal confidence is lowest.

Being Alone or With Peers.   How much time do adolescents actually spend with peers, with their families, or alone? In a fascinating study, teenagers carried pocket-sized electronic paging devices during their normal daily activities. Every so often the experimenters would buzz the subject, asking them to report what they were doing.

The investigators found that the subjects spent more of their waking time (44 percent) with "friends and acquaintances" than they did with family (20 percent) or alone (29 percent).

When the subjects were with their friends, they seemed least likely to want to change what they were doing. The experimenters asked the subjects whether they would like to be doing something else. The teenagers indicated less desire to change what they were doing when they were spending time with their peers.

The teenagers in the sample also sought out a certain amount of time alone. Interestingly, the proportion of time the teenagers spent alone was not affected by the number of friends the person had, the size of the family, or even the presence of a private bedroom.

Solitude for adolescents was associated with reading, studying, and homework. Solitude was associated with reports of better concentration, but a less happy mood. The teenagers studied reported they felt less happy, cheerful, and sociable when they were alone. There was a drop-off in mood when they left the company of others. When these teenagers were alone on Friday and Saturday nights, feelings of loneliness were highest. Such findings underscore the vulnerability that many young people experience in regard to the need to be with others and to be accepted.

THE CONCERNS OF ADOLESCENCE

We have discussed several important aspects of the adolescent experience: dramatic physical changes, a movement away from the family, and the heightened influence of one's peers. How do adolescents react to these experiences? What are the things they are most concerned about? Psychologists and sociologists have asked teenagers questions like this. Here is an example.

Joseph Smith conducted a survey of young people, average age about 16, in a mixed urban-rural area of Pennsylvania. He asked open-ended questions about the kinds of things they were concerned about. The most frequently mentioned concerns were school grades and dating. What seemed to concern these teenagers most was how they were progressing in school and how they were getting along in male-female relationships. Other concerns they mentioned were related to their friends, parents and siblings, money, and what the future held.

If we look at later adolescence (such as the problems college students report they are facing), we find some of the same issues are still a matter of concern. For example, in one study of college men, 54 percent of the difficult social situations reported concerned dating. In a study Roland Tanck and I carried out with students at an urban university, we found that problems related to school performance were reported by 55 percent of the students. The students still reported conflicts with parents (25 percent of the students) and problems relating to self-identity (34 percent of the students). The issue of the future loomed largest, as 60 percent of the students reported problems about career choice.

When the Transition Is Rocky.   The relaxation of parental control may not be a smooth, gentle transition. As Tanck and I found, one-fourth of the young college students that we surveyed were still reporting "conflict with parents."

Here is an example of a possible conflict situation used in a study of adolescent girls carried out by Lisa Gaffney and Richard McFall. If you were the person involved (we'll call her by the initial S), which of the alternatives would you pick: 5, 4, 3, 2, or 1?

> You've had a crush on Steve for the longest time. You finally got up the nerve today to talk to him during free hour about a class you're both taking. You had a good talk together and when the free hour was over Steve said, "Why don't you call me later tonight and we'll talk some more." You want to, but when you mention this to your mother later in the day she says, "No. Girls do not call boys. If he wants to talk to you. let him call you." What do you say or do now?

> 5—S does not call Steve, either because she agrees with her mother or because she is obeying her mother. S may indicate that she will explain to Steve the next day why she did not call him.

> 4—S gives her mother reasons why she should call Steve, for example, that she and Steve are just friends, that Steve does not have her phone number, or that times have changed since her mother was in school and that girls do call guys now.

> 3—S shows that she is willing to discuss the issue. ("Why don't you think I should call Steve?") OR S calls a girlfriend and has the girlfriend call Steve and tell Steve to call S. . . .

> 2—S calls Steve, either when her mother is or is not close by ("I'm calling him and you can't stop me. . . .") OR, "I'd tell her I was calling a girlfriend and call Steve instead."

> 1—S yells at her mother or threatens physical violence.

Imagine a home in which the teenager usually reacted to her parents with responses like 1 or 2. Here you would have a situation of open conflict with parental authority. When you have family relationships like this—when the movement from dependence to independence begins to resemble a rebellion rather than an easy relinquishing of control—the chances are greater that the teenager will become involved in activities the parents cannot control and would disapprove of. Such activities include drug use, early sexual activity, and delinquency.

Earlier and more extensive use of drugs is associated with a rebelliousness in teenagers. A number of studies have shown that young marijuana users felt more negatively about their parents, were less content with family life and wanted to get out on their own. The marijuana users also tended to be less conservative, less interested in organized religion, and more apt to be sexually active.

Some research has suggested there is a relationship between parent-adolescent conflict and the level of sexual experience of the teenager. One of the risks of sexual activity is, of course, unwanted pregnancy.

When pregnancy occurs, the teenage girl is forced into an often difficult decision-making process. What should she do? One might guess that she would consult her parents at this point. However, the girl's problem with her family can be so great that, in one major study it was found that in nearly half of the cases, the girl's mother had no influence on her pregnant daughter's decisions. The girls' fathers were even less involved. Only 30 percent of the girls' fathers had any influence on the girls' decisions about the pregnancy.

Conflict with parents as well as conflict with most forms of authority seem to be related to delinquency. In the study by Gaffney and McFall (page 108), the researchers presented problem situations like the one illustrated to teenagers living in an institution for delinquent girls. The problem situations involved parents, teachers, police, and other authority figures. The girls arrested for delinquent acts were more likely to choose alternatives like 1 or 2 than a control group of girls living in the community.

THE LURE OF THE CULT

A very different hazard lying in wait for the adolescent who is experiencing an uncomfortable transition toward adulthood is the so-called religious cult. Perhaps the ideal subject (many would use the term victim) for these cults is the lonely adolescent who may feel rejected and depressed, badly needing reassurance of his or her self-worth and acceptance. The cults may work on this vulnerability. One technique that has been described is called "love bombing." According to published reports, the sequence of events may go something like this:

The unwary young person may be invited by a cult "recruiter" to his home—perhaps to a dinner party. Here the potential recruit is warmly welcomed, given loads of attention, and made to feel like he is part of a family. At this stage, the real purposes of the group are kept under wraps. The young person is then invited to additional sessions which continue to be warm and accepting. As time goes by, he may be invited for an extended stay in a retreat, in a more remote setting where he finds himself surrounded by group members.

Massive social-psychological pressure may now be exerted on the recruit to reject his former values and to accept the values of the cult. The person may be told his previous life was a sham and the "truth" of the cult and its inspirational leader are pointed out and repeated by the group members. Being psychologically vulnerable in the first place—one against many, isolated from one's normal social supports, and subjected to continuous propaganda—this can be an overwhelming experience. Those who give in are then encouraged to completely isolate themselves from their families. Then they may be subjected to weeks of further indoctrination where they absorb the ways and values of the cult.

Some former cult members reported that they lived under wretched conditions and spent a lot of time "begging" to bring in money to support the cult and its leaders who, incidentally, lived quite well.

Because cults may be established as religious organizations, they can present a problem for democratic societies. Religious freedom in democracy protects the right of individuals to decide whether they want to join a religious organization. Still, the tactics that have been used by cults raise questions for adolescents and their parents.

DATING, MARRIAGE AND DIVORCE

In our society, dating usually begins in adolescence or preadolescence and continues into adulthood. Dating involves stages: meeting someone, asking the person out (or being asked out), and the development of a relationship. Then there is often a fourth, often very uncomfortable, stage: breaking up.

Dating usually carries with it some personal risks. The first risk is not being asked out or not finding anyone to ask out. This means being alone, feeling lonely, and possibly comparing oneself with other people who are enjoying dating relationships. Recall the unhappiness of the adolescents who were alone on Saturday night.

There is a risk also in asking someone out. The person might say no. Being rejected for many people is an unpleasant, sometimes painful, experience. It can make a person feel less worthwhile and attractive.

To illustrate the power of fear of rejection, let's consider a question. In choosing someone to ask out, what does a person consider? On what basis does he or she make a decision? You might say, "Well, physical attractiveness is very important." If you did, there would be a lot of evidence to support you. However, there is more to it than that. If you showed a group of photographs of young men to a young woman and asked her which of the men she would like to date, the odds are she would pick some of those she felt were more physically attractive. However, research suggests she might not pick the *most attractive*. What seems to happen is the arousal of feelings something like this: These very attractive men may not want to go out with me, and I don't want to risk rejection. So our chooser may not risk trying to get what seems unattainable, and may settle for something in the middle.

This feeling (the very attractive person will probably reject me) seemed to be operating for males in a study carried out in a singles bar. The researchers stationed themselves in the evenings in singles bars and recorded how many times women of different levels of attractiveness were approached by men. They found that the most attractive women were not approached any more than women judged less physically attractive.

So both men and women may hesitate to seek out the fairest of the opposite sex. There are many people who are shy and fearful to the point that the experience, or even the anticipation, of asking *anyone* out raises anxiety to near-paralyzing levels. Some psychologists have tried to develop procedures to reduce this anxiety by teaching dating skills.

The idea behind these programs is that dating skills should be as teachable as anything else. Successful experiences can reduce anxiety.

Indeed there is evidence that those who have more confidence and satisfaction in their dating are those who have the most dating experience, starting earlier in life and doing more of it.

In dating skills training sessions, the students (usually college students) meet with a trainer and practice role-playing dating situations. Role-playing is a little like being in the theater without a script. You take the part of somebody and make up your lines as you go along. An example might be for a boy to role-play asking a girl out on a date. To make the situation realistic, the trainer could obtain the help of a girl to play the other party. The trainer provides feedback to the student showing him what might be a more effective approach.

Students who participate in dating skills training often report they feel less anxious about making dates. The real test, of course, is picking up the phone and dialing that certain someone who has been in and out of your mind.

MEETING THAT SOMEONE

In high school and college, the opportunities to meet potential dates are very good. In the smaller schools, particularly, one can get to know many people as part of daily living and classroom interaction. Extracurricular activities and clubs provide additional opportunities.

The college mixer is a dance set up specifically to allow boys and girls to meet each other. Unfortunately, these dances may not turn out to be all that pleasant for the participants. Researchers observed five mixer dances at Yale University and interviewed nearly 100 young men and women at them. Many of the students reported they felt tense and experienced frequent rejection. Mixers may place too much emphasis on first impressions and physical attractiveness, and simply not permit other personal qualities to be noticed.

For the person who is no longer in school, there may be less opportunity to meet potential dates. Clubs based on interests like music or hiking, organizations set up by churches or synagogues, and parties and dates arranged by friends have served as vehicles for bringing people together. In recent years, singles clubs, singles bars, and computer dating have come into vogue. Perhaps the ultimate method that our society has fashioned is direct advertising. In some of our more chic magazines, there are now pages of "personal" ads. You might find something like this:

> Handsome, successful male, age 27, enjoys boating, tennis, concerts, and good restaurants. Looking for young woman who is warm, sensitive, caring, and wants lasting relationship.

DATING AND SEX

Surveys of sexual behavior have become rather popular since Alfred Kinsey's pioneering report in the late 1940's. There have been at least 20 surveys carried out on adolescents alone. The results of these surveys clearly point to an increase in premarital sexual activity through the years in both teenagers and adults.

There seems little doubt that society has relaxed its prohibitions on sex before marriage.

Sex, a topic that was once rarely discussed in an open way, is currently a steady feature of women's magazines that once seldom printed articles on subjects more spicy than new ways of cooking chili.

This change in sexual attitudes and behavior has been welcomed by some and deplored by others, who feel strongly that it represents a breakdown in morality. In addition to moral issues, there are significant health risks that arise with increased sexual activity, including the spread of AIDS. There are also higher numbers of unwanted pregnancies. Still it is clear that the change does represent a different kind of solution to the dilemma posed by adolescence in a society in which marriage takes place well beyond the age of sexual maturity. With the strong prohibitions of earlier eras relaxed, many young people have become sexually active.

One of the arrangements that some young people have entered into is living together as an unmarried couple. Among the arguments advanced for the arrangement are that it provides an opportunity for an exclusive, meaningful relationship without the pressures of marriage. Among the arguments advanced against it are that it is a cop-out, an avoidance of responsibility.

What do young people think about this type of arrangement? How would they compare it to marriage? Over 300 college students were asked to rate their willingness to take part in different types of marriages and living together arrangements. The top choice for both males and females was marriage. The kind of marriage they chose was one in which there was equality and sharing—not a male- or female-dominated marriage. The young men had a more favorable attitude toward living together than the young women.

There has been some research on the effects of living together on the success of subsequent marriages. For example, a team of researchers studied a sample of married couples, comparing those people who had had such a premarital experience with those who had not in terms of how well they related to their spouses. The researchers could find very little difference. In this sample, the earlier living together experience did not have a clear-cut impact on the chances of a good marital relationship.

HAPPINESS IN MARRIAGE

Let us move ahead in time through a period of years. Two young people have gone through a period of dating, forming relationships, breaking up, trying again with someone new, finally meeting and committing themselves to a person who seems very special. Our couple becomes engaged and marries. What's in store for them?

Let us see what students of family life say. Some family therapists speak of developmental stages that families go through. Michael Solomon, for example, sees the first "task" of a marriage as the couple's shifting of their primary attachment from their own parents to each other and the new marriage. A second stage occurs with the birth of the first child—the couple now assumes the role of parents. There is a change here from focusing just on each other to including the child, and this can create difficulties between the spouses. A third stage is individual development within the family—the various family members develop their unique needs, personalities, and interests. A new stage begins when the children depart and the parents and children try to readjust their relationships.

There are many potential stumbling blocks (one might even say land mines) along this route, and one wonders what factors tend to be related to a happy marriage. Let's begin by inquiring about the differences between happily and unhappily married people.

Have you ever watched a young married couple together? Researchers suggest you may be able to tell something about how happy they are by the way they respond to one another. How far apart do they sit? How much eye contact do they have? Do they touch each other? If these researchers' observations are correct, you will find the happier married couples are close together physically and responsive to one another, while the couples who don't get along well are not.

Studies of married couples do suggest that the happier ones enjoy their interactions more. Happy couples report more positive behaviors such as paying attention to each other, approval, concern, humor, smiling, and positive physical interactions than couples who aren't getting along. The happily married couples rate their emotional and sexual relationships and their ability to communicate higher than the couples reporting marital distress.

Research suggests that wives in less happy marriages often want more attention from their husbands: more time together, more conversation, and more appreciation for what they do. For their part, husbands in less happy marriages often want their wives to pay more attention to sexual needs.

The unhappily married person tends to be critical of the spouse and is unreceptive to his or her suggestions. In one study, it was found that the unhappily married person had troubles recognizing positive events in the marriage even

when they occurred. The bleak marital relationship seemed to cast a shadow over everything.

Studies further suggest that people in unhappy marriages seem to *overreact* to the irritants and annoyances that come with marriage. People in stable marriages seem to maintain more of a sense of perspective. Happily married people are less likely to be thrown by the ups and downs of daily events. Their perception of the value of the marriage is less likely to be buffeted by shifting events.

POWER RELATIONSHIPS AND MARITAL HAPPINESS

One of the factors that seems to make a difference in the happiness of marriage partners is the power relationships within the marriage. As you look at a marriage, you might ask: Who seems to be the dominant partner? Is it the husband? The wife? Or is there some kind of sharing or equality in decision making? In which cases would you expect men to report they are happiest? The women?

A summary of 20 studies that have been carried out on this question reports that, in general, marriages in which the wife is dominant seem less happy. Let's speculate why this is so. We know the expectation in western society is for the husband to take a leadership role. When he fails to do this, it may lead to lowered self-esteem in the man who feels he has not lived up to this expectation. When the wife moves in to fill the leadership vacuum, she may not be happy doing so. Being the leader in the marriage may not be what she wanted or expected, and this may lead to disappointment and loss of respect for her spouse. The situation may become more uncomfortable if she tries to force her husband into a more active role.

Research suggests that the marriages in which the partners are happiest are those in which there is a sharing of power and decision making. This sharing may take the form of active discussion by the partners in which they make a joint decision, or consultation by one partner with the other before making decisions. Perhaps the keys here are that consultation maintains the feeling that the individual is being treated with respect, and that joint commitments have considerable strength and staying power.

DISCORD IN MARRIAGE

We have described some of the perceptions of spouses whose marriages are not happy. One of the factors in marital problems (and this is probably true of other human relationships as well) is that marriage partners are not very accurate observers of each other's behavior. In one study, married couples were given a checklist of behaviors (for example, "spouse complimented me, "we watched television together") and asked to indicate whether the spouse had performed them during the past 24 hours. The results? The marriage partners only agreed about half the time as to whether an event had happened. When a sample of couples seeking marriage counseling was used, the agreement rate fell to 38 percent.

When a person is that unaware of or insensitive to what another person is doing, the potential for misunderstanding builds. You can almost hear the argument beginning. "I asked you to do ____ and you didn't do it," says one spouse. "What do you mean I didn't do it?" replies the other.

When people cannot agree about easily observable behaviors, it is not a very long jump to feeling misunderstood, to a perception that one is being treated unfairly, and to feelings of hurt, disappointment, and anger. When such feelings are frequent or persist, the marriage may be in trouble.

One does not have to go very far to find an unhappy marriage where the spouses are angry at one another. Sometimes there are heated verbal exchanges and sometimes physical violence. Or the partners may suffer in silence with deep resentment.

Physical violence in marriage occurs far more often than one might imagine. One estimate based on survey data is that perhaps five million American wives have been the targets of chronic physical abuse by their husbands.

The use of alcohol is often associated with this violence. Studies of the abusive husband suggest that he tends to be a person who was abused himself as a child and who witnessed spouse abuse in the family in which he grew up. It may be that these husbands have modeled their behavior on their fathers'.

Troubled marriages are often the source of considerable stress for both partners. In addition, research has shown that marital conflict is associated with psychological and behavioral problems in the children. Where the marital conflict takes the form of open hostility, the effects on the children seem to be greater.

Interestingly, the effects of marital discord seem to be more evident on boys than on girls. The boys' problems often show up in lack of control in school (conduct disturbances, aggressiveness). The girls may experience the same distress as the boys, but are more able to keep it inside themselves.

THE EFFECTS OF DIVORCE

Divorce in the United States has become so frequent that the odds are close to even that a marriage will end in divorce. Statistics indicate that among young women the chances for marital disruption are higher for those who marry early (in their teens or early twenties), have less education, and come from broken homes.

Divorce involves the shattering of hopes and the splintering of attachments. Divorce usually subjects all those involved to a period of great stress. This stress follows on the heels of the stress already experienced because of the discord in the marriage. The misery of loss and loneliness follows the misery of argument and acrimony.

Both wives and husbands are likely to experience feelings of depression. The divorced mother may find herself faced with many responsibilities and fewer resources to meet them. She may be forced to lower her standard of living. The father may find himself alone, at loose ends, with a feeling of being shut out. Men with broken marriages seem especially vulnerable to emotional or mental illness. One investigator reported that men with broken marriages were nine times more likely to enter psychiatric hospitals for the first time than men with intact marriages.

The effects of divorce on children can be quite marked, particularly during the first year or so. Researchers report reactions of intense longing for the departed parent, anxiety, depression, lowered self-esteem, poor performance in school, difficulties with peers, antisocial acts, and strong feelings of anger toward the parents.

Once again, the most noticeable effects seem to be on boys. Boys living with their divorced mother often have an especially hard time making a satisfactory adjustment. Perhaps it is the loss of the role model of the father or perhaps it is finding oneself in the ambiguous position of being the male in the family without any real authority or status.

While many children are able to make a good recovery from the effects of divorce, data suggest that others may experience long-term negative effects. These children may be unhappy and have a variety of personal, social, or school problems.

Divorce may make children more vulnerable to problems with interpersonal relationships. Studies suggest that girls who come from divorced families are more often sexually active at an early age. It may be that this early sexual activity represents an attempt to fill an emotional void created by the loss of the father. Or the early sexual activity may be a symptom of the lack of control and discipline that can occur after the breakup of a family.

What can be done to reduce the intensity of the emotional problems following divorce? Some research suggests that regular visits with the separated parent may help some parents and their children. Another factor that may make a difference is the level of post-divorce conflict between the parents. Research indicates that when such conflict is low, the children make a better post-divorce adjustment.

Judith Wallerstein, who has closely studied the problems encountered by children of divorced parents, believes that children must deal with six "tasks" in coping with the difficul-

ties caused by the divorce. The first task is to acknowledge the reality of the divorce, to see it for what it is, and not blow it out of proportion with wild fantasies or deny its existence with defense mechanisms.

The child's second task is to put some psychological distance between herself and the conflict going on between the parents. The child needs to "remove the family crisis from its commanding position in his or her inner world." The child should resume her own usual activities.

The third task, and the one that Wallerstein feels may be the most difficult, is to resolve the loss caused by the divorce. The child must "overcome his or her profound sense of rejection, of humiliation, of unlovability, and of powerlessness, which the one parent's departure so often engenders." This task may take many years.

The fourth task is to resolve the anger caused by the divorce. The child may blame one or both parents, or perhaps herself, and this anger spills over into other areas of life.

The fifth task is to accept the permanence of the divorce. Children of divorced parents often fantasize that their parents will be reunited.

The final task for the child is to reach the point where she can take a chance on entering relationships that will let love into her own life. The young person must overcome the fear that what happened to her parents will necessarily happen to her or she will be left with inhibitions that will prevent her from taking the risks needed to form enduring relationships.

AGING

Now we are going to speed up the passage of time. We are going to pass rapidly through the usually productive middle years of a person's life when family life and career may be in full bloom, moving on to the time when the person has to deal with the realities of declining capabilities.

Drawing a rough analogy, one might think of an athlete like a baseball pitcher. In the early part of his career he may have a blazing fast ball that he can blow right past the batters. As the years pass, the speed of that pitch will diminish. As the saying goes, he has "lost something" off his fast ball. If the pitcher is to continue his career, he has to develop other pitches (curves, sliders, fork balls, etc.). He also has to learn to pinpoint his pitches around the corners of the plate to offer the batter less of a target, and to mix up his pitches to keep the batters off balance. He is now substituting experience for raw athletic ability.

Something like this happens as we grow older. Certain abilities decline. Speed of reaction and short-term memory are good examples. The 70-year-old may not react as quickly in a car or be able to absorb and remember new information as well as the 17-year-old. But if she can draw on her vast experience, the 70-year-old may still get along quite well.

As we have suggested, there is a noticeable decline in the aged in certain types of intellectual and motor performance. We mentioned memory. Almost any way you want to measure it, the memory of older adults is usually poorer than that of younger people. This is true in tests of outright recall of new information and in tests using recognition as the standard. These age differences in memory have been found in studies using a variety of materials: sentences, nonsense syllables, prose passages, pictures of objects, and photographs of faces.

Delayed recall is often a particular problem for older adults. In a study where subjects were asked to remember addresses, people over 75 did much worse than younger students. Good advice for many elderly people is "write it down!" One exception to the generalization that memory tends to decline with age is performance on tasks involving implicit memory. Older subjects continue to do quite well on such tasks.

Older and younger people have been compared using standard intelligence tests. Older people do least well on tasks which involve nonverbal (performance) aspects of intelligence. For example, the older people will usually not do well on a task that requires them to put ob-

jects (like a puzzle) together under the pressure of time. The decline in ability, however, is likely to be less noticeable for measures of intellectual ability that use the person's experience. On tasks that involve the use of information or vocabulary, the older person may continue to do very well indeed. Verbal skills stay with one. Older subjects also continue to do well on tests of arithmetic skills, on tasks involving reasoning, and on tests of spatial perception.

When we talk about decline in performance, we must remember that there are still great differences among individuals. There are many examples of elderly people who continue to perform at exceptional levels. In music, for example, the composer Richard Strauss composed some of his finest music in his eighties. The pianist Arthur Rubinstein continued to dazzle audiences with his skill when he was even older.

The older person faces a number of difficult problems. In addition to the decline in certain intellectual capabilities, there are decreased physical capabilities (for example, less stamina and less acute hearing). There are often medical problems (for example, arthritis or high blood pressure) that have to be kept under control. Retirement and the fact that the children have left the home often leave elderly people with less structure in their life—fewer clear-cut ways to spend the days. Loved ones and friends may have died, leaving the elderly person feeling isolated. And there are the basic economic requirements for survival. Elderly people must pay for food and shelter on incomes that may be fixed in times of generally increasing prices.

Over 200 elderly people in Detroit were interviewed about the things they were afraid of in the future. They were concerned about such things as possible deterioration of their neighborhood, being victims of street crime, financial insecurity, losing their independence because of disabling illness, being a burden to others, and the possibility of having to live in a nursing home.

One might suspect that with these problems, there would be high rates of depression among the elderly. While many elderly people do experience loneliness—and this can be made more severe by poor health and inadequate financial resources—community surveys have shown that most elderly people do not appear to be noticeably depressed. In one study, for example, 73 percent of the elderly subjects surveyed reported that their mental health was good or excellent. Loneliness and depression happen to those in all age groups, not just the elderly.

As they slow down physically, elderly people often prefer to adopt a more tranquil lifestyle. For example, in a study of elderly people in Minnesota, the subjects were compared at two points in time, 1947 and 1977, when the mean age was 77. The subjects were asked to give yes or no answers to an identical series of statements on both occasions. In 1977, they were more likely to say no to items such as "work under much tension," "when I get bored, I like to stir up some excitement," "like to go to parties and other affairs where there is a lot of loud fun."

Researchers and others who have worked on the problems of the aged often stress the importance of older people maintaining goals and meaningful activities. Purposeful, rewarding daily activities, including time spent with friends, may be a key to maintaining the best possible level of physical and mental health in the elderly.

Some Questions and Activities

1. Have you ever wanted to write an advice column? Here's your chance. Imagine you write a weekly column in the school paper. Your job is to write replies to the students who have sent you the following letters.

   Dear Gabby:

   I am 14 years old. While I've been to parties with my friends, I have never been on a real date before. A boy I like has asked me out. I'm real nervous about it. I don't know what to say or what to do. How should I act? Please give me some hints.

   Signed,

   Inexperienced

   Dear Gabby:

   I'd really like to ask Betty S. out. I think about her all the time. She's pretty, smart, and lots of fun. She's a cheerleader and I'm sure she wouldn't have anything to do with a guy like me. I'm a pretty ordinary looking guy, though I am a good student. What should I do?

   Signed,

   In Love

   Dear Gabby:

   The kids I hang around with are getting sexually active and pressuring me to do the same. I am not ready for this sort of thing. However, I don't want to seem like a nerd. What do you suggest?

   Signed,

   Unwilling

2. People who marry when they are very young (for example, in their teens) are more likely to divorce than people who marry when they are older. Why do you think this happens?

3. Imagine you are a counselor. Parents come to see you because their child is having emotional problems at home and difficulties in school. In your interview you find out that the parents often have loud fights that the child can hear. If you were giving the parents advice, what would you tell them?

4. Can you think of any special programs or classes that could be included in the high school curriculum that might be especially useful for teenagers?

5. What are the personal qualities you would look for in forming lasting relationships with a person of the opposite sex?

6. Imagine that you have been asked to set up role-playing exercises for students who have anxiety about dating. Make up some problem situations. For example, a boy wants to date the girl who sits across from him in algebra class but doesn't know how to go about it.

7. Bowlby believed that attachment is a fundamental form of behavior and that breaks in attachment could lead to serious emotional reactions. When Bowlby wrote this, he was working with children. Think about adolescents and adults for a moment. Can you think of situations where breaks in attachments lead to emotional difficulties in adolescents and adults?

8. Poor communication is a common problem in unhappy marriages. Can you think of some concrete steps spouses could take to improve the quality of their communication?

9. Is there a senior citizens' center in your community? If there is, visit it one day. What kinds of services does it provide for the people who use it? What kind of services do you think might be valuable to add?

Test Your Knowledge

Read each statement and decide whether it is TRUE or FALSE. **Write your answers on a separate sheet of paper.**

1. Cultures around the world react to adolescence in the same way.

2. Studies have found that adolescents usually spend more time with their families than with their friends.

3. Adolescence is usually characterized by rapid physical growth.

4. Studies suggest that adolescents who are involved in multiple drug use tend to have problems at home.

5. Studies suggest that the influence of the peer group rises steadily throughout adolescence, reaching its peak in early adulthood.

6. Surveys indicate two of the primary concerns of adolescents are school performance and dating.

7. During adolescence both boys and girls grow rapidly.

8. Delinquency in adolescents is not related to conflicts with parents.

9. Performance in high school and participation in extracurricular activities are both related to future entrance into college.

10. Researchers who have studied cults report that cults are completely straightforward in the way they approach and recruit young men and women.

11. Studies of dating behavior show that people always choose the most attractive person available as a possible date.

12. Research to date suggests that marriages in which there is a sharing of power tend to be viewed by the spouses as happier than marriages in which either party is "on top."

13. The effects of divorce are usually more noticeable on boys than on girls.

14. Research indicates that spouses are usually very accurate observers of each other's behavior.

15. Depression is a frequent reaction of people going through a divorce.

16. Happily married couples tend to report less ability to communicate than couples experiencing marital distress.

17. The children of couples who quarrel openly are generally better adjusted than the children of couples who deal with their disagreements discreetly.

18. There is usually some decline in memory in aged persons.

19. Intelligence test scores for aged persons usually show a greater decline for verbal skills than for other kinds of performance.

20. Surveys indicate that most aged people tend to be very depressed.

CHAPTER 9

Abnormal Psychology

Even a machine doesn't always run on an even keel. Sometimes your car will hum along like it's brand new and other times it will sputter, make strange noises, or not even start. Like that car, the moods of human beings go up and down, shift around, and sometimes seem to come to a dead stop. How many times have you felt frustrated or irritated? How about feeling anxious or worried about something? Or how about feeling disappointed or sad—a case of the blues? All of these feelings can be very normal emotions that we all experience at one time or another. While such moods may come over us, they usually go away.

When we begin to discuss abnormal psychology, it is not always clear where the normal ends and abnormal begins. Some of the problems or symptoms we shall describe may sound like feelings you may have experienced at one time or another. Sometimes, the reader may react with the question, *is this me*, he's talking about? There is a tendency among beginning medical students, while learning about one disease after another, to feel they're coming down with everything they're reading about—to become hypochondriacs. Almost everyone experiences psychological problems from time to time, but that hardly means one is heading for an emotional or mental illness.

We will start with three basic terms which are important to consider: *normality, neurosis,* and *psychosis*. We have seen that the normal

range of behaviors allows for ups and downs of moods, periods of joy and sorrow, and a wide range of individual differences in personality. Not everyone is alike. Wouldn't it be a very dull world if we were? What passes for normality also depends on the environment or culture where you live. The behavior of a monk who seeks long periods of silence and meditation is normal in a monastery but might be considered unusual or abnormal in the daily world of business. The concept of normality, then, is somewhat elastic, not a definition for all times and all places.

A **neurosis** is an emotional disorder that has symptoms which can be painful or distressing and can interfere with effective behavior. Neurotic behavior is different from normal, but usually not so different that it is beyond understanding. In some instances, a neurosis seems like an exaggeration of normal behavior. All of us become anxious or depressed at times, but people with neuroses tend to be more so, more often, and in situations which may not seem to make good sense to outsiders. In one type of neurosis, **phobias**, people experience severe anxiety in "normal" situations, such as riding in an elevator.

In discussing neuroses, it's useful to refer to the *Diagnostic and Statistical Manual of Mental Disorders* published by the American Psychiatric Association. This standard reference is what psychiatrists and psychologists often use in diagnosing their patients. In describing neuroses, the manual talks about symptoms that are distressing to the individual, but do not basically interfere with the person's ability to deal with reality. This is an important point because in psychoses, the ability to "test reality" is sometimes markedly impaired. The manual also points out that neuroses are enduring problems, not transitory reactions, and that there is no observable physical cause for the symptoms.

Psychoses are more extreme forms of mental and emotional disorders. Some forms of psychotic behavior such as hallucinations and delusions seem strange and bewildering to outside observers. The loss of the ability to test (deal with) reality is a principal sign of a psychosis and may be so extreme that the patient has to be hospitalized. Among the most often occurring psychoses are schizophrenia, paranoid disorders, psychotic behavior following brain damage, and some depressive problems which may include psychotic symptoms.

In our exploration of abnormal psychology, we will begin with a discussion of anxiety and depression in everyday life. Then we will consider more lasting depressive problems, certain types of neurotic behaviors, and psychoses.

Anxiety and Depression in Everyday Life

Feelings of anxiety and depression are frequent and understandable reactions to the many problems of everyday life. For example, when an exam is scheduled, the normal reaction is to anticipate the event and to develop some concern about it. This concern usually helps mobilize one to deal effectively with the problem. As we indicated earlier, however, if anxiety becomes too intense, it may prove to be a hindrance rather than a help.

Feelings of being sad or blue are normal reactions to disappointments, when things haven't gone well or when one's expectations are dashed. When there is a loss in one's life— the breakup of a relationship, the loss of a job, or the loss of some hopes—people often react by

feeling depressed. This down feeling is sometimes accompanied by physical complaints, trouble in sleeping, and loss of appetite.

Most of us have ways of coping with transitory feelings of anxiety or depression. We have ways of reducing these feelings and pretty soon get back on an even keel. Roland Tanck and I conducted a study of the way college students usually coped with tension. In the table on page 121 is a list of coping techniques used by the students. The most frequent behaviors reported by the students were those which attempted to analyze the problem causing the tension and do something about it. Also high on the list was approaching other people, seeking their advice and company. When you're miserable, find a friend!

Not all of the coping techniques reported seem effective. Becoming irritable or worrying endlessly do not sound particularly helpful. Using marijuana and alcohol may serve to lower tension for a while, but there are dangers of dependency with frequent use of such substances. Our study did point out that young people seem to try to solve their problems by themselves or with the aid of friends. The college students did not often seek professional guidance or rely on medicine.

PERSISTENT DEPRESSION

When feelings of anxiety or depression are not intense or quickly disappear, there seems little to be concerned about. Such feelings become a problem when they are strong or persist over time. Persistent feelings of anxiety or depression can be a problem that requires attention.

Persistent depressions are a major and widespread problem. In a 1975 survey carried out by the National Institute of Mental Health, it was found that 17 percent of the people admitted to inpatient (hospital) or outpatient care in mental health facilities were diagnosed as depressed. This was higher than any other single category of mental illness. These people, plus depressed people being treated by private practitioners and many people not being treated

Table 1

Rank*	Coping Behaviors Used to Diminish Feelings of Tension
1	Try analyzing the problem
2	Take direct action to deal with source of problem
3	Talk the problem over with friends or family
4	Seek company
5	Become irritable and easily angered
6	Spend endless hours thinking about things
7	Daydream or fantasize
8	Just bear with the discomfort until it goes away
9	Take long walks
10.5	Engage in vigorous exercise
10.5	Watch TV or go to a movie
12	Seek sexual comfort
13	Seek complete isolation
14	Pray
15	Eat constantly
16	Just become ineffective—stop functioning well
17	Use marijuana
18	Drink alcohol
19	Take a trip or vacation
20	Meditate
21	Take tranquilizing medicines
22	Seek professional help

*Rank 1 is the coping behavior most often reported; Rank 2, the next most often, and so on. Rank 22 would be the coping behavior reported least often.

at all, suggest the number of depressed cases is very large indeed. And indeed, surveys of households in selected communities in North Carolina, Maryland, California, Missouri, and Connecticut carried out during the 1980's indicated that about five percent of adult Americans had at some time in their lives experienced a major depression and three percent had experienced a prolonged period of moderate depression. That translates into millions of people.

Studies in psychiatric institutions and community surveys indicate that depression seems to occur more often among women than men. No one knows for sure why this is the case.

The Diagnostic and Statistical Manual of Mental Disorders describes enduring periods of **depression** (or what might be called a *depressive neurosis*) as a "loss of interest or pleasure in all, or almost all, usual activities and pastimes . . . . The depressed mood may be characterized by the individual as feeling sad, blue, down in the dumps, or low." Such feelings should persist for a long time before being considered a neurosis. Some typical symptoms of depression are insomnia, low energy level, decreased concentration, social withdrawal, and brooding.

Let's look at a case study. Sheila is 18 years old. After graduating from high school, she enrolled in a large midwestern university. Here she felt like she was being buffeted by problems from every direction. Sheila had to work hard at a job to earn money and did not have time enough to do schoolwork. Inwardly she felt great pressure to get high grades, remarking, "I would be so unhappy if I didn't make high grades." Her social life had fallen into shambles; she had broken up with her boyfriend. She complained about having "no time for herself." The problems began to spill over from one to the other; she began to feel everything was going wrong. She began to take a closer look at herself and didn't like what she saw. Once she compared herself with a girlfriend and said, "I just wish I could be like her, look like her." She complained that she just didn't know how to act around others, remarking that she couldn't express her true feelings and always said the wrong things in a group.

She began to experience feelings of anger and alienation. She began to feel that people didn't care about her, that she was unpopular. Once she was stood up by a date and this really hurt her. She began to withdraw from people and said she "didn't care." As the semester moved on, her mood became chronically depressed. Her ability to study and concentrate on her schoolwork fell off dramatically. She developed a host of physical symptoms: dizziness, weakness, diarrhea, and had trouble eating and sleeping. Her roommate urged her to see someone at the university counseling center.

You probably have known people like Sheila who have become depressed and you may have wondered why this happens. We are not sure, but there are several current theories about depression that seem promising. Some of these theories are biological, focusing on the actions of the neurotransmitters in the brain. Recall that the neurotransmitters are chemicals that seep across the gaps between nerve cells enabling signals to move through the brain and nervous system. Certain of these neurotransmitters such as norepinephrine and serotonin appear to play a role in depression. Studies suggest that many people who are depressed may have too little of these chemicals in the central synapses or that there may be too much activity. Some researchers have suggested that the action of these neurotransmitters may not be properly regulated, something like an automobile engine out of sync. How the neurotransmitters affect depression is currently an important area of research.

In addition to biological explanations for depression, there are also promising psychological theories. Let us take a look at three of these theories.

One theory of the cause of depression is identified with the work of Martin Seligman. The theory has been called the *learned helplessness* theory of depression. The basic idea goes something like this: If a person repeatedly faces uncomfortable situations and finds he is unable to do anything about them, he gradually accepts the notion that he is powerless. He cannot control events and becomes passive. As the person becomes increasingly helpless, he begins to ask why. There is a search for a cause—to place the blame somewhere. According to the theory, if the person blames himself rather than looks for causes in the external world, it increases the likelihood of depression. If he views the cause of his problem as a stable, enduring situation rather than as something that can change, this, too, will help promote depression. Finally, if the situation is viewed as a widespread one affecting much of his life rather than a narrow problem, the chances of depression are increased.

Another current theory about the cause of depression involves the idea of reinforcement, or in this case, the lack of it. Imagine a person who goes along in her usual daily routines, seldom receiving any reinforcement for what she is doing. Perhaps there is little reinforcement to be had, or perhaps she just does the wrong things to bring feelings of gratification. But whatever she does fails to produce reinforcement. According to the theory's chief spokesperson, Peter Lewinsohn, a lack of reinforcement following her efforts—a scarcity of "pleasant events" in her life—is associated with depression. If Lewinsohn is correct, then changing one's behavior to improve one's effectiveness in bringing success or gratification can be an important part of coping with depressed feelings.

The third theory, proposed by Aaron Beck, has also stimulated a great deal of interest among psychologists. In Beck's view, the person who becomes depressed usually has a pattern of negative thoughts. He may think such things as he is being treated unfairly, that he is short on abilities, that no one really likes him, and that he has failed to do anything meaningful in life. When the person constructs a set of beliefs like this (a set of negative cognitions), it's hard for him to feel good about anything. His mood plummets and he becomes depressed. In using Beck's theory, one of the therapist's jobs is to go over these beliefs with the patient, attempting to help the patient realize that many of these ideas really don't hold water.

In regard to belief patterns, many therapists feel that *perfectionistic* attitudes help bring on depression. Perfectionistic attitudes are some-

thing like this: If a task is to be done, it must be done perfectly or you've failed. There is no tolerance for a merely good performance or for making mistakes. The problem with perfectionistic attitudes is that nobody's perfect. People with such attitudes set themselves up for repeated experiences of failure because there is little possibility of success.

Don Hamachek provides a good illustration of perfectionist attitudes in a statement from a client in therapy. "It really bugs me that I can't really get into something unless I can be more or less perfect at it. For instance, I'd love to learn how to play the piano, but it would take years and years to be any good. My dad was the same way. He always said, "If you can't do something right, then don't do it at all.""

Therapists have also felt that the "I must do" attitude rather than the "I like to do" attitude and tendencies to think in terms of extremes—things are either black or white— also tend to set one up for depressive reactions.

Another thinking pattern that some therapists believe may promote depression is constantly comparing oneself with others. People have many different characteristics and abilities. You are likely to do some things better than some of your friends and some things not as well. If you set your standards in terms of what other people are accomplishing rather than your own goals, you may always feel you are second best. As an example, I once treated a woman who developed a successful business, but was convinced she was a failure because she compared herself constantly with another woman whose business was more successful.

Looking at these three theories—learned helplessness, lack of reinforcement, and negative thinking patterns—you can see that there are probably a number of causes for a person becoming depressed. The theories, of course, raise many other questions. What kind of family environments produce learned helplessness? Why does a person keep doing things that produce no feeling of reward? Why do some people tend to develop negative thinking patterns while others do not? These are just a few of the questions that need further research.

MAJOR DEPRESSIONS

We talked about occasional feelings of depression almost everyone experiences and about persistent depressions that may require professional attention. Sometimes depressive problems can become very severe, requiring intensive outpatient care or hospitalization.

Some of the symptoms of a major depression are feelings of sadness and hopelessness, a sense of personal worthlessness, self-reproach and guilt, insomnia, chronic fatigue, brooding, and thoughts of suicide. In addition to this despairing mood, the ability to concentrate is usually lowered and there may be some reduction in short-term memory.

A major depression can happen at any age and can often reoccur. There is some tendency for major depressions to occur more often within the same family.

The *manic-depressive* disorder is one form of severe depression. What happens in this disorder is that there are periods when the person acts in ways which seem to be the very opposite of depressed. These periods are called **manic** periods. Manic periods are characterized by an extremely positive mood and sometimes frantic activity. The patient's self-esteem may be very high and his speech may flow like a rushing river. He is impulsive, calls up old friends in the middle of the night, goes on buying sprees, and, in a word, is "on a tear." The manic episode is something like a car that's racing its engine, then shuts off abruptly.

People who go through manic episodes often experience episodes of serious depression as well. Sometimes the depressed period may directly follow the manic period or vice versa. When patients experience periods of extreme mood swings, the disorder is called a *bipolar* depression. A depression which does not have a manic phase is called a *unipolar* depression.

As an example of the dramatic contrasting moods in bipolar depression, let's draw on a case study. The case study was part of a study of young people who were showing bipolar symptoms, but had not been hospitalized for the problems.

The subject, a young woman of 18, began to develop bipolar symptoms by the age of 12. When she was in a manic episode, she felt "hyper," and laughed and joked all the time. People said "she ought to slow down," and that "she was wearing them out." She had an intense need for excitement and began new activities enthusiastically, then quickly lost interest. At times she could hardly sit still. Her thoughts moved so fast she could "say only one half of a thought and then it was gone." She talked so fast she stumbled over her words. She spent money she couldn't afford for trips and was sexually active. She drove recklessly, going through red lights and stop signs. In contrast, during her depressed periods, her expression was downcast and she cried frequently. She felt tired and worn out. Her concentration was poor and she suffered from insomnia and a variety of physical complaints. She felt pessimistic about her future and had thoughts of suicide. Feeling cut off from other people, she needed a great deal of reassurance.

The researchers in this study found that the periods of symptoms—either manic or depressive symptoms—lasted on the average about three to six days. The episodes occurred fairly often. Typically, about two to six episodes per year were reported for both manic and depressive symptoms.

The treatment of severe depression involves antidepressive drugs and psychotherapy. The particular drugs prescribed will probably depend on the type of depression that is diagnosed. Lithium salts are often given for manic-depression with good results. A class of drugs called *tricyclics* is often prescribed for major depression. Studies have shown that tricyclics are effective with most patients who take them. One of the problems with these drugs, as well as lithium, is unpleasant side effects. Some possible side effects of tricyclics are dizziness, blurred vision, sedation, and weight gain. The search for better-tolerated antidepressants has led to the development of new medicines including a drug called *fluoxetine hydrochloride,* which is more familiar under the brand name Prozac™. Studies indicate that this drug is as effective as the tricyclics and is less likely to cause side effects.

Psychotherapy is also an effective treatment for depression. Research indicates that short-term therapy is as effective as drug treatment for people who are mildly to moderately depressed. In addition to avoiding the side effects caused by medicines, psychotherapy has the advantage of teaching patients better ways of coping with the stresses in their lives that may trigger depressive reactions. Some patients find it helpful to use medications and undergo psychotherapy as well.

ANXIETY AND PHOBIAS

Have you ever experienced a feeling of extreme anxiety? You can feel your heart race, your breathing is difficult, you begin to sweat, your legs may become shaky, your whole system mobilizes to a fever pitch? Sometimes people feel this way when they are on stage about to give a performance. This feeling of stage fright is very uncomfortable, almost disabling. If you stick it out, the intensity of the anxiety reaction usually diminishes and you will be able to carry on, sometimes very well. But the memory of the event may be quite unpleasant and you may be reluctant to put yourself in such a situation again. This sequence of events could be one of the causes of phobias.

The Diagnostic and Statistical Manual describes a phobia as a "persistent and irrational fear of a specific object, activity, or situation that results in a compelling desire to avoid the dreaded object, activity, or situation (the phobic stimulus)." Three of the more common types of phobias are *agoraphobia* (fear of being away from one's home, exposed to the real and imagined dangers of being in public places), *claustrophobia* (fear of confinement in small places), and *acrophobia* (fear of high places). People also have phobic reactions to animals, such as dogs, spiders, or snakes, to being in the water, to flying in airplanes and to a variety of other things. There are quite a few papers written on the subject of school phobia! Some children experience intense anxiety and physical symptoms, such as headaches and abdominal pains, at the thought of leaving home and going to school.

A study was carried out with women in Alberta, Canada, trying to learn something about the incidence of phobias. It was found that severe phobias were uncommon but that nearly 20 percent of the women sampled had fears which were strong enough to cause them to avoid certain situations.

Many phobias are not much more than nuisances. If you have a fear of snakes, it is easy enough to avoid the average cobra by staying away from the jungles of India. But what happens if you have agoraphobia and feel a sense of dread at the thought of going to the supermarket, or even taking a walk to the corner? That can become an extraordinary problem. First of all, agoraphobics can't do very much; they find themselves more and more restricted in their lifestyle. Every time they experience panic in public they may want to do even less. Second, try explaining to someone else that you're afraid to leave your house and see how much sympathy you get. Agoraphobia often causes great problems in a person's life, both for the person and for those around him or her.

There are some treatment programs for controlling phobias which are helpful for many sufferers. Behavioral therapies which we shall discuss in the next chapter are one of the most efficient ways of treating phobias. Certainly these treatments are worth trying and many people who suffer from phobias can be helped to live more normal lives.

Another kind of intense anxiety reaction is called **post-traumatic stress disorder**. That sounds complicated. Let's look at what the words mean. Post means *after*. Traumatic means a *terrifying or horrifying* experience. Stress means *feeling very anxious or uncomfortable*.

Imagine for a moment a situation like combat or bombing raids, or being in a town hit by a tornado, or being physically assaulted or held hostage. Such experiences may arouse intense fear. When the experience is over, the memory may linger on. Sometimes the person who has been through such experiences suffers from recurrent nightmares, flashbacks, or phobic avoidance reactions. With combat veterans, these post-traumatic stress disorders can occur years after the traumatic events actually happened. Neuroses following combat are an old and sometimes tragic story. In World War I, soldiers spent months in mud-filled trenches, listening to the sounds of artillery bombardment. The resulting anxiety neurosis was called "shell shock."

Mental health professionals were very concerned with developing better programs to aid veterans with post-traumatic stress disorders resulting from the war in Vietnam. To illustrate the disorder among Vietnam veterans, we will present some excerpts from a case history reported by Herbert Hendin.

The veteran, in his mid-thirties, was under treatment years after the end of the war. He had been using marijuana heavily, trying to reduce the severity of the nightmares he was experiencing. He also reported he was having a great deal of trouble getting along with people and became easily enraged.

As a soldier in Vietnam, he had been with an infantry division operating north of Saigon. He had been in combat. In one skirmish he had killed an armed Vietcong woman. He had also been ambushed by a North Vietnamese army unit. During the fighting he killed two enemy soldiers with grenades. Then he stepped into a booby-trapped area and was wounded by the explosion. Unconscious, he was left for dead by the enemy. It took a month for him to recover from the concussion and leg wounds.

In treatment he reported three recurrent nightmares. In the first nightmare, he found himself in Vietnam, walking through an area of thick grass. A head suddenly appeared in front of him. He sliced it off.

The second nightmare was terribly frightening and seemed so real, he wasn't sure whether it was really happening. He was carrying the body of a dead woman, searching for a place to hide it.

In the third nightmare he was under attack on a hilltop. In the dream, his wife and his family were with him.

One of the treatment approaches that was developed for veterans who suffer from these disorders like the one above is to get them together with other veterans who have the same problem. They meet in "rap groups" where they are able to share some of their experiences with people who really understand what they have gone through.

PSYCHOSOMATIC PROBLEMS

Many of the patients physicians see in their routine medical practices have complaints that are, at least in part, emotional in origin. Some physical symptoms can be caused or made worse by psychological stress. That is why many physicians now talk about the need to treat the whole person, rather than look at the patient's problems as a collection of symptoms.

Feelings of stress and depression are both associated with physical symptoms. Roland Tanck and I carried out two studies in which college students filled out a specially prepared psychological diary for periods of a week or more. In the diaries, the students kept a record of physical complaints (for example, headaches, weakness, nausea, dizziness, skin flare-ups), the level of interpersonal stresses they were experiencing, and their levels of depression. We found that students who reported more stress had more physical complaints. The same was true for those students with feelings of depression.

It seems clear that both feelings of stress and feelings of depression are related to physical complaints. It is also likely that other psychological factors may be associated with physical symptoms. There is some evidence, for example, that feelings of resentment and anger may be associated with symptoms. Think of the person with a barely submerged boiling point. A case in point would be the disease called neurodermatitis—skin problems without any observable cause. A number of studies have found that people with neurodermatitis tend to show higher levels of anger on psychological tests than control subjects.

Another psychological pattern that has been found in some patients, particularly those with ulcers, is a pattern of passive dependency. Think of the kind of person who tends to be walked on, treated like a doormat.

One very important psychological pattern which has been related to coronary heart disease has been called *Type A behavior*. Imagine a person who is aggressive, competitive, never lets up, and is always concerned with meeting deadlines. Researchers have found that people who fall into this category tend to have elevated levels of cholesterol and triglycerides in their blood. Both are associated with an increased risk of heart attacks. Further studies have confirmed that this competitive, impatient, almost hostile behavior is indeed a risk factor for coronary heart disease.

While we still have much to learn about the causes and treatment of psychosomatic problems, our current information certainly indicates that emotional factors are linked to physical symptoms. A careful review of over 50 studies carried out on this problem concluded that the psychological states that most frequently preceded the development of physical symptoms were resentment, frustration, depression, and helplessness.

Obsessive-Compulsive Disorders

Obsessive-compulsive disorders involve obsessions or compulsive behaviors. Let's see what this means. An obsession is an idea that takes hold of a person and is hard to shake off. One type of example would be obsessive jealousy. A man has the idea that his girlfriend is going out with someone else, doing all kinds of things, and he can't get it off his mind. He tells himself the idea is senseless; she's doing nothing of the sort. Still, he finds it hard to convince himself. The man may have good reality contact otherwise, but he may get stuck on this idea and brood about it.

A fairly common kind of obsession is doubt about whether you have actually done something. Did you really mail the letter? Did you turn off the gas stove? Is the baby all right? Some people may return to check on such possibilities, not once, but repeatedly. Such checking is an example of compulsive behavior. Compulsive behaviors have a "must do," often powerful urgency. In the case of repeated checking, the behavior may reduce anxiety that something is wrong.

In discussing neuroses, we mentioned that the sources of anxiety among neurotics sometimes seem strange to outsiders. Like phobias, compulsions can provide good examples of this. One case study reported on a man who had an obsession that his face had changed every time he chanced to look in a mirror. He had to go through a checking procedure lasting anywhere from several minutes to over an hour to convince himself that everything was all right and his worries were unfounded.

Like many obsessive-compulsive cases, the patient knew that his fears were senseless but he felt unable to control them.

Compulsions are often ritualistic in the way the behavior is carried out. An example might be people who take forever to get dressed, because they have developed a ritualized dressing procedure that they must go through, almost like a computer program, or they would feel very uncomfortable. Have you ever been in the house of a compulsive cleaner? Dust dare not settle!

Compulsions are sometimes thought of as things one does to avoid unpleasant consequences. On that level, compulsions have something in common with superstitions. The baseball manager who brings a particular object into the dugout each day, thinking that this will keep a winning streak alive, is being both superstitious and compulsive.

A frequently observed compulsion is repetitive hand washing. Such people often have a fear of contamination from dirt. Touching dirt may produce anxiety and discomfort. Washing repeatedly helps restore a feeling of cleanliness and reduces anxiety. While most people who go through compulsive hand-washing rituals realize their obsessive fears make little sense, one sometimes encounters people who really believe in the necessity of what they are doing. An example of such a case is provided in an interview reported by Edna Foa.

T: I understand that you need to wash excessively every time you are in contact, direct or indirect, with leukemia.

P: Yes, like the other day I was sitting in the beauty parlor, and I heard the woman who sat next to me telling this other woman that she had just come back from the Children's Hospital where she had visited her grandson who had leukemia. I immediately left, I registered in a hotel, and washed for three days.

T: What do you think would have happened if you did not wash?

P: My children and my husband would get leukemia and die.

T: Would you die too?

P: No, because I am immune, but they are particularly susceptible to these germs.

T: Do you really think people get leukemia through germs?

P: I have talked with several specialists about it. They all tried to assure me that there are no leukemia germs, but medicine is not that advanced: I am convinced that I know something that the doctors have not yet discovered. There are definitely germs that carry leukemia.

T: What is the probability that if you didn't wash after the incident in the beauty parlor your family would get leukemia?

P: One hundred percent. They might not get it immediately, these germs could be in their bodies for five or even ten years. Eventually they will have leukemia. So you see, if I don't wash, it's as if I murdered them.

Perhaps the most famous hand-washing-like ritual was described in Shakespeare's *Macbeth*. It's the scene where Lady Macbeth is sleepwalking. She rubs her hands together, trying to get rid of the smell of blood from the murder she urged her husband to commit.

It seems likely that many compulsions are ways of decreasing anxiety. Therefore, to treat the compulsion, it would seem important for the therapist to uncover the meaning of the compulsion and to deal with the anxiety underlying it.

ANOREXIA NERVOSA

This is a disorder that occurs mainly in young people, primarily girls in their teens. It's not as common a problem as, say, depression: **anorexia nervosa** happens to only about 1 in 200 teenage girls. Anorexia nervosa involves an overconcern about body size and a preoccupation with weight loss, sometimes to the point where the situation becomes life-threatening. What happens is that the person becomes very concerned about her appearance, becomes very fearful about gaining weight, and starts markedly reducing the amount of food she eats. To further lose weight, she may begin periods of self-induced vomiting. Interestingly, while not eating much herself, she may prepare fancy meals for others. Many people with anorexia often continue to have a good appetite while their body weight shrinks and deny anything is wrong. Eventually weight loss becomes profound; medical complications such as dizzy spells and hypothermia develop and treatment must begin to prevent a fatal result.

Anorexia is not usually a conscious attempt at suicide. It is a process in which people may not fully understand what they are doing and what is really happening to them. The precise causes of anorexia are not known, but certainly medical care and psychotherapy would seem to be very important for people who have started down this potentially dangerous path.

Multiple Personality

Multiple personality is a rare disorder in which the person assumes two or more distinct personalities in everyday life, sometimes completely unknown to each other. The personalities may be very different from each other, even complete opposites, and these selves may take turns in controlling the person. In one case, for example, the patient it was a 17-year-old girl who had been suffering from episodes of amnesia. In the first therapy session, the girl's initial personality was that of a friendly, giggly person. Later on, however, she showed up as a resistant, defiant person who did not even recognize her therapist. She appeared to be a different person.

Multiple personality was considered to be related to or perhaps a form of hysteria and attracted the attention of French psychiatrists around the turn of the twentieth century. Many cases of multiple personality were described in the books of the period. Interest waned over the years, however, and multiple personality has faded from the mainstream of psychiatric concerns. This is probably due to its rare occurrence. However, when a documented case does occur, it can be very dramatic as illustrated by the book and movie, *The Three Faces of Eve*.

The Schizophrenias

Schizophrenia is one of the more widespread forms of mental illness. Along with depression, it accounts for more admissions to mental health facilities than any other type of illness.

Schizophrenia is a psychosis. It is one of the most bewildering forms of mental illness. There may be no richer source of some of the more bizarre symptoms of schizophrenia than Eugene Bleuler's classic book written in 1911, *Dementia Praecox or The Group of Schizophrenias*. Here are some examples of the strange thoughts and actions of some of his hospitalized patients:

A patient heard confusing and persistent voices. He believed there was a group of men under his window who wanted to burn him and behead him. They would wait for him, threaten to climb the walls, and hide under his bed. He believed there were others who wanted to help him. Sometimes God was his protector. At other times, he thought God was part of the plot.

Another patient ripped his clothes to shreds, fully aware of what he was doing. He wanted to do this but he didn't know why.

There was a Miss Muller who counted "Mr. Mullers" as if she were counting the number of Mr. Mullers in the room.

A patient did not move for months at a time. He was so rigid that one could move the patient as if he were a piece of wood.

Another patient thought that his inventions were stolen from his mind while he slept.

While many schizophrenic patients may not approach this level of impairment, you can see from these examples how severe the loss of reality can be in schizophrenia.

The symptoms of schizophrenia have been recognized for ages. Descriptions of schizophrenic behavior can be found in Hindu writings of some thirty-four centuries ago. In the nineteenth century, European physicians began to classify these symptoms into different categories. Some types of symptoms (such as incoherence, silliness, grimaces, oddities) were called **hebephrenic**. Other types of symptoms (extreme passivity, rigid posture, decreased awareness of environment, stupor) were called **catatonic**. Toward the end of the nineteenth century, Emil Kraepelin developed a more general disease category called *dementia praecox* under which these various classes of symptoms would fit. Kraepelin did not invent the term dementia praecox, but he worked out systematic ways of describing the disorder and in a real sense put the disease on the map.

The term dementia praecox suggests a state of premature or early mental deterioration. The term was prompted by the observation that many relatively young people appeared to be experiencing symptoms of mental deterioration. The term dementia praecox failed to win long-lasting acceptance and was replaced by the term "schizophrenia." Kraepelin's pupil, Eugen Bleuler, who wrote the book we drew our examples from, named the disease schizophrenia because he felt the disease was often marked by the splitting of different psychological functions. The thinking process, emotions, and activities of the schizophrenic patient did not operate in an integrated way. It's important to remember that schizophrenia is not the same thing as multiple personalities discussed earlier.

Kraepelin and Bleuler talked about several types of schizophrenia These included *catatonia* (catatonic symptoms), *hebephrenia* (hebephrenic symptoms), *simple* schizophrenia (only the basic symptoms), and a type called *paranoid* (delusions of persecution). This early classification has given way to somewhat different views now, but some terms, like paranoid, are still very much a part of both our clinical and everyday vocabulary.

Let us now look at more current views of schizophrenia. Once again, we will turn to the *Diagnostic and Statistical Manual* for our description of the disease. One of the characteristics of schizophrenia is a decline or *deterioration* in functioning. For example, a person might be a very good worker, then his performance begins to fall off. Behavior may become erratic and hard to explain. His social relations may deteriorate and he may take less good care of himself. People begin to notice that something is wrong.

A second characteristic of schizophrenia is disturbances in thought. One striking example of this is **delusion**. Delusions are clearly false ideas that the patient nevertheless believes to be true. Some examples of delusions are "The communists are after me." "There's a snake crawling around in my stomach." "I am the son of the Virgin Mary." The patient may firmly believe these ideas even when everyone tells him he is wrong. When the delusions are of persecution ("The mailman is spying on me." "They're trying to poison me."), the delusion is called paranoid.

Some delusions appear way-out and bizarre. One example is a woman who believed that when a United States spacecraft soared through the rings of Saturn, her picture was telecast throughout space and she was declared queen of the galaxy.

Delusions differ in how organized they are. Sometimes delusions seem to be no more than a series of unrelated ideas; sometimes they form an organized picture. An example of the former is a young woman who expressed the following delusional ideas, all in one interview. (1) Her parents had leukemia. (2) She was being turned into a homosexual. (3) People below were being killed in a torture chamber and their bodies put into food. (4) A special machine was changing her face into a man's face. (5) Secret injections of experimental drugs were being used to poison her.

A third characteristic of schizophrenia is *hallucinations*. A hallucination is perceiving an event that really isn't happening. Typically, the patient "hears voices." Someone is speaking to the patient that no outside observer can see. The voices may be commenting on the patient's behavior, may be even ordering him to do something. This, of course, could be dangerous. For example, a schizophrenic patient was asked what his conscience was and what it did. The patient replied it was a voice that told him to jump out of the window. In addition to hearing voices, patients may feel things like electric or burning sensations or experience visual hallucinations.

A fourth characteristic of schizophrenia is blunted emotion or what's technically called *flattened effect*. What this means is the patient doesn't respond to people or situations with the normal emotions you would expect. Sometimes the patient's voice lacks expression and the tone seems monotonous.

In some cases of schizophrenia there is a tendency to withdraw from the world. In its extreme form, such withdrawal has been called **autism**. Here the patient seems to be living in his or her own world.

While schizophrenics may show blunted emotions and withdrawn behavior, their dreamlife is often extremely threatening. The dreams of schizophrenics are often overwhelming; sometimes the dreamer may be viciously attacked, even destroyed.

These then are some descriptions of schizophrenic symptoms. What do we know about schizophrenia? The answer is a lot, but not nearly enough. Most importantly, we are really not sure of the cause or causes of schizophrenia, though in view of the bizarre symptoms of the disorder one would suspect that there might be abnormalities in the brain. Researchers have used a variety of high-tech imaging techniques to study the brains of schizophrenic patients. A review of research indicated that about one half of the patients studied showed evidence of brain abnormalities. Many patients had enlarged ventricles; these are cavities filled with fluid within the brain. Since many schizophrenic patients do not show brain abnormalities, the question of the role of brain abnormalities in this disorder is still unsettled.

There is also reason to believe that there is a genetic involvement in the disorder. Children of schizophrenic parents run a higher risk of developing schizophrenia than the general population. This seems to be true even if the children are raised by adoptive parents who are not schizophrenic. Studies of identical twins suggest that if one of the twins has schizophrenia, the other twin has about one chance in two of also developing the disorder. Since the heredity of twins is identical and the chances of becoming schizophrenic are only about 50-50, environmental factors would also seem to play a role in schizophrenia. Investigators have been looking at such factors as the parent-child relationship and the impact of stress situations. Some researchers have reported that the symptomatic outbursts of some schizophrenics are triggered by periods of stress.

Sociologists have found that schizophrenia seems to occur more often in the lower socio-economic stratas of society than it does in the middle. While researchers have speculated on why this is so, no one really knows for sure. Psychologists have found that schizophrenics tend to have difficulty in processing information and often have slowed reaction time. Schizophrenic patients do not show much impairment in simple tests of recognition memory, but have difficulty with the more demanding tests of outright recall. One theory is that schizophrenics have problems dealing with complex stimulation from the environment. Their capacity to deal with complexity is overloaded.

Schizophrenia often begins in adolescence or young adulthood. Men are first hospitalized for schizophrenia younger than women are. The peak risk age for men is in their twenties, perhaps less than age 25, while for women, the peak risk age is higher, in their thirties. People who make the best recovery from schizophrenia are those who are in better emotional shape to start with. The person who has settled down in life, who has developed a stable relationship such as marriage, is working, and has a place in the community is the one most likely to "shake off" the illness and return to active life. The patients with the poorest outlook are those who have shown an early, gradual, continuous deterioration.

Individual psychotherapy seems to be of little value for schizophrenia The most effective treatment for schizophrenia today appears to be antipsychotic medications. Using these medicines, many patients who would have formerly spent a long time in the hospital are now able to return to their homes. Before the mid-1950's, the schizophrenic patient usually was hospitalized for several years. Now the average stay is about a month. It should be noted, though, that symptom outbursts requiring periods of rehospitalization are fairly common—perhaps in 40 percent of the patients. Still, the improvement in getting patients out of mental hospitals has been dramatic.

Paranoid Disorders

Sometimes **paranoia** is viewed as a type of schizophrenia, sometimes as a different type of illness. The schizophrenic patient typically develops symptoms in adolescence or early adulthood; many paranoid patients develop symptoms in middle or later adult life. The paranoid patient's intellectual abilities are not usually impaired, as the typical schizophrenic patient's abilities are, and the paranoid patient is often able to work capably.

The major symptom of paranoid disorders is delusions of persecution. These delusions are more systematic and less bizarre than the typical schizophrenic delusion. Typical paranoid delusions are that the person is being spied upon, followed, or poisoned. Paranoid people are often angry and suspicious, and sometimes think about taking legal actions against people whom they imagine are causing them problems. The term *paranoia* refers to a fixed, unshakable delusion.

Kenneth Colby, who has been interested in the causes of paranoid disorders, noted that certain events have sometimes preceded paranoid reactions. Some examples of these events or situations are being socially isolated, having language difficulties, and increasing deafness. These conditions would make a person less able to accurately interpret what's going on in the world and might result in increased suspiciousness. Colby also noted that failure in work, school, or in romance seems to precede symptoms in some patients. Perhaps the person's self-esteem is reduced and the paranoid-prone person may lash out as a defense rather than look within herself for causes of her problems.

Organic Brain Disorders

When we discussed neuroses, we talked about psychological difficulties that occurred without any known organic cause. When we discuss psychoses like schizophrenia, we think there very well might be genetic and biochemical factors involved in the causes of these diseases, but we're not exactly sure what they are or how they operate. When we talk about **organic brain disorders**, the situation is different. Here the biological causes can often be demonstrated and are believed to be the causes of the observed psychological disturbances.

What happens is that people start behaving in unusual ways—they may have problems with memory and concentration; they may experience hallucinations or delusions—and the causes lie in the fact that the brain is not working normally. In some instances, the problem may be temporary. This can happen when the person is acutely intoxicated by alcohol or under the influence of mind-distorting drugs

such as LSD. In other instances, the problem may be chronic. This happens when the person suffers from a brain disease and the abnormalities usually get worse over time.

A widespread type of brain disorder is called *senile dementia*. One type of this disorder is **Alzheimer's disease**, which afflicts people over the age of 65. Some of the important early symptoms of Alzheimer's disease are losses in short-term memory and difficulties in concentration. These problems get worse as the disease progresses, until it reaches the point where the person can hardly do anything alone and finally needs full-time care. Alzheimer's disease is caused by brain atrophy. This can usually be demonstrated by medical tests such as a CAT (Computer-Assisted Tomography) scan. It's important to run these tests and make an accurate diagnosis because some elderly people may develop symptoms similar to Alzheimer's disease (such as poor scores on tests of memory) as part of a major depression. Depression can usually be treated with much more success than Alzheimer's disease. At the present time, there is little treatment for Alzheimer's disease other than good family or nursing home care.

We have explained some of the emotional and mental problems that are part of the field of abnormal psychology. There was a time when these problems were poorly understood and were viewed with fear and ignorance. It was considered to be a disgrace to have someone in the family who was mentally ill, and if someone had a "nervous breakdown" (which is a vague, popular term for mental illness), it was often hushed up. The stigma attached to mental and emotional problems has diminished as our knowledge has increased. Developments in both drug therapy and psychotherapy offer increased hope for the afflicted, and continued research on abnormal psychology offers still better prospects for the future.

Some Questions

1. Have you ever seen mental illness portrayed on television or in the movies? If you have, what concepts or ideas about mental illness do you remember?

2. Why do you suppose people had a more negative view of mental illness ("keep it quiet when it happens") than, say, a disease like heart disease?

3. What do you think would be some of the reasons for depression among people in their teens?

4. The table on page 121 lists a number of behaviors used to diminish tension. Based on your own experience, which of these behaviors would you say might be most effective?

5. Do you know anyone who has ever had a strong phobia about some specific situation? If you do, what was the situation? Was he or she able to do anything about the situation?

6. Women seem to be more vulnerable to depression than men. Why might this be so?

7. Type A personalities run a higher risk of heart disease. If you were a counselor, what advice would you give such a person?

8. Multiple personality is a very rare disorder, schizophrenia a much more common disorder. Yet people confuse the two disorders. Why do you think this is so?

9. What are some of the more hopeful things you might tell a friend who was concerned about someone who developed schizophrenia?

Test Your Knowledge

Read each statement and decide whether it is TRUE or FALSE. **Write your answers on a separate sheet of paper.**

1. A psychosis is generally considered a more serious disorder than a neurosis.

2. A bipolar depression has a manic and a depressive phase.

3. When a person feels anxious occasionally, it means he or she has an emotional illness.

4. Anorexia nervosa is a problem that involves excessive weight loss.

5. Claustrophobia is a fear of animals like spiders or snakes.

6. Physical complaints and insomnia are often associated with depression.

7. One of the symptoms of schizophrenia is delusions.

8. Multiple personality is a very common form of mental illness.

9. Dementia praecox was an early name for the disease schizophrenia.

10. Depression is a problem that occurs in men more often than in women.

11. The public has always taken a sympathetic, supportive attitude towards mentally ill people.

12. Delusions of persecution are called paranoia.

13. The person with Type A behavior is typically very relaxed and low-key.

14. Stress is often associated with physical complaints.

15. There are currently very effective treatments for Alzheimer's disease.

16. Some of the symptoms of Alzheimer's disease are problems with short-term memory and concentration.

17. Hallucinations occur only in the disease schizophrenia.

18. Extreme social withdrawal is called autism.

19. Post-traumatic stress neuroses are only found during wars.

20. The average length of stay for hospitalization for schizophrenia has been increasing since the 1950's.

21. Imaging studies of schizophrenic patients have found no evidence of brain abnormalities.

22. Research indicates that biological factors play no role in depression.

Psychotherapy

For some time now, Jack has been feeling anxious and depressed. He's been having trouble falling asleep. Sometimes he lies awake at night just thinking about things. Much of the time he feels lonely. His mood is pessimistic and sometimes things just seem hopeless.

He's tried talking about his problems with his friends, but it hasn't helped that much. He's reached the point where he feels he just can't cope with things himself. He decides he needs professional help. He wants to go into therapy.

Jack doesn't know much about therapy, and he doesn't know how to find a therapist. He asks around. A friend says he saw a psychiatrist briefly—she has an office in that large downtown medical building. Jack glances through the yellow pages of his telephone directory. He calls up the local psychological association. A woman answers and gives him the names of three members of the association who are licensed by the state and do therapy. He sees an advertisement in the newspaper for a social worker who does therapy.

Questions run through his mind. Therapists come from different backgrounds—psychiatry, psychology, social work. Do they all do the same thing? How can he pick out a "good" therapist? What will the therapist expect of him? What should he expect of the therapist? What benefits can he reasonably expect from therapy?

There are thousands of people like Jack facing this kind of situation. They recognize they need therapy and must find and choose a therapist. They may make a decision knowing very little about therapy.

Perhaps the first thing to recognize about psychotherapy is that it is not as standardized as, say, medicine or dentistry. There are many different approaches to psychotherapy. One therapist may have the client lie down on a couch and encourage the client to talk about whatever is on his mind. Another therapist might teach the patient techniques of deep muscle relaxation. Still another therapist might engage the patient in confrontations over his ideas and beliefs. And there are some therapists who do things which sound "way out." Have you ever heard of "primal therapy" or the "primal scream"?

In this chapter we are going to look at several types of psychotherapy that are now being practiced. Then we will examine data about the effectiveness of psychotherapy. We will close with a look at group therapy.

Psychoanalytic Therapy

Treatment of people with emotional and mental problems goes back a long way in history. But psychotherapy as we think of it today begins with Freud. You will remember that Freud developed a theory about the causes of certain types of neurotic symptoms. Freud believed in an unconscious part of the mind that held unacceptable thoughts and impulses striving for release. A censor kept these thoughts and impulses out of awareness. Sometimes these thoughts got out in the disguised form of symptoms.

As an example, Freud mentioned a patient who felt a wish to marry her brother-in-law at the time when her sister was dying. The wish was clearly unacceptable and was repressed. The thoughts, however, gained expression in the form of hysterical symptoms.

If the Freudian view is correct, then therapy should be aimed at bringing the cause of the symptoms (the unacceptable thoughts and impulses) to awareness. Once the patient has recognized and accepted these thoughts as his own, the pressures from them should be relieved. The symptoms, which are expressions of this pressure, should disappear. As Freud put it in his early writings, when all the memories had been restored, the illness would clear up and would not reoccur.

So the aim of Freudian psychoanalysis was to bring to awareness the unconscious thoughts and impulses of the patient—to try to get unconscious ideas past the censoring forces into consciousness.

Freud tried to accomplish this objective in a number of ways. In his early work, he tried hypnosis. One of the reasons he gave up hypnosis was probably that he was not very good at it. In *Studies on Hysteria*, Freud wrote: "I soon began to tire of issuing assurances and commands such as 'you are going to sleep!' and of hearing the patient, as so often happened when the degree of hypnosis was light, remonstrate with me: 'But, doctor, I'm *not* asleep. . .'

For a while Freud tried another method of bringing forth memories; he pressed the patient's forehead, urging her to remember. This procedure apparently did not work too well either. Freud then hit upon a very important discovery, the method of **free association**, which became the primary tool of psychoanalysis. Instead of urging the patient to remember things, the analyst encourages the patient to suspend her critical judgment and report every-

thing that passes through her mind, even if the ideas are painful or embarrassing or seem unimportant. The patient is told to hold nothing back.

Freud would say something like this to a patient: "You will notice that as you talk ideas will come to you which you will hesitate to express. You'll be inclined to think that the ideas have no connection or are unimportant to the process. Don't give in to these feelings." Freud viewed attempts at withholding as signs of resistance to the analysis.

In traditional psychoanalysis, the patient lies down on a couch, the analyst sits behind the patient, and the patient begins to talk.

When free association works—and many patients are unable to do it well—a chain of ideas may get started, perhaps from one of the day's experiences, perhaps from a dream the patient had during the night. The chain of ideas may take the patient well back into childhood.

The psychoanalytic procedure for free association with dreams is particularly interesting. The analyst hears the dream in its entirety, then brings up one thought from the dream at a time to the patient, asking for her associations. Frequently, these associations are past experiences of the patient that suggest unresolved, troubling problems. Freud saw dream association as a "royal road to the unconscious" that would help unearth the repressed material that he believed sustained neurotic symptoms.

While the patient talks, the analyst listens, tuning into the patient's stream of thought. The analyst says little. He tries to take a neutral position, neither praising nor blaming the patient and not revealing much of himself. At times, he'll offer an interpretation. The analyst tries not to tell the patient what to do. Psychoanalysis is a slow, often painful, process of self-discovery that may take years to complete.

As the years went on, Freud continually revised his ideas. He recognized that simply bringing out unconscious materials didn't always make patients better, and that sometimes cures were not permanent. While Freud struggled with these problems, other psychoanalysts began to move away from the original Freudian techniques. Some well-known psychoanalysts, such as Jung and Adler, developed different approaches to both theory and practice.

For a number of years, psychoanalytic therapy dominated psychotherapy. The technique was fascinating and had a considerable mystique. The problem with the method, however, was that it took a great deal of time to complete an analysis, and carefully controlled studies that would show that the technique was indeed effective were lacking. The search for alternatives began.

Nondirective or Client-Centered Therapy

Perhaps the first serious outside challenge to the dominant position of psychoanalytic therapy came from the work of Carl Rogers. Rogers began writing about therapy it the 1930's, discussing the treatment of problem children. Gradually, he began to develop a method of therapy called *nondirective therapy*, and later *client-centered therapy*. One of Rogers' basic ideas was that it was *not* the therapist's responsibility to direct the flow of the therapeutic interview, to advise the patient, or even to interpret. Rather the therapist should use techniques which *reflect* back to the client the client's own feelings. This will help the client recognize more clearly what his own feelings, attitudes, and reaction patterns are.

Rogers believed that as the client became aware of and expressed his feelings, he would develop insights—new ways of looking at himself, his relationships, and his goals. He would achieve better self-understanding and more self-acceptance. In Rogers' view, such insight would be followed by actions implementing the new goals. In addition, the client would be more capable of solving his own problems in the future.

In helping the patient move toward increased insight and self-acceptance, a Rogerian therapist acts something like an ultrasensitive mirror. The therapist talks little, listens sensitively, and tries to give back to the client the essence of what the client is saying—not so much ideas as feelings.

According to Rogers, the therapist who can best assist the client in this exploration of self is a person who the client sees as genuine, and who doesn't evaluate or pass judgment on the client. Perhaps most important, the therapist must be able to listen empathetically, that is, must be able to stand in the client's shoes and feel what the client is feeling. Rogerian therapists must be able to communicate to their clients the sense that they are thinking, feeling, and exploring along with them.

Here is an example of the client-centered approach taken from Rogers' early book *Counseling and Psychotherapy*. The client, Paul, is talking about his schoolwork, which is not going well, and his expectations about his parents' reactions.

Paul: . . .Oh, I don't know if they're going to sort of condemn me. I think so, because that's what they've done in the past. They've said, "It's your fault. You don't have enough will power, you're not interested." That's the experience I've had in the past. I've been sort of telling them that I improved in this respect. I was—I was all right the first quarter. Well, I wasn't entirely all right, but I just got worse. (*Pause.*)

Counselor: You feel that they'll be unsympathetic and they'll condemn you for your failures.

Paul: Well, my—I'm pretty sure my father will. My mother might not. He hasn't been—he doesn't experience these things; he just doesn't know what it's like. "Lack of ambition" is what he'd say. (*Pause.*)

Counselor: You feel that he could never understand you?

Paul: No, I don't think he is—is capable of that, because I don't get along with him, don't at all!

Notice how the counselor is reflecting back the feelings of the client. The client then explores deeper into his own feelings.

Rogers saw a great deal of growth potential in his clients. His client-centered method of therapy was a careful, low-key, gradual approach to bringing it out. Its aim was discovery by the patient, assisted, but never forced, by the therapist.

For a while, the choice of a type of psychotherapy came down to some form of psychoanalysis or the Rogerian client-centered approach. Both approaches to therapy put the therapist in a relatively passive role. Then there was an explosion in psychotherapeutic techniques. All kinds of new approaches to therapy emerged. The old rules governing what a therapist should or should not do have been seriously questioned. We will now look at three of the newer approaches to therapy: **cognitive therapy, Gestalt therapy,** and **behavioral therapy.**

Cognitive Therapy

The word *cognitive* has to do with beliefs or understandings. In our discussion of the causes of depression, we mentioned Beck's theory that depression was associated with a pattern of negative thoughts. The person might believe that he was inadequate in various ways, or that the cards were stacked against him, or that the future was hopeless; the result was that his mood sank in despair. If beliefs such as these were part of the depressive problem, then perhaps it might be possible to alter such beliefs during therapy and thus lessen or eliminate the depressive symptoms. The basic idea behind cognitive therapy is to bring out and make clear what the client's beliefs are and to assist the client in trying to change them.

The cognitive therapist looks for patterns such as perfectionistic ideas and black-and-white thinking. She searches for harmful patterns in the client's thinking. Does the patient blow things out of proportion, overgeneralize, take things personally? The therapist looks for irrational ideas that, if believed, may set the patient up for depression and other symptoms.

How does the cognitive therapist go about this? She tries to get the patient to pay attention to his thoughts, particularly those thoughts which occur around the time he is experiencing symptoms. For example, if the patient reports he is unable to sleep, the therapist might say, "Tell me what you were thinking about when you were lying awake. Imagine there was a tape recorder taking down your thoughts. Tell me as clearly as you can what your thoughts were."

When the cognitive therapist has recorded enough of the patient's thoughts, she will work with the patient, trying to put these thoughts together and find a pattern. She will try to point out the beliefs the patient operates under in his daily life.

To illustrate the cognitive approach, we will present a case study.

Alan is a senior in a suburban prep school. He began therapy because he was feeling depressed. During therapy he made statements like, "I spend hours studying, I hardly ever have any fun"; "I work hard, but I'm not getting good grades"; "I was not accepted into the better of the colleges I applied for"; "My father always tells me, if you work hard enough, you can do anything you want"; "He tells me I have to give 110 percent effort." After listening to many statements like these, the therapist noted that Alan was trying to live up to his father's expectations, not his own, and that he was operating under the belief that "hard work guaranteed success in life." In Alan's case, it hadn't worked out that way. If this belief were correct, then Alan had failed in his own eyes. Alan agreed, saying that he thought he had failed.

The therapist suggested that maybe the belief was the problem, not Alan's performance. She began to work with Alan to challenge the belief. She pointed out that hard work was very important, but was only one ingredient in success. Aptitudes, skills, and talents were also important. She reminded him of basketball players who worked very hard trying to make a professional basketball team but lacked the speed and quickness to play professional ball. It wasn't for lack of effort, she said. The therapist asked Alan whether he would criticize someone who was trying as hard as he could. Alan replied no. The therapist asked, "Isn't that what you're already doing in school?"

Gestalt Therapy

Psychoanalysis focuses on thought processes, aiming to lead the patient back through a chain of associations to the distant past. Gestalt therapy, in contrast, focuses on the immediate flow of experience, on what is felt here and now, moment by moment. Psychoanalysis—and this is true of most psychotherapies—is intellectual. Most therapies involve talking and thinking about feelings, experiences, and problems. In contrast, Gestalt therapy involves dramatics; it is like being in the theater. Gestalt therapy is like role-playing; you write your own script as you go along. But this time you play *all* the parts. The therapist is something like a stage director.

Let's illustrate briefly the essentials of the technique. Imagine that the patient reports a dream: she is in an airplane during a violent rainstorm and she is afraid of crashing. The Gestalt therapist does not ask for associations to the dream as a psychoanalyst would. Instead she points to an empty chair and says, "There is a storm. Act the part of the storm. Be the storm. What is it saying?"

The patient moves over to the empty chair. She acts as if she is the storm. She throws her hands forward. Her voice becomes angry. She says, "I'm going to terrify you. I'm going to attack your airplane with lightning and rain and wind. I'm going to destroy the airplane!"

The therapist says to the patient, "Now talk back to the storm."

The patient returns to her own chair. Her voice is meek: "Why do you want to hurt me? What have I done?"

The patient changes chairs again. Her voice is scornful. "Because you're weak. You let people walk all over you. You're just getting what's coming to you."

You can see that the patient has begun to project her own feelings about herself into the dialogue between herself and the storm. A conflict about aspects of her own behavior is beginning to emerge.

Imagine that the dialogue continues. The patient takes the part of the airplane that is carrying her safely through the storm. The patient also takes the part of the weakness she feels in dealing with others and the anger that is directed at the weakness. There is a dramatic dialogue in which the patient plays all the parts.

The Gestalt therapist views aspects of the dream (for example, the feelings of weakness and anger) as parts of the self the client is uncomfortable with. In Gestalt therapy, the client learns how to accept such feelings and make them part of the self.

In his research on Gestalt therapy, Leslie Greenberg spoke of one of the two chairs as the "experiencing chair." This chair represents the experiencing part of the person, the self that is conducting an inner exploration. The other chair is filled with alien parts of the personality and with the person's projections on other people and objects. In the earlier stages of Gestalt therapy, statements from the other chair may be harsher and more critical. This harshness may diminish as therapy progresses and self-acceptance grows.

Greenberg provides an example of such a change in the following excerpts from the case of a young woman. In the excerpts, *Other* is the client when she is playing the part of her mother, and *Experiencing* is the client when she takes the part of herself. *T* is the therapist. The client changes chairs when she changes roles.

(Early stage of therapy)

Other: Do you want to go to hell? You must want to—couldn't you even do it just for us? What can I do—how can I be your mother and have such a daughter?

Experiencing:	I want you to love me because of who I am. . . . I feel no guilt for the way I have lived. I have made mistakes but I feel positive about my life in the last few years. You feel negative, that they are lost years. You have not believed me in the past which has been really hard for me [soft voice].
(Later stage of therapy)	
Experiencing:	You see me through your eyes and according to your rules.
T:	Come over here. How do you see her? Be those eyes. What do you see over there?
Other:	I see a sad girl [focused voice].
T:	So tell her this.
Other:	I see a lonely girl. . . . I don't know how you could be happy. I feel sad when I see you unhappy. I want to do something but I don't know what to do. I want to see you make a decision on what to do next, a good decision. . . .
(Still later stage of therapy)	
Experiencing:	I'm sad that I had to spend so much time untangling. That's what I'm sad about and I'm actually pretty good these days and I'm still a little lost but I'm really enjoying finding my way. I'm really enjoying it. . . .

Greenberg points out that the client has moved from criticizing herself in the other chair, to feeling compassion, to increased acceptance when she says she is finding her way.

Gestalt therapy was the brainchild of Fritz Perls, a refugee who fled Europe during the rise of Nazi Germany and eventually settled in the United States. Perls had psychoanalytic training, but turned his back on Freud's methods. He expressed the opinion that free association was like a game to avoid what is really happening and that you could "chase your childhood memories to doomsday, but nothing will change."

Perls believed that a person's personality was incomplete because the person had disowned parts of the self. Unacceptable feelings were rationalized away or repressed. The result was a shrinking of the person's energy and capabilities. In Perls' view, therapy should provide the patient with the opportunity to discover these missing parts and to integrate them with the self.

Perls distrusted intellectual approaches to therapy. In working out his own methods, he drew on his early training in the theater. The result is a dramatic approach to therapy that is well illustrated in his book *Gestalt Therapy Verbatim.*

Behavior Therapy

The psychoanalytically oriented therapist looks for explanations for symptoms caused by repressed impulses from early childhood. The cognitive therapist looks for explanations in distorted beliefs about the self and the world. In both instances, to deal with symptoms, the therapist and client search for causes and attempt to deal with the causes. The behavioral therapist has a different approach: focus on and treat the symptoms directly.

For example, take the problem of a person who is very overweight. The psychoanalytic therapist might look for the causes of overeating in frustrations that happened in infancy or early childhood. The cognitive therapist might say something like, "I think you're overeating because you're depressed and you're depressed because you believe you haven't accomplished as much as you felt you should have." In contrast, the behavioral therapist might say, "I want you to record what you eat at every meal, and in between. This procedure of monitoring what you are eating will help you cut down your food intake."

The behavioral therapist might take a position something like this: "In therapy, you're interested in changing behavior. So, let's go about *changing behavior*. If a person is tense, don't spend a lot of time figuring out why he is tense, teach him how to relax!"

The critics of behavioral therapy scoffed at such ideas. They made statements like, "Behavioral therapy is just a quick fix"; and, "You might get rid of one symptom but another symptom will develop to take its place." The behavioral therapists replied, "What's wrong with doing things quickly?" and "The idea that new symptoms will appear is just a theory, not a fact." And so the debate raged, and will only be finally settled by clinical studies demonstrating what behavioral therapy can and cannot do.

Among the early successes of behavioral therapy has been the effective treatment of phobias. One method used is called **systematic desensitization**. The patient is first taught a procedure called deep muscle relaxation. Here, the person is taught to relax the muscles of her body, one at a time, until she feels almost limp. In this relaxed state, the client then imagines brief scenes involving the feared stimulus. The client begins by imagining the least threatening scenes and gradually works up to more threatening scenes. If she experiences anxiety while imagining these scenes, she stops the procedure and backtracks slightly. If the phobia is fear of heights, for example, the first scene she imagines might be standing on the bottom step of a ladder. A much later scene might be looking out of a window from a tall building.

This pairing of anxiety-evoking scenes with a relaxed state tends to reduce the fear connected with the scene. People undergoing this treatment often show a marked reduction in fear when exposed to the real life situation.

Behavioral therapists have found that relaxation training itself can be useful in dealing with a number of problems. Difficulties in falling asleep (sleep-onset insomnia) can often be helped by relaxation training. Some studies suggest that the amount of time needed for such

people to fall asleep may be cut in half. Relaxation training can also be useful as a treatment for certain types of headaches.

Another behavioral approach is the careful use of reinforcements to modify behavior. This technique is often useful in institutions to change behavior in ways which are considered desirable. For example, in some schools for retarded children, the children can earn "tokens" if they behave in approved ways. Later these tokens can be turned in for desired rewards like candy, trinkets, or privileges. Another setting where token reinforcements have been used successfully is the psychiatric ward. Here, the tokens are used to improve the patient's self-care, work performance, and social interactions.

As an example of how a token reinforcement program works, let's turn to a case study provided by Patricia Sand and her coworkers. A child, aged seven, entered the rehabilitation center of the university hospital. He had suffered a brain injury from an accident at age four, and afterwards developed behavior problems. When he was asked to do something he didn't like, he would throw tantrums, screaming, spitting, hitting, kicking, and biting. During the first week of treatment, these tantrums occurred as many as six times a day. To control this behavior and thus make it possible to begin rehabilitative work on the physical problems resulting from the brain injury, the hospital staff used two strategies. (1) Because it was believed that the attention the child received during the tantrum reinforced this tantrum behavior, the child was promptly removed to his room as soon as he began a tantrum. (2) The nurses and therapists started giving the child tokens when he did what they asked him to. At the end of each day the child could purchase treats with these tokens, such as small toys, candies, and extra fruit juice. These two procedures markedly reduced the number of tantrums. The boy's interest in learning picked up. By the time he left the hospital, he was described as a cheerful child whom the staff enjoyed working with.

Assertiveness training and the teaching of social skills are other examples of direct approaches to changing behavior. Imagine, for example, that a person comes into therapy complaining that he is too passive, a doormat everyone walks over. A traditional therapist would probably want to know how this all came about. She might spend a great deal of time exploring the client's developmental history. In contrast, a behavioral approach might be to practice a series of role-playing exercises in which the client learns to make more assertive responses. The therapist might say something like this: "Imagine you're in a restaurant. You've been waiting a long time to be served. The waiter begins to serve another couple that came in after you. Now, the waiter is about to pass you by again. What do you say to him?" The client will practice responses which, while not belligerent, are assertive enough to enable him to stand up for his own rights.

Eclectic Approaches

With the variety of approaches to therapy now available, the reader may be wondering if it is possible for a therapist to offer a variety of approaches to draw on those he or she feels are best suited to the needs of the individual client. The answer is clearly *yes*. Many therapists consider themselves *eclectic*. Eclectic approaches are those in which therapists borrow what they feel is useful from different methods of therapy for use within their own therapy.

Common Features of Psychotherapies

As we have seen, psychotherapy is presently being practiced in a number of quite different ways. There are, however, some common features running through most forms of psychotherapy. These common features start with the fact that the client typically enters the process of psychotherapy in a demoralized state. If it is to accomplish anything, psychotherapy has to restore hope to the patient. If the patient can be mobilized to start doing things, there is a chance that he or she can begin to make the

changes necessary to correct the problems that brought on this demoralized state.

This restoration of hope may begin when the client enters the therapist's office and sees that he or she is dealing with a professionally trained person. The client soon begins to realize that there is someone there who is seriously paying attention to the problem. Moreover, the client will often leave the encounter with the belief that the *therapist feels* that something can be done. In these initial sessions, hope is often rekindled, the first vital step toward the client's getting better.

Secondly, the therapist offers a special relationship to the client. This relationship is something apart from the strains of daily living where the client has to be on guard as to what he or she says, and to whom. The client can trust the therapist to maintain confidentiality, and can turn to the therapist when he or she is feeling down and out and troubled.

The therapist-client relationship is an important part of most psychotherapies. Psychoanalytic therapists often view the relationship as one in which the client puts the therapist in a role rather like that of a parent. The client then reexperiences and works through earlier, unresolved conflicts.

The fact that therapists are confidential, usually try to be good listeners, and do not jump on the client for admitting weaknesses or expressing anger provides a special environment for the patient. Under these conditions, clients have a real opportunity to get things off their chests, to verbalize feelings and thoughts that have been pent up. Letting out these pent-up feelings in a safe, nonjudgmental atmosphere is a relief to many clients. This experience, common to most therapies, is called a **catharsis**.

Third, most psychotherapies offer some kind of definition or diagnosis of the client's problem. Labeling the problem, saying: "This is what you've got," "This is what is bothering you," is a first step in giving the patient a feeling that the problem can be brought under control.

Fourth, most psychotherapies offer clients an opportunity to learn more about their problems and themselves. This understanding can be useful in helping the person make changes in behavior or lifestyle.

EFFECTIVENESS OF PSYCHOTHERAPY

The question has often been asked: is psychotherapy effective? Does it do any good? A statistical review of 475 separate studies compared people given psychotherapy with people in a control group who were not given therapy. The authors concluded that the average person in these studies who had received psychotherapy was indeed better off than the average person in the control group who had not. Further studies carried out since this review have continued to confirm the conclusion that psychotherapy is often helpful to emotionally troubled people.

Researchers have also asked the question, "Which types of psychotherapy are most effective?" Many studies comparing the effectiveness of different types of psychotherapy have been carried out. The general conclusion seems to be that there is not much difference in the effectiveness of different types of therapy. When one is choosing a therapist, concerns about the types of therapy offered may be less important than the qualities of the individual therapist.

Another question one might ask about psychotherapy has to do with its long-term effects. Do the benefits from therapy last, or do they wither away after the treatment ends? A review of 67 studies in which follow-up assessments were made of clients concluded that the gains made in therapy seemed to be maintained over time.

SOME THOUGHTS ON CHOOSING A THERAPIST

When choosing a therapist, it makes sense to look into the type of therapy the therapist practices. Clients should find out whether the therapy is going to be of a type that they feel they need and expect. Also, since the relationship aspects of psychotherapy seem to be of great importance, clients should select therapists whom they feel comfortable working with. Cost

factors are also important. Psychotherapy can be very expensive. Some therapists in private practice maintain a sliding scale of fees in order to make it possible for people to get the help they need. One can also find psychotherapy offered at affordable rates in community mental health centers and university counseling centers. Local psychological, psychiatric, and mental health associations are good places to begin inquiries.

Group Therapy

In individual therapy, the therapist typically meets with the patient for about 50 minutes, takes a break, then meets with another patient. Working this way, the therapist can only see a handful of patients during a normal working day.

Group therapy is one way of getting around this limitation. A therapist—sometimes there may be co-therapists—may meet with five, six, seven, or even more patients at a time. The session might be extended to an hour and a half, two hours, or even longer.

Group therapy can be a useful growth experience, but does differ in important ways from individual therapy. The client does not have the therapist's undivided attention for a set period of time. Each client's problems will be examined for only a fraction of the total time, and these are likely to be unequal fractions, for some clients will seek center stage with what's bothering them, while others will hold back. Moreover, the client is no longer alone with a therapist, engaging in a safe, confidential dialogue. Group therapy is a more open, less-controlled situation where other clients watch, listen, and get involved. The group members will comment about and discuss each other's behavior.

Group therapy offers a number of potential advantages. For one thing, group therapy provides a setting where people can learn from each other's experiences. Finding out that one is not alone in having problems is often reassuring. Learning about the problems of others can be something like taking a short psychology course.

If one's problems involve difficulties in relating to other people, the group situation offers a setting where these difficulties can be clearly pointed out. The group may serve as a kind of miniaturized social world. The therapist and group members may provide feedback to other members about what they are doing, particularly about inappropriate and ineffective behaviors. By listening to these comments, clients can begin to see themselves as others see them.

The client also has a chance to try out and practice new ways of behaving in this relatively protected setting. In individual therapy, a client can talk about different ways of behaving; in a group setting, they can be tested.

Finally, the members of the group can offer support to each other. Many of the group members may be going through difficult periods in their lives and the group members often act to bolster each other. Irvin Yalom, who has been both a therapist and researcher on group psychotherapy, points out that the feelings members develop for each other and the group are very important. The more the group comes together as a "cohesive unit," the more likely it is that the members will report therapeutic benefits from the experience.

In addition to group therapy sessions run by professional therapists, there are self-help *groups* which may be beneficial for many people. Sometimes these groups are set up to deal with particular problems, such as alcoholism or bereavement. Alcoholics Anonymous is probably the best known example of a self-help group. AA groups usually meet once a week. A meeting usually includes narratives by the members, relating how they became alcoholics and how they found their way back to sobriety. AA offers a spiritually oriented message to its members on how to maintain sobriety. Support of one member by another in the effort to stay away from alcohol is an essential element of AA programs. AA can point to a host of successes in keeping its members from using alcohol.

Some individuals may be in psychotherapy and self-help groups at the same time. Both experiences may be very valuable to a person. At times, however, the person may get different messages in the different situations. For example, two researchers described the case of a young man who was going to a psychiatrist and also was a member of AA. The psychiatrist wanted to keep the young man on medicine for a schizophrenic condition. Some friends at AA who were helping him with his alcoholic problem were trying to pressure him to drop the medication and live a drug-free life. The man was put into a conflict situation when he tried to use both the professional and self-help approaches at the same time.

We will close this chapter with a word about **encounter groups**. Encounter groups are not the same as group psychotherapy. Encounter groups are generally larger, the members may include people who are drawn from the ranks of the normal rather than the troubled, and the leader may not be a licensed psychotherapist. Encounter sessions may last for hours at a time; sometimes group members may spend whole days together in close contact. The members may be encouraged to reexamine their values, to disclose their inner selves, to "let it all hang out." The pressures exerted by this group experience on individual members can be considerable; the encounter can be an intensely emotional experience. The idea behind the encounter group is to promote "personal growth" and indeed some participants have been motivated to seek positive behavioral changes in their lives. On the other hand, some people have suffered emotional disturbances after being in an encounter group. Clearly, encounter groups are not for everyone.

Some Questions and Activities

1. We have described several types of therapy: psychoanalytic, cognitive, Gestalt, behavioral, and eclectic. If you have reason to see a therapist, which of these types of therapists would you be most interested in seeing? Why?

2. Counseling is a term that has a wider meaning than therapy. Counseling can be done by a lawyer, a minister, or your counselor at school. What are some of the things that would prompt a student to make an appointment to see the guidance counselor at school?

3. Psychiatrists have an M.D., which allows them to prescribe medicine. Can you think of some cases where the use of medicine might be important?

4. If you were a psychologist and felt your patient needed medicine, what steps could you take to see that the patient got it?

5. Suppose you saw an advertisement in the newspaper for someone holding group sessions to promote "inner growth" and "better relationships." If the advertisement sounded interesting and you called the leader, what questions would you ask about the leader and the program?

6. Imagine you are a behavioral therapist. A client comes to see you, stating that he has a terrible fear of dogs. He has had this fear since he was frightened by a dog as a small child. He had learned about the systematic desensitization procedure for treating phobias and would like to try it. After you've trained the client in the technique of deep muscle relaxation, you and the client plan to work out a series of seven scenes involving the client and dogs, ranging from least threatening to most threatening. To see how you might go about this, try making up a series of such scenes yourself.

7. Reread the next-to-last paragraph of this chapter (page 144, column two). If you knew the man receiving conflicting advice, what would you suggest he do?

8. Choose a volunteer in the class to call up the referral service of your local psychological society to find out what kind f information they will give you about therapists. Will the service just provide you with names of a few therapists or will it give you additional information about the types of therapy they provide?

Test Your Knowledge

Read each statement and decide whether it is TRUE or FALSE. **Write your answers on a separate sheet of paper.**

1. Psychotherapy is a highly standardized procedure that all therapists follow closely.

2. One of the important methods of psychoanalytic therapy is free association.

3. In client-centered therapy, the therapist takes the lead in directing the flow of the conversation.

4. In client-centered therapy, the therapist tries to reflect back the patient's feelings.

5. Only a handful of studies have thus far shown that therapy is effective.

6. One of the features of Gestalt therapy is that clients dramatize aspects of their problems rather than just talking about them.

7. Psychoanalytic therapy is the only brand of therapy that deals with dreams.

8. The behavioral therapist spends most of his or her time exploring the client's early childhood looking for causes of symptoms.

9. Systematic desensitization is a technique used to treat phobias.

10. One of the common features of various types of therapy is the tendency to rekindle hope in demoralized people.

11. Psychoanalysis is a relatively short-term type of therapy.

12. Cognitive therapy attempts to modify faulty patterns of thinking.

13. Both Freud and Rogers recommended that therapists feel free to give the patients advice during therapy.

14. The only advantage of group therapy is that it is less expensive than individual therapy.

15. In group therapy, group members are asked not to comment about each other's problems during the therapy session.

16. Self-help groups such as AA are always run by professionally trained therapists.

17. Encounter groups sometimes produce emotional distress in individuals attending the sessions.

18. Studies have shown that some of the different types of psychotherapy now being offered have about the same level of effectiveness.

19. The experience of letting out pent-up feelings in therapy is called a catharsis.

20. The therapist-client relationship is generally felt to be an unimportant aspect of psychotherapy.

CHAPTER 11

Concluding Remarks

In this book we have introduced some of the major topics that make up the field of modern psychology. We have discussed perception, memory, learning, motivation, personality, human development, abnormal psychology, and psychotherapy. While we have covered a great deal of territory, there was much we had to leave out. Psychology is an expanding field with a rapid growth of information.

One may ask: what are some of the topics at the vanguard of psychology today? Before we address this question, we should mention two factors which influence and sometimes limit what psychologists can do. The first factor is the availability of sound techniques to study particular types of problems. Researchers can't study a problem adequately unless there is an effective way to do it. A good example of this limitation is the study of unconscious processes. While this is a fascinating problem area, we simply don't have adequate ways to study it. Until better techniques are devised to study unconscious processes, our knowledge about these processes will continue to be sketchy.

A second factor that shapes the direction of psychological inquiry and research is public policy. This effect can sometimes be seen clearly in the way the available funds for psychological research are allocated (divided up). It is usually easier to carry out research when funds are available. Funds will pay for such needs as student assistants and special equipment. Funding often comes from government agencies in the form of research grants. The granting agencies may choose to target these funds towards specific problems. If there is a great deal of public concern, for example, to try to do something about the problems of drug abuse or schizophrenia, funds are likely to be directed to research in that area rather than other areas. Researchers are likely to design research in areas likely to receive funds.

Recognizing such influences, let's look at some of the problems that are of major concern to psychology today.

The Study of Social Issues

One tendency seems pretty clear. Many psychologists have moved out of academic laboratories and are spending a great deal of time studying the real-life problems that confront our society. Let's examine some of the ways they are doing this.

First, psychologists have become increasingly involved in matters of medicine and public health. Some examples of this are the efforts to control heart disease and cancer. A number of risk factors have been identified that increase one's chances of developing heart disease or cancer. High blood pressure, overweight, and smoking are among the risk factors for heart disease, and smoking is a risk factor for lung cancer. Since some of these factors can be controlled by the patient's behavior, psychologists have tried to apply their special knowledge about behavior to these problems.

We have already discussed the possibility of using biofeedback as a means of exerting some control over blood pressure. In regard to overweight, psychologists have helped develop behavioral modification techniques, which appear promising as a part of overall weight control programs. Psychologists are doing a lot of research and evaluating different techniques to help people stop smoking. These techniques include hypnotic suggestion, aversion therapy (combining the act of smoking with unpleasant consequences), and behavioral modification.

In controlling habits like overeating and smoking, the problem is not so much getting people to make some immediate change, like going on a diet. The problem is getting people to *stay with* these changed behaviors. Behavioral modification plans may be particularly helpful in accomplishing this. This is certainly suggested by statistics. According to published reports, the dropout rate in many traditional self-help or commercial weight-loss programs ranges from 20 percent to 80 percent. The dropout rate for behavioral programs is less than this. An estimate based on a review of 17 studies indicated a mean dropout rate of 14 percent. The behavioral approach seems to help people stick with these control programs.

As you might imagine, psychologists have joined with other scientists to help in the effort to control the spread of AIDS, one of the most serious public health problems of our times. Among other activities, psychologists have participated in survey research to monitor the level of high-risk sexual behaviors that increase chances of infection with the HIV virus. This survey data helps public health officials assess the effectiveness of educational programs that promote preventative behaviors such as abstinence, use of condoms, and exclusiveness in sexual relationships.

Another example of a social issue that has drawn the attention of researchers in psychology is the changing role of women in society. Psychologists have been interested in understanding these changes and the implications they have for both women and their families. We have already discussed studies of the effects of day care on the emotional development of children. Psychologists are also looking at the effects of careers on women and their marriages. Researchers are investigating such questions as: What does a career do for a woman's self-esteem? What seems to determine the quality of marriage for a dual-career couple? What determines the choice of career for a woman?

Some additional examples of social issues that have drawn the attention of psychologists are the effects of TV viewing on children, the effects of unemployment on mental health, the effects of homelessness, and the decision-making process of juries. It is hoped that this latter information will be useful in giving us a better understanding of how our legal system works.

Finally, psychologists are giving considerable attention to the problem of violence in our society. Research is being carried out on a range of violent acts including rape, wife battering, and child abuse. Psychologists are helping to explore the questions of what causes aggression and what can be done to curtail acts of violence. Some examples of recent studies include how people respond to verbal aggression, the relation of temperature level to acts of overt aggression, and the effectiveness of treatment programs for spouse batterers.

Basic Research

While many psychologists have turned their attention to applying their skills to the problems of society, other psychologists continue to do basic research, expanding our basic knowledge of psychology. Such basic research goes on in university laboratories, hospitals, and clinics throughout the world. Often this research is carried out jointly with psychiatrists and scientists from other backgrounds. Psychologists are certainly indebted to the work of their colleagues in medicine and pharmacology.

Some of the most exciting basic research

being carried out today has to do with the biological foundations of behavior. Scientists are gaining a better understanding of the influence of genes on mental disorders, of the important role of the neurotransmitters, and of the effects of different areas of the brain on behavior. New, exciting technical advances have made it possible for researchers to better understand the structure and functioning of the brain, both in normal individuals and people who are experiencing severe psychological difficulties. Computer-assisted tomography (CAT) and nuclear magnetic resonance (NMR) provide cross-sectional views of areas of the brain. Positron emission tomography (PET) and single photon emission tomography (SPECT) provide measures of activity in different parts of the brain. It is now possible for scientists to obtain sensitive measurements of the brain and its activity that would have been in the realm of science fiction not so long ago.

Psychologists continue to carry out basic research on problems ranging from perception to personality. In closing, however, we would just like to mention one more type of investigation as an example of the creative kinds of research that have caught the public's attention. This is the successful attempt to teach communication skills to chimpanzees. These efforts, which have been underway for some years now, threaten to revolutionize our thinking about the communication capabilities of other species. Using sign language, chimps have been taught well over one hundred different signs in communicating with humans. The possibility of generations of chimps teaching each other to communicate using a human-developed language is an idea that just may emerge from the realm of science fiction into reality.

The experiments of R. Allen Gardner and Beatrix Gardner at the University of Nevada at Reno are particularly interesting. They taught American Sign Language to several chimpanzees. They even devised a vocabulary test to see how well the chimps were doing. You might be wondering how one could manage this. Imagine a sliding door with a latch. When the chimp touched the latch, the sliding door opened exposing a picture on a projection screen. It might be a picture of a bird, apple, or flower. If the chimp made the correct sign for the picture, she was marked correct by the observer. How did the chimps do? They made their share of errors, but they didn't do badly either. I would be tempted to give them a passing grade, if not a gold star, or better yet a banana.

Are scientists just working with chimpanzees? No, they have been working with other animals, including parrots and those intriguing, aquatic acrobats, dolphins. In testing the vocabulary of chimps, the Gardners remarked that the success of the endeavor depended on the good humor of the chimps. Imagine the problems in testing an animal whose inclination might be to take a dip in the cold water.

Further Reading in Psychology

As we conclude this book, you may be wondering, "Where can I turn to learn more about psychology? What sources are available to me?"

Your public library probably has a variety of textbooks written on specific areas of psychology. Books on such subjects as abnormal psychology, developmental psychology, and tests and measurement are usually written by experts in the field. You will usually find the evidence for the author's conclusions clearly presented. Psychology textbooks are a convenient source of dependable information.

There are also "popular" books written on psychology. Such books are often much easier to read than textbooks, but they may not present much evidence for their conclusions. You should always ask, does the author cite studies to document her conclusions and do these studies meet the scientific standards we have discussed?

Two very readable, well-researched books are William Dement's book on sleep research, *Some Must Watch While Some Must Sleep*, and Janet Malcolm's book on psychoanalysis, *Psychoanalysis: The Impossible Profession*.

You may be wondering about magazines and journals. The professional journals in psychology and psychiatry are an excellent source of information, but are written in technical language. One has to have a knowledge of statistics and research procedures to fully understand them. In regard to articles dealing with psychological topics which appear in popular magazines, we suggest that you apply the same standards we have mentioned for popular books. Always ask yourself, "What is the evidence that is presented to support the points that are made?"

The author and publisher hope that this book has stimulated your interest in psychology. We hope you will read further in the field and welcome your reactions to this book.

Glossary

achievement motive—A desire to accomplish, excel, win recognition.

Alzheimer's disease—A brain disorder most likely to occur in elderly people.

anorexia nervosa—A disorder in which there is an overconcern about body size; food intake is reduced and the patient may lose a dangerous amount of body weight.

anxiety—Feelings of discomfort often brought on by the anticipation of some unpleasant event.

aptitude—A particular kind of ability, such as musical, artistic, or mechanical ability.

autism—A condition of extreme social withdrawal.

aversive control—A disagreeable or painful stimulus applied to modify behavior; punishment.

axon—A long fiber extending from the cell body of the neuron.

behavioral therapy—An approach to therapy which tends to focus directly on changing behavior rather than searching for underlying causes of the problem.

biofeedback—A technique for providing information about bodily functioning to the individual on a continuous basis; during the procedure, the individual learns to develop some control over the process that is being monitored.

catatonia—Schizophrenic symptoms which include being unresponsive and in a stupor.

catharsis—Expression of feelings and thoughts that have been held back; letting out of pent-up emotions, followed by a feeling of relief.

cerebrum—The largest part of the brain.

client-centered therapy—An approach to therapy developed by Carl Rogers in which the therapist does not direct the flow of the interview. Instead, the therapist tries to reflect back the feelings of the client.

collective unconscious—The storehouse of ancestral memory, wisdom, and experience of humankind; defined by Jung.

cognitions—Our thoughts, beliefs, and understandings about ourselves and the external world.

cognitive therapy—An approach to therapy which tries to identify and change belief systems which are causing the patient difficulty.

conditioning, conditioned reflex—A procedure developed by Pavlov in which a neutral stimulus is paired with a stimulus that can already bring on a response. The pairing enables the neutral stimulus to elicit the response on its own.

conflict—The presence of wishes, desires, or goals which seem to contradict one another.

correlation—The extent to which two measures are related.

defense mechanism—An unconscious process which helps prevent the arousal of excessive anxiety.

delusion—A clearly false perception that a person nevertheless believes to be real.

dendrites—Short fibers attached to the neuron that receive the incoming nervous impulse.

denial—A defense mechanism in which the person refuses to admit realities and acts as if things were otherwise.

depression—An emotional state characterized by a sad mood and feelings of despair, often accompanied by lowered activity level, sleep disturbances, and physical symptoms.

ego—In Freud's view, the executive agency of the personality.

encounter group—A group of people meeting, often for many hours at a time, with the aim of enhancing the personal growth of the participants.

experiment—A scientific procedure in which changes are introduced into a situation under carefully controlled conditions and the effects of the changes are carefully noted. The experiment is the scientific procedure most likely to reveal cause-and-effect relationships.

extinction—The weakening of a conditioned response by the repeated presentation of the conditioned stimulus without the unconditioned stimulus. The term extinction is also used in reinforcement theory. Here, it refers to a condition of not reinforcing a response that has previously been reinforced.

extrasensory perception—Acquisition of information without the use of any of the known senses.

extrinsic motivation—Motivation that comes from sources outside the self, such as pay for a job or the demands of others.

figure—A concept of Gestalt psychology. When one looks at something, the part one attends to is called the figure. The background in which the figure is seen is called the **ground**.

free association—A technique developed by Freud in which the patient reports whatever comes into his or her mind, no matter what it is.

frustration—The psychological state that exists when obstacles block one from attaining one's goals.

galvanic skin response (GSR)—A change in the electrical conductivity of the skin. The GSR is often used as a measure of emotional reaction.

Gestalt psychology—A school of psychology that stresses perceptual organization and insight in the explanation of behavior.

Gestalt therapy—A form of therapy associated with Fritz Perls. Gestalt therapy uses dramatics and the two-chair technique in an attempt to integrate disowned parts of the self.

group therapy—Therapy in which a number of patients meet at the same time with a therapist.

hallucination—A perception that something is happening that is not really happening, such as hearing voices when there are none.

hebephrenia—Schizophrenic symptoms such as grimacing, acting silly, and using speech that doesn't make sense.

hypothesis—A specific prediction that something will happen under certain conditions. In research, the hypothesis is tested and either supported or not supported.

hysteria—A disorder in which symptoms such as paralysis and insensitivity to pain occur without any organic (physical) basis.

id—In Freud's theory, the part of the personality that is made up of instincts and primitive impulses.

inferiority complex—An idea developed by Adler, who said that all people experience feelings of inferiority. Striving to overcome this sense of inferiority is a key to achievement.

insight—An understanding of a situation, a relationship, or the way something works.

insomnia—Difficulty in sleeping.

intrinsic motivation—Motivation that comes from within the self, such as the pleasure of watching a good movie.

introspection—Paying careful attention to and analyzing one's own conscious experience.

introversion-extroversion—A concept of Jung's which is an important way of describing personality. Extroverts tend to seek and enjoy the company of others, while introverts seem more oriented toward the self.

kinesthetic sense—Sensations from one's body about movement or position.

level of aspiration—The level of the goals one sets for oneself; more challenging goals indicate a higher level of aspiration.

locus of control—A concept identified with the work of Julian Rotter, who asked where people see the control of reinforcement in their lives. Reinforcement can be seen as being controlled by external sources or under one's own control.

long-term memory—The last stage in the memory storage process; information that has been fixed in the memory and stored for long-term use is in long-term memory.

manic—Describes an emotional state in which people act in an elated, frantic, even reckless manner.

maturation—Physical development of the organism as it grows.

mean—A measure of the average found by adding the scores of a group and dividing this total by the number of scores used in the calculation.

median—A numerical value which divides a list of scores in half.

mode—The most frequently occurring score in a group.

motive—Specific type of motivation, such as achievement, sex, affiliation. Motives have a driving force, impelling the individual toward action.

multiple personality—A disorder in which the person appears to have two or more distinct personalities, often unknown to one another.

myelin sheath—Fatty white covering found on some nerve fibers.

neuron—The nerve cell.

neuroses—Emotional disorders with symptoms that distress the individual. The individual's ability to "test reality," however, remains intact.

neurotransmitter—Chemicals involved in the transmission of the nervous impulse across the synapse.

nonsense syllable—Three-letter syllable with little meaning devised by Ebbinghaus for the study of memory.

obsessive-compulsive disorder—Disorder featuring obsessions and/or compulsive behaviors. Obsessions are ideas that keep recurring and are hard to shake off. Compulsive behaviors have a driving, must-do quality and are often performed in a ritualistic manner.

Oedipus complex—A concept of Freud's, related to his belief that boys have sexual feelings toward their mothers and girls toward their fathers.

organic brain disorders—Psychological disturbances caused by brain damage.

paranoia—A disorder characterized by delusions of persecution.

parasympathetic division—One of the two divisions of the autonomic nervous system; the other is the sympathetic division. The parasympathetic division maintains normal bodily functions.

partial reinforcement—A condition in which reinforcement is not given after every response but only intermittently.

perception—The process in which the brain gives meaning to the stimulation registered by the senses.

personality—Enduring traits and characteristics of an individual.

phobia—Fear of a certain object or situation leading to a strong desire to avoid it.

polygraph—An instrument that records continuous measures of blood pressure, breathing, and the galvanic skin response.

post-traumatic stress neurosis—Anxiety that is traceable to being in a terrifying situation such as combat. Such anxiety may occur years after the terrifying experience.

proactive inhibition—A process in which previously learned material interferes with the learning of new material.

projection—A defense mechanism in which desires and feelings unacceptable to oneself are attributed to others.

projective tests—Personality tests that use unclear or ambiguous materials. In responding to these materials, subjects draw on their own background and experience, revealing aspects of their personalities.

psychiatrist—Person with a medical degree and a specialization in psychiatry, a field of study concerned with mental and emotional disorders.

psychoanalysis—A theory of human behavior developed by Sigmund Freud and his followers. It's also a method of therapy based on Freud's ideas.

psychologist—Person who has completed training in psychology. A psychologist normally holds a Ph.D. (doctor of philosophy) degree in psychology.

psychosomatic illness—Physical symptoms or disease that is in part emotional in origin.

psychotherapy—Psychological treatment of emotional and mental problems, often referred to simply as therapy.

psychoses—Mental disorders characterized by loss of contact with reality.

rationalization—A defense mechanism in which a person provides acceptable reasons for failures and shortcomings.

reaction formation—A defense mechanism in which unacceptable wishes are transformed into their opposites.

recall—Unaided memory of information that the subject has previously been exposed to.

recognition—Aided recall. The subject is asked to identify information when it is presented. An example is picking out the correct answer from alternatives, as in a multiple-choice test.

reinforcement theory—An approach to understanding learning and behavior which sees the occurrence of reinforcement as of central importance.

reliability—The extent to which a measuring instrument consistently and dependably records information.

replication—Repetition of a study to see if the results obtained the first time can be obtained again.

repression—A defensive process central to Freudian theory in which unacceptable impulses and ideas are excluded from consciousness.

retroactive inhibition—A process that takes place when learning of new material interferes with recall for previously learned material.

role-playing—A technique used in therapy and in group situations in which a person is asked to play a specific part. Unlike a play, there is no script and the participants make up their lines as they go along.

Rorschach test—A projective technique that uses a series of standardized inkblots. Subjects are asked to report what they see in the blots.

sample—A group of subjects used in a study. A sample is often carefully selected to be representative of a larger population about which the researcher wants to draw conclusions.

schizophrenia—A mental disorder that is characterized by loss of contact with reality. Symptoms include delusions, hallucinations, blunted emotion, and deterioration in performance.

self-concept—The individual's view of himself or herself as a person.

sensory-information storage—The beginning stage of the memory process. Much information is held, but only for a fraction of a second.

shaping—A technique for modifying behavior. Initially, approximately correct responses are reinforced. Then reinforcement is given only for responses which are closer to the desired target.

short-term memory—The second stage of the memory storage process, during which a small number of bits of information are held for a few seconds.

standard deviation—A measure of variability based on how far each score in the group is from the mean.

stimulus—Anything that can or does cause a response (plural: **stimuli**).

subliminal perception—Reaction to stimuli at or below threshold levels.

superego—In Freud's theory, the part of the personality that represents social standards and conscience.

sympathetic division—One of the two divisions of the autonomic nervous system; the other is the parasympathetic division. The sympathetic division responds when the individual deals with stress-provoking or emergency conditions.

synapse—The point at which neurons come into contact.

systematic desensitization—A procedure developed by behavioral therapists and used in the treatment of phobias. The procedure pairs muscle relaxation with imagination of increasingly threatening scenes relating to the phobia.

Thematic Apperception Test—A projective test in which subjects are asked to make up stories while viewing a set of drawings.

theory—An explanation that accounts for observations. In science such explanations are stated in precise, formal language and permit deductions which can often be tested by research.

threshold—The point at which a subject can just make out (identify) a stimulus.

unconscious—A concept advanced by Freud and others. They believed that part of the mind contains ideas and wishes of which we are unaware. These wishes may continue to operate with active force even though they are out of awareness.

validity—The degree to which a measure actually measures what it is claimed to measure.

variability—The extent to which scores are spread apart in a sample.

Answer Key

Chapter 1, p. 10:

1. F	6. T	11. T	15. F
2. T	7. F	12. F	16. F
3. T	8. F	13. T	17. T
4. T	9. T	14. T	18. T
5. F	10. T		

Chapter 2, p. 24:

1. T	8. T	14. F
2. F	9. T	15. T
3. F	10. T	16. T
4. T	11. F	17. F
5. T	12. F	18. T
6. F	13. T	19. T
7. T		

Chapter 3, p. 35:

1. T	6. T	11. T	16. F
2. F	7. F	12. T	17. T
3. T	8. T	13. T	18. F
4. T	9. T	14. F	19. F
5. F	10. F	15. F	20. T

Chapter 4, pp. 59–61:

Perception, p. 59:	Memory, p. 60:	Learning, p. 61:
1. F	1. T	1. F
2. T	2. T	2. F
3. T	3. F	3. T
4. F	4. T	4. T
5. T	5. F	5. T
6. F	6. T	6. F
7. F	7. F	7. T
8. T	8. F	8. T
9. T	9. T	9. F
	10. F	10. T
	11. F	
	12. F	

Chapter 5, p. 73:

1. T		3. F		5. F		7. T		9. T		11. F		13. T
2. F		4. F		6. T		8. T		10. T		12. F		14. F

Chapter 6, p. 90:

1. F	8. F	15. T
2. F	9. F	16. T
3. F	10. T	17. F
4. F	11. F	18. T
5. F	12. F	19. T
6. T	13. T	20. T
7. T	14. F	21. F

Chapter 7, p. 102:

1. T	3. T	5. F	7. T	9. T	11. T
2. F	4. T	6. F	8. T	10. T	12. F

Chapter 8, pp. 117-118:

1. F	6. T	11. F	16. F
2. F	7. T	12. T	17. F
3. T	8. F	13. T	18. T
4. T	9. T	14. F	19. F
5. F	10. F	15. T	20. F

Chapter 9, p. 134:

1. T	7. T	13. F	18. T
2. T	8. F	14. T	19. F
3. F	9. T	15. F	20. F
4. T	10. F	16. T	21. F
5. F	11. F	17. F	22. F
6. T	12. T		

Chapter 10, p. 146:

1. F	6. T	11. F	16. F
2. T	7. F	12. T	17. T
3. F	8. F	13. F	18. T
4. T	9. T	14. F	19. T
5. F	10. T	15. F	20. F

References

Chapter 1

Flugel, J. C., and West, D.J. *A Hundred Years of Psychology.* New York: Basic Books, 1964.

Fowler, R. D. "Though Number of Women in Field has Grown, Still Room for More!" *American Psychological Association Monitor,* 1991, Vol. 22, p. 3.

Jones, E. *The Life and Work of Sigmund Freud.* Volume l. New York: Basic Books, 1953.

Murphy, G., and Murphy, L.B. *Western Psychology.* New York: Basic Books, 1969.

Neugebauer, R. "Medieval and Early Modern Theories of Mental Illness." *Archives of General Psychiatry,* 1979, Vol. 36, pp. 477–483.

Sokal, M.M. "Origins and early years of the American Psychological Association, 1890–1906." *American Psychologist,* 1992, Vol. 47, pp. 111–122.

Spanos, N.P., and Gottlieb, J. "Demonic Possession, Mesmerism, and Hysteria: A Social Psychological Perspective on Their Historical Interrelations." *Journal of Abnormal Psychology,* 1979, Vol. 88, pp. 527–546.

Stapp, J., and Fulcher, R. "The Employment of 1979 and 1980 Doctorate Recipients in Psychology." *American Psychologist,* 1982, Vol. 37, pp. 1159–1185.

Chapter 2

Anastasi, A. *Psychological Testing.* Fourth Edition. New York: Macmillan, 1976.

Buros, O.K. *The Eighth Mental Measurements Yearbook.* Highland Park, NY: Gryphon Press, 1978.

Garvin, A.D. *Applied Statistics.* Portland, ME: J. Weston Walch, 1981.

Lipsey, M.W., and Wilson, D.B. "The Efficacy of Psychological, Educational, and Behavioral Treatment: Confirmation from Meta Analysis." *American Psychologist,* 1993, Vol. 48, pp. 1181–1209.

Chapter 3

Borkovec, T.D., Lane, T.W., and Van Oot, P.H. "Phenomenology of Sleep Among Insomniacs and Good Sleepers: Wakefulness Experience When Cortically Asleep." *Journal of Abnormal Psychology,* 1981, Vol. 90, pp. 607–609.

Coursey, R.D. "Electromyograph Feedback as a Relaxation Technique." *Journal of Consulting and Clinical Psychology,* 1975, Vol. 43, pp. 825–834.

Erwin, B.J., and Rosenbaum, G. "Parietal Lobe Syndrome and Schizophrenia: Comparison of Neuropsychological Deficits." *Journal of Abnormal Psychology,* 1979, Vol. 88, pp. 234–241.

Freedman, R.R., and Sattler, H.L. "Physiological and Psychological Factors in Sleep-Onset Insomnia." *Journal of Abnormal Psychology,* 1982, Vol. 91, pp. 380–389.

Gatchel, R.J., and Proctor, J.D. "Effectiveness of Voluntary Heart Rate Control in Reducing Speech Anxiety." *Journal of Consulting and Clinical Psychology,* 1976, Vol. 44, pp. 381–389.

Gorenstein, E.E. "Frontal Lobe Function in Psychopaths." *Journal of Abnormal Psychology,* 1982, Vol. 91, pp. 368–379.

Kinsbourne, M. "Hemispheric Specialization and the Growth of Human Under- stand- ing." *American Psychologist,* 1982, Vol. 37, pp. 411–420.

Larner, G., Jr. "Agencies Get Green Light for Lie Tests." *Washington Post,* October 20, 1983.

National Institute of Mental Health, Dept. of Health Education and Welfare. *Research on Sleep and Dreams.* Publication No. (ADM) 76–244. Government Printing Office, Washington, DC, 1965.

Regestein, Q.R. "A Clinical Framework for Insomnia." *Massachusetts Journal of Mental Health,* 1973, Vol. 4, pp. 4–15.

Sperry, R.W. "Hemisphere Deconnection and Unity in Conscious Awareness." *American Psychologist,* 1968, Vol. 23, pp. 723–733.

Szucko, J.J., and Kleinmuntz, B. "Statistical Versus Clinical Lie Detection." *American Psychologist,* 1981, Vol. 36, pp. 488–496.

Williamson, D.A., and Blanchard, E.B. "Heart Rate and Blood Pressure Biofeedback." *Biofeedback and Self-regulation,* 1979, Vol. 4, pp. 35–50.

Chapter 4

Bloom, K.C., and Shuell, T.J. "Effects of Massed and Distributed Practice on the Learning and Retention of Second-Language Vocabulary." *Journal of Educational Research,* 1981, Vol. 74, pp. 245–248.

Boice, R. "Observational Skills." *Psychological Bulletin,* 1983, Vol. 93, pp. 3–29.

Brown, A.S. "A Review of the Tip-of-the-Tongue Experience." *Psychological Bulletin,* 1991, Vol. 109, pp. 204–223.

Byrne, D. "The Effects of a Subliminal Food Stimulus on Verbal Responses." *Journal of Applied Psychology,* 1959, Vol. 43, pp. 249–252.

Cohen, A. R. "Cognitive Tuning as a Factor Affecting Impression Formation." *Journal of Personality*, 1961, Vol. 29, pp. 235–245.

Cowart, B.J. "Development of Taste Perception in Humans: Sensitivity and Preference Throughout the Life Span." *Psychological Bulletin*, 1981, Vol. 90, pp. 43–73.

Ebbinghaus, H. *Memory; A Contribution to Experimental Psychology.* Toronto: Dover Publications, 1964.

Goldstein, M., and Davis, D. "The Impact of Stimuli Registering Outside of Awareness upon Personal Preferences." Journal of Personality, 1961, Vol. 29, pp. 247- 257.

Greeno, J.G. "Psychology of Learning, 1960-1980: One Participant's Observations." *American Psychologist*, 1980, Vol. 35, pp. 713–728.

Hilgard, E.R. *Theories of Learning.* New York: Appleton-Century-Crofts, 1948.

Köhler, W. *The Mentality of Apes.* London: Kegan, Paul, Trench, Trubner & Co., 1927.

Kraut, R.E. "Verbal and Nonverbal Cues in the Perception of Lying." *Journal of Personality and Social Psychology*, 1978, Vol. 36, pp. 380–391.

Kroger, W. S., and Douce, R. G. "Hypnosis in Criminal Investigation." *International Journal of Clinical and Experimental Hypnosis*, 1979, Vol. 27, pp. 358–374.

Loftus, E.F., and Loftus, G.R. "On the Permanence of Stored Information in the Human Brain." *American Psychologist*, 1980, Vol. 35, pp. 409–420.

Miller, L.L., and Cornett, T.L. "Marijuana: Dose Effects on Pulse Rate, Subjective Estimates of Intoxication, Free Recall and Recognition Memory." *Pharmacology, Biochemistry & Behavior*, 1978, Vol. 9, pp. 573–577.

Miller, N.E. "Studies of Fear as an Acquirable Drive. I. Fear as Motivation and Fear-Reduction as Reinforcement in the Learning of New Responses." *Journal of Experimental Psychology*, 1948, Vol. 38, pp. 89–101.

Murray, H.A., and Wheeler, D.R. "A Note on the Possible Clairvoyance of Dreams." *Journal of Psychology*, 1937, Vol. 3, pp. 309–313.

Penfield, W. "Consciousness, Memory and Man's Conditioned Reflexes." K. Pribram (Ed.), *On the Biology of Learning.* New York: Harcourt, Brace & World, 1969.

Schacter, D.L. "Understanding Implicit Memory: A Cognitive Neuroscience Approach." *American Psychologist*, 1992, Vol. 47, pp. 559–569.

Schoenfeld, W.N. "Reinforcement in Behavior Theory." *Pavlovian Journal*, 1978, Vol. 13, pp. 135–144.

Skinner, B. F. "Pigeons in a Pelican." *American Psychologist*, 1960, Vol. 15, pp. 28–37.

Smith, M. C. "Hypnotic Memory Enhancement of Witnesses: Does It Work?" *Psychological Bulletin*, 1983, Vol. 94, pp. 387–407.

Squire, L.R., Knowlton, B., and Musen, G. "The Structure and Organization of Memory." *Annual Review of Psychology*, 1993, Vol. 44, pp. 453–495.

Zuckerman, M. "The Effects of Subliminal and Supraliminal Suggestion on Verbal Productivity." *Journal of Abnormal and Social Psychology*, 1960, Vol. 60, pp. 404–411.

Zuckerman, M., and Cohen, N. "Sources of Reports of Visual and Auditory Sensations in Perceptual-Isolation Experiments." *Psychological Bulletin*, 1964, Vol. 62, pp. 1–20.

Chapter 5

Asch, S.E. *Social Psychology*. New York: Prentice-Hall, 1952.

Batson, C.D., Coke, J.S., Chard, F., Smith, D., and Talliaferro, A. "Generality of the 'Glow of Goodwill': Effects of Mood on Helping and Information Acquisition." *Social Psychology Quarterly*, 1979, Vol. 42, pp. 176–179.

Burnstein, E. "Fear of Failure, Achievement Motivation, and Aspiring to Prestigeful Occupations." *Journal of Abnormal and Social Psychology*, 1963, Vol. 67, pp. 189–193.

Buss, A.H. "Physical Aggression in Relation to Different Frustrations." *Journal of Abnormal Psychology and Social Psychology*, 1963, Vol. 67, pp. 1–7.

Dollard, J., Doob, L.W., Miller, N.E., Mowrer, O.H., and Sears, R.R. *Frustration and Aggression*. New Haven: Yale University Press, 1939.

Efran, J.S., Goldsmith, D., McFarland, III, P.J., and Sharf, B. "The Effect on Endurance of a Verbal Commitment Versus Exhortation, Task Information, and Monetary Incentives." *Motivation and Emotion*, 1979, Vol. 3, pp. 93–101.

Griffiths, T.J., Steel, D.H., and Vaccaro, P. "Relationship Between Anxiety and Performance in Scuba Diving." *Perceptual and Motor Skills*, 1979, Vol. 48, pp. 1009–1010.

Katzell, R.A., and Guzzo, R.A. "Psychological Approaches to Productivity Improve-Merit." *American Psychologist*, 1983. Vol. 38, pp. 468–472.

Lamb D.H. "On the Distinction Between Physical and Psychological Stressors: A Review of the Evidence." *Motivation and Emotion*, 1979, Vol. 1, pp. 51–61.

Locke, E.A., Shaw, K.N., Saari, L.M., and Latham, G.P. "Goal Setting and Task Performance: 1969–1980." *Psychological Bulletin*, 1981, Vol. 90, pp. 125–152.

Maslow, A.H. *Motivation and Personality*. New York: Harper & Row, 1970.

Reitman, W.R. "Motivational Induction and the Behavior Correlates of the Achievement and Affiliation Motives." *Journal of Abnormal and Social Psychology*, 1960, Vol. 60, pp. 8–13.

Warden, C.J., *Animal Motivation: Experimental Studies on the Albino Rat*. New York: Columbia University Press, 1931.

Weinberg, R.S. "Anxiety and Motor Performance: Drive Theory vs. Cognitive Theory." *International Journal of Sports Psychology*, 1979, Vol. 10, pp. 112–121.

Chapter 6

Adler, A. *What Life Should Mean to You*. New York: Capricorn Books, 1958.

Bennet, E.A. *What Jung Really Said*. New York: Schocken Books, 1967.

Bouchard, T.J., Jr., Lykken, D.T., McGue, M., Segal, N.L., and Tellegen, A. "Sources of Human Psychological Differences: The Minnesota Study of Twins Reared Apart." *Science*, 1990, Vol. 250, pp. 223–228.

Budner, S. "Intolerance of Ambiguity as a Personality Variable." *Journal of Personality*, 1962, Vol. 30, pp. 29–50.

Cole, D., Rodriguez, J., and Cole, S. "Locus of Control in Mexicans and Chicanos: The Case of the Missing Fatalist." *Journal of Consulting and Clinical Psychology*, 1978, Vol. 46, pp. 1323–1329.

Digman, J.M. "Personality Structure: Emergence of the Five-Factor Model." *Annual Review of Psychology*, 1990, Vol. 41, pp. 417–440.

Driver, H.E. *Indians of North America*. Chicago: The University of Chicago Press, 1969.

Eron, L.D. "Prescription for Reduction of Aggression." *American Psychologist*, 1980, Vol. 35, pp. 244–252.

Freud, S. *The Basic Writings of Sigmund Freud*. New York: Random House, 1938.

——— . *The Complete Introductory Lectures on Psychoanalysis*. New York: Norton, 1966.

Hall, C.S., and Lindzey, G. *Theories of Personality*. New York: Wiley, 1957.

Hollender, M.H. "The Case of Anna O.: A Reformulation." *American Journal of Psychiatry*, 1980, Vol. 137, pp. 797–800.

Jones, E. *The Life and Work of Sigmund Freud*. New York: Basic Books, 1953.

Juni, S. "Classical Projection: A Critique of Experimental Methodologies." *Genetic Psychology Monographs*, 1980, Vol. 101, pp. 119–146.

Kluckhohn, C. *Mirror for Man*. New York: Whittlesey House, 1949.

——— . *Culture and Behavior*. New York: The Free Press, 1962.

Leary, T. *Interpersonal Diagnosis of Personality.* New York: Roland Press, 1957.

Malcolm, J. *Psychoanalysis: The Impossible Profession.* New York: Knopf, 1981.

Mesquita, B., and Frijda, N. H. "Cultural variations in emotions: A review." *Psychological Bulletin*, 1992, Vol. 112, pp. 179–204.

Nowicki, S., Jr. "Reported Stressful Events During Developmental Periods and Their Relation to Locus of Control Orientation in College Students." *Journal of Consulting and Clinical Psychology*, 1978, Vol. 46, pp. 1552–1553.

Rotter, J. B. "Generalized Expectancies for Internal vs. External Control of Reinforcement." *Psychological Monographs*, 1966, Vol. 80 (1, whole No. 609).

————— . "Some Problems and Misconceptions Related to the Construct of Internal Versus External Control of Reinforcement." *Journal of Consulting and Clinical Psychology*, 1975, Vol. 43, pp. 56–67.

Sophocles. *Oedipus the King.* In *The Complete Great Tragedies.* University of Chicago Press, 1942.

Strickland, B. R. "Internal-External Expectancies and Health-Related Behaviors." *Journal of Consulting and Clinical Psychology*, 1978, Vol. 46, pp. 1192–1211.

Symonds, P. M. *The Dynamics of Human Adjustment.* New York: D. Appleton-Century, 1946.

Witkin, H. A., Lewis, H. B., Hertzman, M., Machover, K., Meissner, P. B., and Wapner, S. *Personality Through Perception.* New York: Harper, 1954.

Chapter 7

Ball, R. S. "The Gesell Developmental Schedules: Arnold Gesell (1880–1961)." *Journal of Abnormal Child Psychology*, 1977, Vol. 5, pp. 233–239.

Bowlby, J. "Attachment and Loss: Retrospect and Prospect." *American Journal of Orthopsychiatry*, 1982, Vol. 52, pp. 664-678.

Conway, L. P., and Hansen, D. J. "Social Behavior of Physically Abused and Neglected Children: A Critical Review." *Clinical Psychology Review*, 1989, Vol. 9, pp. 627–652.

D'Andrade, R. G. "Sex Differences and Cultural Institutions." In Maccoby, E. E. *The Development of Sex Differences.* Palo Alto, CA: Stanford University Press, 1966.

Dennis, W., and Dennis, M. G. "The Effect of Cradling Practices upon the Onset of Walking in Hopi Children." *Journal of Genetic Psychology*, 1940, Vol. 56, pp. 77–86.

Field, T. M. "Infant Behaviors Directed Toward Peers and Adults in the Presence and Absence of Mother." *Infant Behavior and Development*, 1979, Vol. 2, pp. 47–54.

Gesell, A., Halverson, H.M., Thompson, H., Ilg, F.L., Castner, B.M., Ames, L.B., and Amatruda, C.S. *The First Five Years of Life: A Guide to the Study of the Preschool Child*. New York: Harper & Row, 1940.

Goldsmith, H.H., and Alansky, J.A. "Maternal and Infant Temperamental Predictions of Attachment: A Meta-Analytic Review." *Journal of Consulting and Clinical Psychology*, 1987, Vol. 55, pp. 805–816.

Harlow, H.F. "The Nature of Love." *American Psychologist*, 1958, Vol. 13, pp. 673–685.

Harter, S., Alexander, P.C., and Neimeyer, R.A. "Long-term Effects of Incestuous Child Abuse in College Women: Social Adjustment, Social Cognition, and Family Characteristics." *Journal of Consulting and Clinical Psychology*, 1988, Vol. 56, pp. 5–8.

Holland, V.M., and Rohrman, N.L. "Distribution of the Feature [+ Animate] in the Lexicon of the Child." *Journal of Psycholinguistic Research*, 1979, Vol. 8, pp. 367–378.

Katz, D.E., and Braly, K.W. "Racial Stereotypes of 100 College Students." *Journal of Abnormal and Social Psychology*, 1933, Vol. 28, pp. 280–290.

Koepke, J.E., and Barnes, P. "Amount of Sucking When a Sucking Object Is Readily Available to Human Newborns." *Child Development*, 1982, Vol. 53, pp. 978–983.

Lerner, R.M. "Children and Adolescents As Producers of Their Own Development." *Developmental Review*, 1982, Vol. 2, pp. 342–390.

Levarie, S., and Rudolph N. "Can Newborn Infants Distinguish Between Tone and Noise?" *Perceptual and Motor Skills*, 1978, Vol. 47, pp. 1123–1126.

Lewis, M., and Weinraub, M. "Origins of Early Sex-Role Development." *Sex Roles*, 1979, Vol. 5, pp. 135–153.

Malinosky-Rummell, R., and Hansen, D.J. "Long-Term Consequences of Childhood Physical Abuse." *Psychological Bulletin*, 1993, Vol. 114, pp. 68–79.

Marini, M.M. "Sex Differences in Determination of Adolescent Aspirations: A Review of Research." *Sex Roles*, 1978, Vol. 4, pp. 723–753.

Matheny, Jr., A.P., Dolan, A.B., and Krantz, J.Z. "Cognitive Aspects of Interests, Responsibilities, and Vocational Goals in Adolescence." *Adolescence*, 1980, Vol. 58, pp. 301–311.

Parten, M.B. "Social Participation Among Preschool Children." *Journal of Abnormal and Social Psychology*, 1932, Vol. 27, pp. 243–269.

Piaget, J. *The Origins of Intelligence in the Child*. New York: International University Press, 1956.

Skeels, H.M. "A Study of the Effects of Differential Stimulation on Mentally Retarded Children: A Follow-up Report." *American Journal of Mental Deficiency*, 1942, Vol. 46, pp. 340–350.

Thurnher, M. "Turning Points and Developmental Change: Subjective and Objective Assessments." *American Journal of Orthopsychiatry*, 1983, Vol. 53, pp. 52–60.

Vernon, P.E. "Intelligence Testing and the Nature/Nurture Debate, 1928–1978: What Next?" *British Journal of Educational Psychology*, 1979, Vol. 49, pp. 1–14.

Wachs, T.D., Francis, J., and McQuiston, S. "Psychological Dimensions of the Infant's Physical Environment." *Infant Behavior and Development*, 1979, Vol. 2, pp. 155–161.

Yamamoto, K. "Children's Ratings of the Stressfulness of Experiences." *Developmental Psychology*, 1979, Vol. 15, pp. 581–582.

Yarrow, L.J., McQuiston, S., MacTurk, R.H., McCarthy, M.E., Klein, R.P., and Vietze, P.M. "Assessment of Mastery Motivation During the First Year of Life: Contemporaneous and Cross-Age Relationships." *Developmental Psychology*, 1983, Vol. 19, pp. 159–171.

Zelazo, P.R., and Kearsley, R.B. "The Emergence of Functional Play in Infants: Evidence for a Major Cognitive Transition." *Journal of Applied Developmental Psychology*, 1980, Vol. 1, pp. 95–117.

Chapter 8

Adler, T. "Not All Cognitive Skills Affected by Age." *American Psychological Association Monitor*, 1991, Vol. 22, p. 16.

Beier, E.G., and Sternberg, D.P. "Marital Communications: Subtle Cues Between Newlyweds." *Journal of Communication*, 1977, Vol. 27, pp. 92–97.

Birch, L.L. "Effects of Peer Models' Food Choices and Eating Behaviors on Preschoolers' Food Preferences." *Child Development*, 1980, Vol. 51, pp. 489–496.

Burke, D.M., and Light, L.L. "Memory and Aging: The Role of Retrieval Processes." *Psychological Bulletin*, 1981, Vol. 90, pp. 513–546.

Diepold, J., and Young, R.D. "Empirical Studies of Adolescent Sexual Behavior: A Critical Review." *Adolescence*, 1979, Vol. 14, pp. 45-64.

Elwood, R.W., and Jacobson, N.S. "Spouses' Agreement in Reporting Their Behavioral Interactions: A Clinical Replication." *Journal of Consulting and Clinical Psychology*, 1982, Vol. 50, pp. 783–784.

Emery, R.E. "Interparental Conflict and the Children of Discord and Divorce." *Psychological Bulletin*, 1982, Vol. 92, pp. 310–330.

Foner, A., and Kertzer, D. "Transitions over the Life Course: Lessons from Age-Set Societies." *American Journal of Sociology*, 1978, Vol. 83, pp. 1081–1104.

Gaffney, L.R., and McFall, R.M. "A Comparison of Social Skills in Delinquent and Nondelinquent Adolescent Girls Using a Behavioral Role-playing Inventory." *Journal of Consulting and Clinical Psychology*, 1981, Vol. 49, pp. 959–967.

Glass, C.R., Gottman, J.M., and Shmurak, S.H. "Response-Acquisition and Cognitive Self-Statement Modification Approaches to Dating-Skills Training." *Journal of Counseling Psychology*, 1976, Vol. 23, pp. 520–526.

Glenwick, D.S., Jason, L.A., and Elman, D. "Physical Attractiveness and Social Contact in the Singles Bar." *Journal of Social Psychology*, 1978, Vol. 105, pp. 311–312.

Granick, S., and Patterson, R.D. (Eds.) *Human Aging II: An Eleven-Year Follow-up Biomedical and Behavioral Study.* DHEW Publication No. (ADM) pp. 74–123. U.S. Government Printing Office, 1974.

Gray-Little, B., and Burks, N. "Power and Satisfaction in Marriage: A Review and Critique." *Psychological Bulletin*, 1983, Vol. 93, pp. 513–538.

Gubrium, J.F. "Apprehensions of Coping in Competence and Responses to Fear in Old Change." *International Journal of Aging and Human Development*, 1973, Vol. 4, pp. 111–125.

Herold, E.S. "Variables Influencing the Dating Adjustment of University Students." *Journal of Youth and Adolescence*, 1979, Vol. 8, pp. 73–79.

Hetherington, E.M. "Effects of Father Absence on Personality Development in Adolescent Daughters." *Developmental Psychology*, 1972, Vol. 7, pp. 313–326.

Jacobs, J.W. "The Effect of Divorce on Fathers: An Overview of the Literature." *American Journal of Psychiatry*, 1982, Vol. 139, pp. 1235–1241.

Jacobson, N.S., and Moore, D. "Spouses as Observers of the Events in Their Relationship." *Journal of Consulting and Clinical Psychology*, 1981, Vol. 49, pp. 269–277.

Jacobson, N.S., Follette, W.C., and McDonald, D.W. "Reactivity to Positive and Negative Behavior in Distressed and Nondistressed Married Couples." *Journal of Consulting and Clinical Psychology*, 1982, Vol. 50, pp. 706–714.

Jacques, J.M., and Chason, K.J. "Cohabitation: Its Impact on Marital Success." *Family Coordinator*, 1979, Vol. 28, pp. 35–39.

Larson, R., and Csikszentmihalyi, M. "Experimental Correlates of Time Alone in Adolescence." *Journal of Personality*, 1978, Vol. 46, pp. 677–693.

Leon, G.R., Gillum, B., Gillum, R., and Gouze, M. "Personality Stability and Change over a 30-year Period—Middle Age to Old Age." *Journal of Consulting and Clinical Psychology*, 1979, Vol. 47, pp. 517–524.

Margolin, G., Talovic, S., and Weinstein, C.D. "Areas of Change Questionnaire: A Practical Approach to Marital Assessment." *Journal of Consulting and Clinical Psychology*, 1983, Vol. 51, pp. 920-931.

Mott, F.L., and Moore, S.F. "The Causes of Marital Disruption Among Young American Women: An Interdisciplinary Perspective." *Journal of Marriage and the Family*, 1979, Vol. 41, pp. 355–365.

Perlman, D., Gerson, A.C., and Spinner, B. "Loneliness Among Senior Citizens: An Empirical Report." *Essence*, 1978, Vol. 2, pp. 239–248.

Robbins, P.R. *Marijuana: A Short Course. Update for the Eighties.* Brookline Village, MA: Branden Press, 1983.

Robbins, P.R., and Tanck, R.H. "Sex Differences in Problems Relating to Depression." *Sex Roles*, 1983.

Robinson, E.A., and Price, M.G. "Pleasurable Behavior in Marital Interaction: An Observational Study." *Journal of Consulting and Clinical Psychology*, 1980, Vol. 48, pp. 117–118.

Rosen, R.H. "Adolescent Pregnancy Decision-Making: Are Parents Important?" *Adolescence*, 1980, Vol. 15, pp. 43–54.

Rosenbaum, A., and O'Leary, K.D. "Marital Violence: Characteristics of Abusive Couples." *Journal of Consulting and Clinical Psychology*, 1981, Vol. 49, pp. 63–71.

Roumaniuk, M., McAuley, W.J., and Arling, G. "An Examination of the Prevalence of Mental Disorders Among the Elderly in the Community." *Journal of Abnormal Psychology*, 1983, Vol. 92, pp. 458–467.

Sattler, J.M. "Age Effects on Wechsler Adult Intelligence Scale—Revised Tests." *Journal of Consulting and Clinical Psychology*, 1982, Vol. 50, pp. 785–786.

Schneider, F.W., and Coutts, L.M. "The High School Environment: A Comparison of Coeducational and Single-Sex Schools." *Journal of Educational Psychology*, 1982, Vol. 74, pp. 898–906.

Schwartz, L.L., and Kaslow, F.W. "Religious Cults, the Individual, and the Family." *Journal of Marital and Family Therapy*, 1979, Vol. 5, pp. 15–26.

Schwartz, P., and Lever, J. "Fear and Loathing at a College Mixer." *Urban Life*, 1976, Vol. 4, pp. 413–431.

Shanteau, J., and Nagy, G. F. "Probability of Acceptance in Dating Choice." *Journal of Personality and Social Psychology*, 1979, Vol. 37, pp. 522–533.

Smith, J. A. "A Survey of Adolescents' Interests: Concerns and Information." *Adolescence*, 1980, Vol. 15, pp. 475–482.

Solomon, M.A. "A Developmental, Conceptual Premise for Family Therapy." *Family Process*, 1973, Vol. 12, pp. 179–196.

Strong, L.D. "Alternative Marital and Family Forms: Their Relative Attractiveness to College Students and Correlates of Willingness to Participate in Nontraditional Forms." *Journal of Marriage and the Family*, 1978, Vol. 40, pp. 493–503.

Wallerstein, J.S. "Children of Divorce: The Psychological Tasks of One Child." *American Journal of Orthopsychiatry*, 1983, Vol. 53, pp. 230–243.

Weisfeld, G.E. "An Ethological View of Human Adolescence." *Journal of Nervous and Mental Disease*, 1979, Vol. 167, pp. 38–55.

Wodarski, J.S. "Single Parents and Children: A Review for Social Workers." *Family Therapy*, 1982, Vol. 9, pp. 311–320.

Young, J.W., and Ferguson, L.R. "Developmental Changes Through Adolescence in the Spontaneous Nomination of Reference Groups as a Function of Decision Content." *Journal of Youth and Adolescence*, 1979, Vol. 8, pp. 239–252.

Chapter 9

Abramson, L.Y., Seligman, M.E.P., and Teasdale, J.D. "Learned Helplessness in Humans: Critique and Reformulation." *Journal of Abnormal Psychology*, 1978, Vol. 87, pp. 49–74.

American Psychiatric Association. *Diagnostic and Statistical Manual of Mental Disorders* (3rd ed.). Washington, DC: American Psychiatric Association, 1980.

Blaney, P.H. "Contemporary Theories of Depression: Critique and Comparison." *Journal of Abnormal Psychology*, 1977, Vol. 86, pp. 203–223.

Bleuler, E. *Dementia Praecox or the Group of Schizophrenias*. New York: International Universities Press, 1950.

Characteristics of Admissions to Selected Mental Health Facilities, 1975: An Annotated Book of Charts and Tables. Washington, DC: U.S. Government Printing Office, 1981.

Colby, K.M. "Appraisal of Four Psychological Theories of Paranoid Phenomena." *Journal of Abnormal Psychology*, 1977, Vol. 86, pp. 54–59.

Costello, C. G. "Fears and Phobias in Women: A Community Study." *Journal of Abnormal Psychology*, 1982, Vol. 91, pp. 280–286.

Depue, R.A., Slater, J.F., Wolfstetter-Kausch, H., Klein, D., Goplerod, E., and Farr, D. "A Behavioral Paradigm for Identifying Persons at Risk for Bipolar Depresssive Disorder: A Conceptual Framework and Five Validation Studies. *Journal of Abnormal Psychology*, 1981, Vol. 90, pp. 381–437.

Foa, E.B. "Failure in Treating Obsessive-compulsives." *Behavior Research & Therapy*, 1979, Vol. 17, pp. 169–176.

Gjerde, P.F. "Attentional Capacity Dysfunction and Arousal in Schizophrenia." *Psychological Bulletin*, 1983, Vol. 93, pp. 57–72.

Gottesman, I. "Schizophrenia and Genetics: Where Are We? Are You Sure?" L. Wynne, R. Cromwell, and S. Matthysse (Eds.). *The Nature of Schizophrenia*. New York: Wiley, 1978.

Gruenewald, D. "Multiple Personality and Splitting Phenomena: A Reconceptualization." *Journal of Nervous and Mental Disease*, 1977, Vol. 164, pp. 385–393.

Halmi, K.A. "Anorexia Nervosa: Recent Investigations." *Annual Review of Medicine*, 1978, Vol. 29, pp. 137–148.

Hammachek, D.E. "Psychodynamics of Normal and Neurotic Perfectionism." *Psychology*, 1978, Vol. 15, pp. 27–33.

Harder, D.W., Strauss, J.S., Kokes, R.F., Ritzler, B.A., and Gift, T.E. "Life Events and Psychopathology Severity Among First Psychiatric Admissions." *Journal of Abnormal Psychology*, 1980, Vol. 89, pp. 165–180.

Heinrichs, R.W. "Schizophrenia and the Brain: Conditions for a Neuropsychology of Madness." *American Psychologist*, 1993, Vol. 48, pp. 221–233.

Hendin, H. "Psychotherapy for Veterans with Posttraumatic Stress Disorders." *American Journal of Psychotherapy*, 1983, Vol. 37, pp. 85–99.

Kendler, K.S., Glazer, W.M., and Morgenstern, H. "Dimensions of Delusional Experience." *American Journal of Psychiatry*, 1983, Vol. 140, pp. 466–469.

Lewine, R.R.J. "Sex Differences in Schizophrenias: Timing or Subtypes?" *Psychological Bulletin*, 1981, Vol. 90, pp. 432–444.

Luborsky, L., Docherty, J.P., and Penick, S. "Onset Conditions for Psychosomatic Symptoms: A Comparative Review of Immediate Observation with Retrospective Research." *Psychosomatic Medicine*, 1973, Vol. 35, pp. 187–204.

Raz, S., and Raz., N. "Structural Brain Abnormalities in the Major Psychoses: A Quantitative Review of the Evidence." *Psychological Bulletin*, 1990, Vol. 108, pp. 93–108.

Robbins, P.R. "Personality and Psychosomatic Illness: A Selective Review of Research." *Genetic Psychology Monographs*, 1969, Vol. 80, pp. 51–90.

————. *Understanding Depression*. Jefferson, NC: McFarland, 1993.

Robbins, P.R., and Tanck, R.H. "Further Research Using a Psychological Diary Technique to Investigate Psychosomatic Relationships." *Journal of Clinical Psychology*, 1982, Vol. 38, pp. 356–359.

Rosenberg, H., and Upper, D. "Problems with Stimulus Response Equivalence and Reactivity in the Assessment and Treatment of Obsessive-compulsive Neurosis." *Behavior Research & Therapy*, 1981, Vol. 21, pp. 177–180.

Tanck, R.H., and Robbins, P.R. "Assertiveness, Locus of Control, and Coping Behaviors Used to Diminish Tension." *Journal of Personality Assessment*, 1979, Vol. 43, pp. 396–400.

Zubin, J., and Spring, B. "Vulnerability—A New View of Schizophrenia." *Journal of Abnormal Psychology*, 1977 Vol. 86. pp. 103–126.

Chapter 10

Beck, A.T., Rush, A.J., Shaw, T.D., and Emery, G. *Cognitive Therapy of Depression*. New York: Guildford, 1979.

Carlson, C.G., Hersen, M., and Eisler, R.M. "Token Economy Programs in the Treatment of Hospitalized Adult Psychiatric Patients." *Journal of Nervous and Mental Disease*, 1972, Vol. 155, pp. 192–204.

Breuer, J., and Freud, S. *Studies on Hysteria*. In Strachey, J. (Ed.), standard edition of the *Complete Psychological Works of Sigmund Freud*. London: Hogarth Press, 1955.

Evans, R.I. *The Making of Psychology* (Chapter 17, Carl Rogers). New York: A.A. Knopf, 1976.

Frank, J.D. "Common Features of Psychotherapies and Their Patients." *Psychotherapy and Psychosomatics*, 1974, Vol. 24, pp. 368–371.

Freud, S. *The Basic Writings of Sigmund Freud*. New York: Random House, 1938.

————. *Therapy and Technique*. New York: Collier, 1963.

Garfield, S.L. "What Are the Therapeutic Variables in Psychotherapy?" *Psychotherapy and Psychosomatics*, 1974, Vol. 24, pp. 372–378.

Glass, G.V., and Kliegl, R.M. "An Apology for Research Integration in the Study of Psychotherapy." *Journal of Consulting and Clinical Psychology*, 1983, Vol. 51, pp. 28–41.

Greenberg, L.S. "The Intensive Analysis of Recurrent Events from the Practice of Gestalt Therapy." *Psychotherapy: Theory, Research, and Practice*, 1980, Vol. 17, pp. 143–150.

Katz, R., and Rode, E. "Community Alternatives to Psychotherapy." *Psychotherapy: Theory, Research, and Practice*, 1981, Vol. 18, pp. 365–374.

Malcolm, J. *Psychoanalysis: The Impossible Profession*. New York: Knopf, 1981.

Nicholson, R.A., and Berman, J.S. "Is Follow-up Necessary in Evaluating Psychotherapy?" *Psychological Bulletin*, 1983, Vol. 93. pp. 261–278.

Perls, F.S. *Gestalt Therapy Verbatim*. Moab, UT: Real People Press, 1969.

Rogers, Carl R. *Counseling and Psychotherapy*. Boston, MA: Houghton Mifflin, 1942.

Sand, P.L., Trieschmann, R.B., Fordyce, W.E., and Fowler, R.S. "Behavior Modification in the Medical Rehabilitation Setting: Rationale and Some Applications." *Rehabilitation Research and Practice Review*, 1970, Vol. 1, pp. 11–24.

Strupp, H.H. "On the Basic Ingredients of Psychotherapy." *Psychotherapy and Psychosomatics*, 1974, Vol. 24, pp. 249–260.

Yalom, I.D. *The Theory and Practice of Group Psychotherapy* (2nd ed.). New York: Basic Books, 1975.

Chapter 11

Brownell, K.D. "Obesity: Understanding and Treating a Serious, Prevalent, and Refractory Disorder." *Journal of Consulting and Clinical Psychology*, 1982, Vol. 50, pp. 820–840.

Dement, W.C. *Some Must Watch While Some Must Sleep*. San Francisco: Freeman, 1974.

Gardner, R.A., and Gardner, B.T. "A Vocabulary Test for Chimpanzees (Pan Troglodytes)." *Journal of Comparative Psychology*, 1984, Vol. 98, pp. 381–404.

Herman, L.M., Morrel-Samuels, P., and Pack, A.A. "Bottlenosed Dolphin and Human Recognition of Veridical and Degraded Video Displays of an Artificial Gestural Language." *Journal of Experimental Psychology: General*, 1990, Vol. 119, pp. 215–230.

Limber, J. "Language in Child and Chimp?" *American Psychologist*, 1977, Vol. 32, pp. 280–295.

Malcolm, J. *Psychoanalysis: The Impossible Profession*. New York: Knopf, 1981.

Index

T

Tanck, Roland, 70, 106, 120, 126
temporal lobe, 27
tests, psychological, 5
    achievement, 15
    and performance on by elderly, 113
    aptitude, 15
    intelligence, 15
    interests, 15
    personality, 16
thalamus, 28
Thematic Apperception Test, 16, 42, 65, 88
Thorndike, E. L., 51
Thorndike, Edward, 5, 52
tip-of-the-tongue experiences, 50
tolerance for ambiguity, 79
Tolman, Edward C., 56
tricyclics, 124
tympanic membrane, 26
Type A behavior, 127

U

unconditioned response, 4
unconscious, the, 3, 80

V

variability, measures of, 20
violence in society, 148
Vocational Interest Blank (VIB), 15

W

Wallerstein, Judith, 112
Watson, John B., 5, 51
Wechsler, David, 5
Wechsler Adult Intelligence Scale, 15
Wertheimer, Max, 39
Wheeler, D. R., 43
white matter, 27
Witkin, Herman, 79
word association, 3
Wundt, Wilhelm, 1, 3, 5

Y

Yalom, Irvin, 144
Yarrow, Leon, 95